Tales from the Bridge Table

Contract Bridge 1925–1995

John Clay

CORONET BOOKS
Hodder & Stoughton

First published in Great Britain in 1998
by Hodder and Stoughton
First published in paperback in 1999
by Hodder and Stoughton
A division of Hodder Headline PLC

A Coronet Paperback

10 9 8 7 6 5 4 3 2 1

A CIP catalogue record for this title is available
from the British Library

ISBN 0340 73908 8

Printed and bound in Great Britain by
Mackays of Chatham PLC, Chatham, Kent

Hodder and Stoughton
A division of Hodder Headline PLC
338 Euston Road
London NW1 3BH

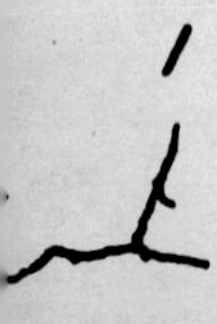

Tales from the Bridge Table

Also by John Clay

CULBERTSON
THE MAN WHO MADE CONTRACT BRIDGE

MEN AT WILDLIFE

JOHN MASTERS
A REGIMENTED LIFE

R. D. LAING
A DIVIDED SELF

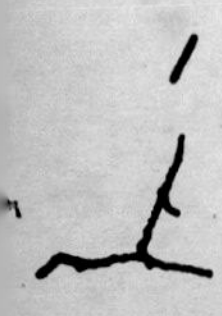

For J.E.M.B.

who crossed many bridges

Contents

♠♥♦
♣

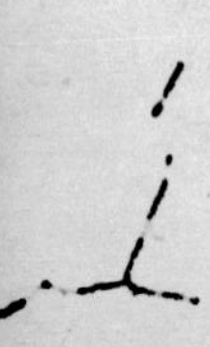

Acknowledgements

The author is grateful for the permission of the following publishers, authors and literary agents to quote copyrighted material from the following works:

Cohen, Ben and Reese, Terence, *The Acol System*, Contract Bridge Equipment Ltd, Leeds, 1946

Dahl, Roald, *Someone Like You*, Michael Joseph, London, 1954. Reprinted by permission of David Higham Associates Ltd.

Fleming, Ian, *Moonraker*, Jonathan Cape, London, 1955. Reprinted by permission of © 1995 Glidrose Productions Ltd.

Francis, Henry G., Truscott, Alan F., Frey, Richard L. and Hayward, Diane (eds), *The Official Encyclopedia of Bridge* (Fourth Edition), Crown, New York, 1984

Macleod, Iain, *Bridge is an Easy Game*, The Falcon Press, London, 1952

Mahmood, Zia, *Bridge My Way*, Faber & Faber, London, 1991

Markus, Rixi, *A Vulnerable Game; The Memoirs of Rixi Markus*, Collins, London, 1988

Maugham, W. Somerset, *The Complete Short Stories*, William Heinemann, London, 1951. Reprinted by permission of A. P. Watt Ltd on behalf of The Royal Literary Fund.

Reese, Terence, *Bridge at the Top*, Faber & Faber, London, 1977

Simon, S. J., *Why You Lose at Bridge*, Nicholson & Watson, London, 1947

Sims, Dorothy, *Psychic Bidding*, Vanguard Press, New York, 1932

Sims, Dorothy, *Curiouser and Curiouser: A Book in the Jugular Vein*, Simon and Schuster, New York, 1940

Sobel, Helen, *Winning Bridge*, Peter Davies, London, 1950

Every effort has been made to trace copyright holders in relation to this book and the author would like to apologise to anyone who has not been found or properly acknowledged. Subsequent editions will include any corrections or omissions notified to the author.

Preface

♠♥♦
♣

My first book on bridge was a biography of Ely Culbertson. I wanted to explore how contract bridge started and how Culbertson, quintessentially a 1930s figure, took charge of this. I came from a card-playing family myself. As a child I watched my parents play bridge before saying goodnight. It all seemed very adult and grown-up, the palpable excitement of the card table apparent even in those days. At my prep school I played the usual card games, rummy, beggar-my-neighbour, racing demon. At public school, Downside, I started playing bridge. It was a Benedictine school and bridge was tolerated by the monks for its educational rather than its spiritual value.

At home the *Sporting Life* accompanied *The Times* at the breakfast table. In order to preserve links with home I continued to back horses, regularly ringing up a bookmaker in Wells on the school telephone. This required sounding my most grown-up, 'Mr Clay speaking', a fourteen-year-old's attempt at insouciance. Downside, as a Catholic school, had several Irish pupils and therefore its own horse-racing fraternity. I can recall the excitement when an Irish pupil backed Never Say Die to win the Derby in 1954 at thirty-three to one. I went to Bath races whenever possible, trying to make it coincide with 'essential' dental appointments. My vivid memories were of seeing the large white five-pound notes bookmakers still handled and of Ras Prince Monolulu, the black tipster with his African head-dress, shouting to his circle of devotees, 'I gotta horse.'

The headmaster discovered my betting activities and summoned me to his office during afternoon games, always a bad sign. A fellow punter at school called 'Archer' Hardy had grassed on me. The headmaster talked in a friendly, patronising way, and I was lulled into believing I had committed a minor misdemeanour in an acceptable schoolboy tradition. Not a bit of it. *Quidquid id est, timeo Danaos et dona ferentes*. He suddenly told me to bend over and caned me on my bare backside. I went back to bridge.

At Cambridge University I played bridge more seriously. I was in a college, Trinity Hall, where there happened to be three or four keen players. Sometimes I played in other colleges after my own college front gates closed and once or twice persuaded a taxi driver to take me back down the lane alongside my college wall to help me climb in by standing on his taxi roof, but it was hazardous – better to remain with the all-night game where bridge concentration and stamina would be tested to the full.

After University I played bridge in London fairly regularly. But the game returned to my life properly when I became an author. I was now in my early forties and began my writing career with short stories, liking the compression and the way of depicting characters through detail. The following summer while staying with friends in Corfu, I watched a fellow guest writing her biography sitting each morning under an olive tree. Perhaps I, too, could write a biography, earn some money and then go back to fiction writing with a financial cushion. Back in England I wondered whom to write about. It needed to be a twentieth-century figure, dead – too risky to write about the living – and with family and friends still around to interview.

I then remembered a short story I had written about a bridge-playing husband and wife, with the husband playing a slam contract – it was his moment of glory in an otherwise hen-pecked existence – and fantasising about being like the Culbertsons, whom I'd dimly remembered as a glamorous 1930s couple, the wife as svelte and elegant as her dinner-jacketed husband. I enquired into Culbertson as a possible biographical subject. Good fortune proved to be on my side. I happened to go out to Spain soon afterwards where my mother had a house. Near her at Sotogrande lived Jaime Ortiz Patino, an international bridge player for Switzerland and President of the World Bridge Federation. I went to talk to him about my idea for a biography of Culbertson. He was immediately interested and gave me names of people to contact in the USA, where Culbertson had spent most of his life. He also told me that Albert Morehead, Culbertson's closest friend and literary executor, had been working on his biography when he had fallen ill and died of cancer. The field suddenly opened up and my book was on.

My first research trip to the USA followed up these introductions. I hoped to contact Culbertson's family, although none of them had any bridge connections, so it wasn't going to be easy. I went to New York where I got in touch with Richard Frey, one of Culbertson's oldest friends and colleagues on his bridge magazine, *The Bridge World.* I rang him on my first evening in New York and he invited me round the next day. As this was my first interview for my first book, I was unsure how to proceed. Should I invite him out to lunch? Should I offer him money? Should I bring a present? I arrived at his apartment on East 87th Street, notebook and tape recorder in hand. He greeted me affably at the door. It was winter and he had a bad cough, and his wife hovered around anxiously. We sat down and talked. In fact he talked non-stop for four hours, opening up a new world for me. I suddenly realised that talking to someone about the thing that had mattered most to him in his life would mean that he would talk at great length and uninhibitedly, a first lesson in biographical strategy. Frey told me much about Culbertson's early years and the inside story of *The Bridge World,* and what tournament life had been like in the 1930s.

Frey suggested I get in touch with Oswald Jacoby, another Culbertson associate and an all-time great of bridge. I rang him in Dallas from the Park Avenue apartment where I was staying. Jacoby seemed more than willing to talk, in fact he talked twenty to the dozen, his mind racing far ahead of his speech. He told me to ring him at six o'clock each morning, his preferred time for conversation. He had a phenomenal memory and could pinpoint hands played over fifty years ago with amazing accuracy. Jacoby suggested I visit him in Dallas. I could go on there from Memphis where I was going to visit the American Contract Bridge League headquarters, whose library held some valuable Culbertson papers, as well as having its own near-complete collection of bridge books and publications.

I went via another introduction – they were beginning to snowball – to have lunch with Sam Fry at the Regency Club on East 67th Street. Fry was another *Bridge World* editor and a good friend and companion of Culbertson. The Regency, the foremost bridge club in New York, gave me a first-hand insight into the upper echelons of New York bridge. It clearly resembled Culbertson's own 1930s club, Crockford's, which he ran with considerable flair on East 65th Street.

Old-timers, such as Frey, Jacoby and Fry, with their remarkable memories, seemed living proof of how well bridge can exercise the mind, the best defence against Alzheimer's. 'We don't stop playing because we grow old, we grow old because we stop playing,' George Bernard Shaw once said. The way these old people – I was also to talk by telephone to Baron Waldemar von Zedtwitz, then well over ninety and living in Hawaii – could recall events from a bygone era was astounding and encouraging.

I went to Memphis, as scheduled, and then on to Dallas where Jacoby met me at the airport in his white Cadillac El Dorado. He drove firmly, but erratically, to the Dallas Country Club where we lunched in surroundings reminiscent of the TV series, with much Southern politeness and references to 'you-all'. We talked about Jacoby's part in the famous Culbertson versus Lenz match. After lunch he drove me to his home to meet his wife Mary Zita, his memory showing no sign of diminishing as the day wore on. 'That was on a Tuesday in March 1932, and I held four spades to the king . . .'

On a second research trip to the USA I finally encountered Culbertson's family. I first met Ely and Jo's son Bruce, christened Ely after his father, but, once clear of his father's dominance, reverting to Bruce. He worked for an aerospace firm near Boston. We dined early, as is the American custom, and I could soon see that holding my liquor was going to be the benchmark of our relationship. We ate, or rather drank, dinner. After a while I realised that my memory would never retain all he was telling me, so I asked if I could use a tape recorder. He grudgingly assented, his scepticism of biographers momentarily relenting. Next morning, when I came to listen to the tape, the sound of cutlery and tinkling glasses obliterated almost all conversation. Still, contact had been made. When I rang to thank him for the evening, he offered me his father's black address book, which turned out to be a biographer's treasure trove. In it, in his own handwriting, Culbertson had marked intimate details of his private life, circling women's names with symbols of presumed intimacy.

For his second marriage, Culbertson married someone much younger than himself. She was Dorothy Baehne, a student at Vassar when she first met him in 1946. Culbertson, by then, had switched most of his interests from bridge to international politics and had developed a system for world peace based on geo-politics, which he called the World Federation Plan. Dorothy had met him when he was talking at a political meeting, then rang him in New York after graduating from Vassar. Culbertson offered her a job and before long they were married. She was self-confident, good-looking, dynamic. She became his Galatea, to be moulded to his wishes as per the Pygmalion story. But their marriage didn't last, Dorothy eventually divorcing him for 'intolerable severity'.

I went to see Dorothy's mother, Hildegarde Baehne, in Vermont at the house where the Culbertsons had lived. She laid on an afternoon bridge game for me. A fellow player was a 103-year-old woman, the redoubtable Gertrude Croker, still smoking and drinking, further testimony to the mind-enhancing qualities of bridge. As snow fell outside, it might have been a scene from Turgenev. Through Hildegarde Baehne, I learnt that Culbertson's last private secretary was Cynthia Koestler, wife of Arthur Koestler. In the early 1950s, Cynthia Jefferies, as she then was, had been in New York at the tail end of an unhappy marriage. Culbertson had interviewed her for the job, telling her the world was divided into two sorts of people, those with two-dimensional minds – he waved these aside with a sweep of his hand – and a select few with three-dimensional minds. Cynthia probably had two and a half, he said, but if she stayed working for him, she might end up with three. She spent two years working for Culbertson before leaving, at Koestler's request, to join him in London where they later got married. I spoke to her on the telephone shortly after returning from my research trip in 1983. We arranged to meet the following week on a Wednesday. I went, as arranged, to the Koestlers' house in Knightsbridge at 3.30 p.m., rang the bell, got no answer, rang again several times, noticed drawn curtains on the first floor which seemed unusual for that time of day, spoke to their basement resident who said that as far as he knew they were in. Still no reply, so I went away very disappointed. Next day I was listening to the morning radio when I heard news of their joint suicide, which must have taken place undetected the night before my visit.

Cynthia knew much of what lay behind the manuscript of Culbertson's unfinished sequel to his autobiography. I'd seen bits of the typescript in the Albert Morehead Memorial Library in Memphis. In it, Culbertson gives a lengthy account of various amours and adventures in between marriages, including an account of being blackmailed by a young woman half his age. Cynthia Koestler knew these secrets and much else besides, yet by then my biographical search was nearly over. My book was completed and came out in 1985.

Here, in this second book on bridge, I want to pick up on themes that move on and across from the earlier book. I want to show the progression of bridge from its early years of auction to its development as contract and into the game that we know today. Personalities have always been important in bridge and I plan to highlight some of the significant players and events that made this happen, particularly the women players whose contribution to the development of the game may have been underestimated. First I begin with the central figures who really put contract bridge on the map. These were Ely and Jo Culbertson, and their first meeting took place in 1922, still in the days of auction bridge.

Jo Culbertson

—♠♥♦—
♣

Jo Culbertson was the leading woman bridge player of her era. It was unusual in the early 1920s – indeed, as it still is today – to find a woman player competing at the highest level. She had been born Josephine Murphy on 2 February 1898, at Bayside, New York, her father Edward Murphy being a civil engineer of Irish extraction. After school she took a business course and became secretary to Pat Powers, the six-day bicycle-race impresario. Later she became secretary to Wilbur Whitehead, leading player at the Knickerbocker Whist Club, and she was for a time his mistress. Whitehead taught her bridge. 'Mr Whitehead used me as his guinea-pig,' she once said. 'He didn't see why women shouldn't play bridge as well as men, even though at that time they restricted their play to "social bridge".'

Through Whitehead she became something of a favourite at the Knickerbocker. Other players tried to help her along with her game and improve her auction bridge, Sidney Lenz in particular. Then, in 1919, she met James Dillon, a Princeton graduate, who had just returned from the war in Europe. He was rather wild but was good-looking, and promised a more glamorous way of life. She was young and impressionable and they were soon married. But he proved unstable – he was a drinker and a drug-taker – and after only a few months of marriage committed suicide. It was a shattering blow to Josephine who withdrew into herself and would not talk about it. Others were left to speculate about the causes of his suicide. She was still marked by the scars of her disastrous marriage when she came across Ely Culbertson.

They met for the first time one night in March 1922. He had gone for the evening to the Knickerbocker Whist Club and ran into Whitehead downstairs who told him they were looking for a fourth player for a game on the third floor. Whitehead and he went upstairs together, and he was introduced to the two other players – Ralph Liebenderfer, a lawyer, and Josephine Dillon. He had already heard about her and was immediately attracted by her. She was quite tall, slender, with large

Irish eyes, a slightly upturned nose and an engaging smile. He noticed her hands particularly, long, narrow and sensitive. She seemed to have an air of relaxed, unhurried calm about her. He sensed she had taken note of him too but was not going to reveal what she felt. They cut for partners and Culbertson drew Liebenderfer. As the cards were being shuffled, Jo turned to Culbertson. 'I hear you're a very lucky player and that you have invented a system. Well, I'm sure it's not all luck. There must be a little skill in it as well.'

It was a promising start. It meant she had heard of him as well. The men played for five cents a point while Jo settled for one cent, which was her limit. The game proceeded as slowly as the traffic on Fifth Avenue outside, largely because Whitehead insisted on lengthy post-mortems after every deal. For him the bridge table was like a dissecting slab for the anatomy of quick tricks. Jo and Liebenderfer seemed unperturbed by this and were obviously used to it. Culbertson was in no hurry, either, captivated by the presence of Jo. His normally astute bridge defences must have slipped, for he soon found himself in a trap of her making. She had twice bid a suit in which she held a void. Culbertson cannot have been listening too closely and doubled; she switched to her real suit, he doubled again, she quickly redoubled and made the contract with a trick to spare. Culbertson had been completely taken in and groaned ruefully. 'I never imagined a woman capable of such a triple-cross.' 'It's the only chance we women have,' Jo replied drily.

Culbertson silently chalked up the humiliation in his 'someday-I'll-show-you' column. He now understood what Liebenderfer meant when he said she had a man's mind. But for all her man's mind, she had, in Culbertson's eyes, another inestimable quality – charm. This emanated from her overall presence, her gestures and dignity and her quiet restraint. For Culbertson she was a challenge – the sort of woman he felt he had to live up to in order to earn her respect. He also felt that there was already something, a sort of unspoken intimacy, between them.

When the game ended, he stayed on at the club, talking to Whitehead, a resident at the club, but his mind was elsewhere. He longed to hear more about Jo, hoping perhaps for some fatherly advice, but Whitehead was entirely preoccupied with the game that had just taken place. Culbertson went home but, try as he might, he found his thoughts coming back time and again to Jo. She was his type all right, but he knew he would have to tread carefully. She was still feeling the effects of her marriage to one glamorous personality and would be wary of another.

He decided upon a waiting game. Instead of pressing his suit, his tactic was to avoid seeing her altogether for the next two weeks. When invited to join a third-floor game at the Knickerbocker Whist Club, he declined, making an excuse that he had a previous engagement. It was the 'Culbertson Pursuit System', New-York-style. No doubt there was a degree of insecurity in it as well. Beneath his outward conceit and brashness, he still could not quite bring himself to believe that an exceptional woman like Jo Dillon would find him attractive on his own account. Jo seemed to have a host of admirers and he could see that, for her, it had not been a case of love at first sight.

Culbertson wondered how he could make his 'Pursuit System' really effective. It all revolved, he said to himself, around three basic precepts: emotion, reason and imagination. He sat in his room at night working it out, sketching out his plan on bits of paper filled with notes and diagrams. The first two were linked. First, arouse her sympathy, then lull her suspicions and quieten her fears. At their next meeting he would seek to present himself in a favourable light, display his sincerity and genuineness. Next he would establish intellectual mastery over her by using his card system, paving the way for admiration. On to the third stage, then, when her imagination would be opened up as she envisaged the endless possibilities of their triumphs and shared life together.

Well, of course, it did not work out like that, the human heart failing to be as biddable as a deck of cards. Jo soon came to personify a sort of prize between Whitehead representing the old order and Culbertson representing the new. He continued to go to the Knickerbocker Whist Club where he was viewed as something of a brash upstart. His ideas on bridge seemed so strange that no one took them particularly seriously, yet he still came out a regular winner. He had evolved his system in opposition to the older, more inflexible methods. His new scientific approach meant analysing every nuance of the cards and each step of the bidding. The old guard remained self-satisfied and saw no need to change. They glorified the 'rules' of bidding and would rather score 200 points by following those rules than 300 by abandoning them. Culbertson kept a 'crime sheet' in which he analysed their bids and plays as well as his own and he felt he could prove to himself that they actually threw away thousands of points when they thought they had played perfectly. He imagined that Jo, too, viewed his theories at that time with faint derision. This was his chance. If he could get to work on her and make her see that his system was perfectly sound and probably superior to others, and that she had been wrong in her original assessment, then stage three of his 'Pursuit System' was on.

Next time he was invited to the third floor, he accepted unhesitatingly. The other two players with Jo were top auction players and Culbertson at first suspected he had been invited out of curiosity. He was right. The other two had been keen to meet him and see him with their own eyes. Every time he made an unusual bid he noticed them exchanging meaningful glances and barely suppressed laughter behind their polite smiles. Jo remained cool and friendly throughout, amused rather than critical. Culbertson went away pleased with their second encounter.

Culbertson made a few converts to his system, though he had to admit they were mostly losers in search of a miracle cure. His main ally and partner was Julio Aceves. They played together at the Tuesday night duplicate games and won a number of substantial bets, struck against them by fellow members who were convinced Culbertson's luck must sooner or later run out. But his winnings put him ahead on the club's championship board by what was then the widest margin in the club's history. Second came Sidney Lenz. Perhaps this was the start of their later rivalry.

One evening after dinner at the club, Culbertson ran into Jo again and tried to persuade her to play his system. She still resisted his theories and remained a Whitehead follower. 'You've got a false sense of loyalty. If my methods are correct, that will only help Whitehead. I'll hand them over to him as I haven't the slightest intention of becoming a bridge writer,' he assured her, keen to win her over at any price.

But Jo was not only thinking of his system of cards. 'It isn't your ideas or your so-called system that makes you win,' she told him. 'What is it, then?' 'It's your knowledge of human nature and your card experience. You'd win with any system.' This was encouraging. She must have been watching him more closely than he imagined. At last he got her to try out his system, not at the club, but at home. She said she would give it a try and for two weeks, almost every evening, he went to her apartment and they dealt out hands together, bidding them first according to traditional auction methods and then again according to the Culbertson System. In the end, Jo was convinced, and converted to his methods. They also became fast friends, and moved on to first-name terms.

Jo was living at the time in a studio apartment which she also used for her bridge teaching. After her teaching sessions, a group of her friends used to gather, Culbertson among them. They would have cocktails and then usually go to the Beaux Arts restaurant next door. This was a legendary speakeasy run by the equally legendary Texas Guinan ('Where the hell would I be without Prohibition?') and it was to be the setting for much of their courtship. Speakeasies, following the advent of Prohibition in 1920, were in their heyday. They were usually detectable only by the tell-tale line of limousines and taxicabs parked outside, and an elaborate procedure, involving the use of passwords or special latchkeys, was required to gain admission. So plentiful were they that many New Yorkers seldom ventured elsewhere, even to the extent of measuring distances, like John O'Hara heroines, by the taxi-fares between speakeasies.

Their romance was not exactly aided by the rather sour-tasting Californian champagne that arrived under a French label, and as time went by they gradually withdrew from the noisier crowd, preferring to be on their own. As spring came and it was warm enough to be outdoors they would sit on a bench in the little park at the back of the New York Public Library on 42nd Street. Jo still could not make Culbertson out. He was such a mixture, open and generous at one moment, secretive and dogmatic at the next. Did he really mean what he was saying, or was it all done for effect? She knew he was a calculating type, always seeking the best way to play the hand, as it were; that much she could recognise. But there was another side to him that gradually became more apparent, an inner loneliness that seemed to be tied up with his Russian background and his feeling that somehow he didn't quite belong in America. She began to see more of that side of his nature when he took her to a Russian restaurant, the haunt of emigrés attempting to re-create the atmosphere of St Petersburg. Jo would listen for hours as he told her about his early experiences in Russia. Another time he took her to hear Chaliapin sing *Boris Godunov* at the Metropolitan Opera. As he talked about Russia, she began to understand how much this had shaped his contradictory personality. It was as if the Russian side, dreamy and visionary, had not yet fused with the more practical, business-like American side.

As they spent more time together, they drew closer and closer.

Culbertson, impulsive and hasty, ignoring the principles of his 'Pursuit System', took this as a sign of a fully established relationship. He was rash enough to show her his diary, partly to gain her approval, and partly to impress her with the depths of his 'soul'. It was a classic mistake and had the opposite effect from what he had intended. It only filled her with misgivings and confirmed her hidden fears that at heart he was not the marrying kind, more a restless, nomadic individual. She was afraid that if they married and set up home together, some day he would go away. For her, this fear was greater than infidelity. Culbertson had failed to notice how fragile Jo was beneath her restrained exterior. The scars of her first marriage were still with her.

Once she had read the diaries, she felt she had to speak to him. 'You're too proud, Ely, too full of strange ideas. You simply refuse to be like anyone else. How can you expect me to build a home on such pride?' She accused him of being a 'nomad at heart' who viewed women as little more than details in his life. If Culbertson was ruled by ideas more than by his heart, how could she rely on him? Set against this was her obvious attraction to him. He was a kindred spirit – determined, not afraid to go it alone. But for the moment she was overwhelmed by mistrust.

Culbertson was taken aback by her perspicacious comments. At first he tried to laugh it off and joke with her. What was marriage after all but a piece of paper? This only infuriated her the more and she threatened to call the whole thing off. 'I want to forget all about you. Please take me home.' Culbertson shrugged his shoulders and without a word did as she said. It looked like the end. He went back to his apartment and tried hard to rationalise the situation. 'She's not the woman for me,' he told himself. 'My ideal woman must follow me everywhere, regardless of consequences.' It was the first time he had gone so far as to ask anyone to marry him, and he had been turned down. He tried thinking of her as just another American girl – spoiled, like the rest of them. He plunged into playing bridge all night, and for much of the next day. In the evening he went to the Knickerbocker Whist Club, half hoping to meet her, but she did not show up. He telephoned her at home, but her mother answered, telling him she had gone to Saratoga for the races and would not be back for some time.

Crestfallen, he returned home and had dinner with his father. He knew he had not seen much of him recently and now he could, at least, try to make up for it. He tried too to put Jo out of his mind, but she kept returning. Give it another week, he told himself, and it will all have blown over. But another week passed and it only became worse. Without her his life was empty. He became fearful of losing her altogether but his pride still held him back and prevented him from getting in touch with her.

He weighed up the pros and cons. At one level he knew that much of what she had said was right. He should give up his wasteful life and settle down and earn a proper living. By marrying Jo there was every chance they could be happy, have children, and he would end up doing something worthwhile with his life. He had only to look at her to see that she was good-looking, practical, had good business sense, and might even be prepared to look after him – what more could he ask for? If the cost was merely that he had to give up some of his philandering and his obsession with nebulous political ideals, surely that was a reasonable price to pay?

Jo had gone to stay with Connie Percy and her husband in Saratoga. Connie had been a friend of Culbertson's too, so he rang her house the next morning. He learned from her, reading between the lines, that Jo had been unhappy these past few days. He asked if he could come up and stay and was thrilled when she said he could. The first night he and Jo went out for dinner to a roadhouse, where in a noisy and impersonal atmosphere they talked things over. Culbertson asked Jo whether she forgave him. He admitted his approach had been arrogant and stupid, and apologised for it. He wanted to assure her of his genuine love for her. Had she changed her mind about their getting married? She refused to commit herself, saying she needed time to convince herself that he was really different. 'Am I on probation, then?' Culbertson asked. 'There you go again, proud as always. I thought you said you had learnt a new humility.'

The week at Saratoga sped by. They managed to avoid going to the racetrack altogether, but they did play bridge one evening against Hal Sims and Charlie Downs who had come up for the races. It was during the course of this game that Culbertson first glimpsed the possibilities of himself and Jo becoming a celebrated bridge partnership. Not only did their respective temperaments seem to complement each other at the bridge table but they already had that essential ingredient to partnership success, a sixth sense or intuitive understanding of each other's bidding and play.

When they returned to New York, they thought they would put it to the test. Culbertson had run into Percy Gregg, a well-known stock-broker and bridge player from Philadelphia. Gregg liked challenge matches, and, fortuitously, also played with a woman partner; he assumed his opponents would consider him to be at a disadvantage for this reason. But the challengers, often overconfident, would be beaten and some hefty side-bets would go Gregg's way. Here then was just the sort of opportunity Culbertson was looking for. They arranged a match together – one hundred rubbers over ten sessions, stakes to be one cent a point for the ladies and ninety-nine cents for the men. Culbertson did not flinch at this. He was confident of his partnership with Jo. They went into training, practising for hours on end to perfect their technique. They knew that because of the high stakes (a dollar a point was extremely high in those days, usually reserved for only a few multi-millionaires) news of this game was bound to get around, and if they won their reputation would be made.

Gregg's partner was Mrs Lillian Peck at whose home the match was to take place. They began on a Sunday afternoon and the contrasting styles of the two sets of players soon became apparent. Gregg was a quick, incisive player and Mrs Peck, despite her nonchalant air, played a very strong game also. Jo and Ely, on the other hand, played slowly and deliberately, relying on their well-tried technique to see them through. It was the old story of professionals against amateurs, of the steady but sure against the brilliant but uncoordinated. Gregg and his partner were bold in places and then unnecessarily cautious in others.

At the end of the first session Jo and Ely were ahead. But, true to their new professionalism, they set to work as soon as the session had ended, analysing the day's hands and seeing if they could have played or bid them better, trying always to assess the percentage of luck and of skill. By the end of the sixth session, they were several thousand dollars up and looked all set to win more. The partnership of Percy Gregg and Mrs Peck was cracking up. In desperation Gregg tried to 'buy' his way out of trouble and resorted to more and more psychic bids ('that form of legitimate dishonesty' as S. J. Simon was later to term them), in the belief that he stood a better chance of fooling two opponents than one partner. But it was not to be. Matters reached a head when Mrs Peck found herself in a high redoubled spade contract looking at a dummy with minimal values in the suits bid. Rather than play the hand, she quit there and then, and the match was over.

But the other match that Culbertson wanted to win above all still eluded him. Throughout that winter, Jo kept him at arm's length. The more he pressed his attentions on her the more she resisted. She still could not be sure of him, sure that she could really trust him. Then in the middle of April 1923 he had to go into hospital for an operation. It was his stomach ulcers playing up, an indication of the nervous strain he had really been under. Jo came to visit him. The shock of seeing him ill and vulnerable and his obvious sincerity in talking to her changed her view of him. As he convalesced in hospital after his operation, she began to understand him better and see that many of his traits, his contrariness and obstinacy, concealed a kinder, gentler side, and many of her fears were removed.

She finally relented and agreed to marry him. They went to see Father Duffy of the Holy Cross Church on West 42nd Street (Jo was a Roman Catholic) and asked him to perform the ceremony. On the night before their wedding they worked out that all they had to start married life with was $50, but in some strange way they relished the challenge of having it all to make. Neither of them would have welcomed a helping hand. They too were linked to the American Dream. They were married on 11 June 1923, by Father Duffy, with Culbertson's father as best man. The only others present were Jo's parents and Connie Percy. After the service they went back to Jo's home for a brief celebration and on the way there in the taxi, Culbertson, not generally given to romantic display, gave Jo a small jewelled box and told her, 'JoJotte, some day I'll make you the happiest woman in the world.' Their honeymoon was twenty-four hours at a hotel at Long Beach – all they could afford as the Gregg match winnings had by now been used up.

Many of Jo's old friends were shocked to hear of her marriage. Culbertson was still an outsider to most of them, and something of an unknown quantity. Few of them could make him out and they were sure the marriage would not last. Whitehead and his Knickerbocker circle were sorry to see her go. They had grown used to her presence, and thought of her as one of them. But just as few knew what Culbertson was like, few probably appreciated the unconventional streak in Jo. From an early age she had struck out on her own. Rather than stick to the traditional areas of work for women, she had taken up competitive bridge, very much a male-dominated world. It was this side of her that was attracted to Culbertson. She sensed in him another unusual, unconventional personality, with whom she could continue along the same path.

But however promising the future, they still had to earn a living. They discussed it together. Jo planned to go on with her bridge teaching for which she had built up quite a clientele and the reputation of being one of New York's best teachers. Jo was keen for Culbertson to write a book putting his bridge ideas into print. After all, he had always claimed he wanted to be a writer. But for the moment he thought he could rely on his gambling to earn them a living. They were young and there seemed to be no hurry.

Rather than confine himself to the five-cents game at the Knickerbocker, Culbertson, with his eye for the main chance, decided to look for something bigger. Through the offices of a friend of his from Paris, Walbridge Taft, the son of former President Taft, he got a letter of introduction to the Whist Club on East 38th Street and was elected a member. This was a very exclusive club, the haunt of bankers, Wall Street brokers and other wealthy businessmen. It was here that he first got to know Charles M. Schwab, President of Bethlehem Steel Corporation, who was later to play an important role in his bridge life. Joseph Elwell had been a member there too before his mysterious murder in 1920. The stakes were high, usually fifty cents a point, or even higher. Wins and losses could run into several thousand dollars a night. But the members enjoyed their bridge in much the same way as they enjoyed bringing off a successful coup at business. They were mostly rugged individualists, who had little time for systems but preferred to rely on their formidable bargaining powers as they strove to reach an optimum contract. It was bridge all right, but of a sort that even Culbertson had not encountered before – full of inconsistencies, brilliant and inspired one moment, calamitous the next.

Like many wealthy men, the members often welcomed the chance to play with an expert, and were happy to pay for the facility. They all knew bridge was Culbertson's sole source of income, while he, in return, repaid them by explaining what he saw as some of the finer points of the game. It was not long before he notched up big winnings as his own methods and his reliance on the early formulations of his Approach System began to pay off. He was able to sail along, as he put it, 'with all sails unfurled in a stiff distributional breeze'. Indeed, a bridge colleague and well-known writer on bridge, R. F. Foster, wrote a series of articles for *Vanity Fair* at this time describing some of his 'magnificent plays' and giving him the title of Mr Culbertson Gettritzki.

In July 1923 he and Jo rented a big, sprawling house on the shores of Lake Mount Arab in the Adirondacks. It was a delayed honeymoon and they were blissfully happy swimming in the lake and walking through the woods.

In September they returned to New York and rented a small apartment on West 55th Street, opposite the Gotham Hotel. The furnishing of this new apartment, their first home together, depended mainly on Culbertson's fluctuating winnings at bridge. But now that they were married they were content to lead an easy-going, relaxed life.

Then Culbertson encountered one of those prolonged runs of bad luck at cards that are an inseparable part of a gambler's life. It seemed never to go away and they even had to pawn some of their valuables and borrow money from friends to keep going. He was forced to leave the high-stake game at the Whist Club and go back to the five-cent tables at the Knickerbocker Whist Club. It was the second winter of their marriage and life became difficult. In the spring of 1925 this culminated in a physical collapse. Culbertson's stomach ulcers were playing up again. They could not afford proper medical treatment or advice. Culbertson was determined to go on playing but it soon became apparent to both of them that what someone of his highly strung temperament needed was complete rest.

At that point his luck turned and on one day he won $350. It was enough for them to put the furniture into store, pay off the back rent – Jo's own earnings helped here – and leave New York. Their destination was Mount Arab, the spot where they had had such an idyllic summer two years previously. This time they decided to rent a small log cabin for $40 per month. They planned to spend three months there and calculated that they had $200 to buy food, pay for medical expenses and whatever else they might need for day-to-day living. The cabin was by no means luxurious, but it suited their purpose. While they were there they celebrated their second wedding anniversary. All they could muster were some wild flowers plus two volumes of Dostoevsky and Anatole France that Ely had bought in a second-hand bookshop in New York.

The remoteness and seclusion of Mount Arab gave Ely plenty of time to reflect. He would sit for hours on the porch turning things over in his mind. He knew he had been forcing the pace too much, spending too long at the card table, to the exclusion of all else. He would lapse into deep reverie. Jo would do her best to snap him out of these moods. Reassured by Jo's faith in him, Culbertson pronounced that he would become the agent of his own cure. He had devised a 'Culbertson System of Self-Cure'. This entailed changing direction, not so much in their way of life but by what he termed 'psychic rest', exchanging the humdrum, day-to-day worries of making a living playing cards for other, more intellectual preoccupations with what he saw as the destiny of America and the mysterious forces arising in Europe.

By September he felt well again, his stomach pains had virtually ceased and he felt refreshed and mentally invigorated. It was Jo's turn to fall ill. She had borne the main burden of his illness all through the summer and now found herself with excruciating abdominal pain. At first she laughed it off and claimed that they were sympathetic pains, caused by trying to share some of his illness. But on the evening of Labour Day, Jo suddenly collapsed while washing dishes. She passed out for a full ten to fifteen minutes, and when she regained consciousness it was clear she was in considerable pain. Culbertson was in a panic. There was no telephone in the house, so he had no choice but to leave Jo and paddle across the lake to their nearest neighbour's house, where fortunately there was a telephone and a doctor could be summoned within minutes.

The doctor made a quick examination of her and recommended that she go straight away to New York to see a specialist – there was a train leaving in an hour that they could catch. Jo was feeling very weak so they rigged up a stretcher to take her to the station. Meanwhile Culbertson had got in touch with Connie Percy to ask her to contact a gynaecologist and prepare for Jo's arrival.

Doctors had told Jo before her marriage that it would be difficult for her to have children, but she had wanted to try all the same. It was a fifty-fifty chance, and to her mind that was 'as good as a finesse'. But this time it had not come off. She had had a miscarriage. When they arrived at the Roosevelt Hospital in New York, the doctors told Culbertson her condition was very serious. She would have to have an immediate operation and the result of it would not be known until she came out of the anaesthetic later that evening. In the meantime the doctor told Culbertson he would only be in the way if he stayed. Ely went straight to the Knickerbocker Whist Club. The other players were glad to see him and commented on his fine tan. 'You want to play?' 'That's what I'm here for.' His only thought was of the hospital expenses.

He played all that afternoon, had his dinner brought on a tray alongside the table, and continued into the night. He played as hard and as effectively as he had ever played. From time to time he went to the telephone to enquire about Jo. The hospital told him she would not come round until after midnight. He went on playing. That afternoon had been the low point of his and Jo's life. Now the tide was turning. When he rang the hospital after midnight and learnt that she was all right, he knew his presentiment had been correct.

It had been a salutary lesson for Ely. Here was his wife prepared to risk her life on their behalf and all he was doing was living in the vague expectancy that one day he might become a writer or an expert on social systems in line with his student days in Paris. So far he had failed to give her the stability and way of life he had originally promised. For the first time he really began to look hard at what a card player's life was about, particularly now that he could see it through another person's eyes. Its constant ups and downs, hopes and confusions, were hardly the basis for a constructive future. He should listen more to Jo, remember what she said about giving up gambling, and become a bridge teacher like her. Then he could make a decent living, and give her the security and happiness she deserved.

But the pull of the gambler was still strong, at times dominating all else, and somewhere at the back of his mind there remained his long-held resistance to a bourgeois existence. He decided to give himself another six months of professional card playing and see if he could accumulate some capital. At the same time he set about becoming a teacher of auction bridge, getting a business card printed: Mr Ely Culbertson, Bridge Instructor. He deliberately omitted his address on 55th Street, as the area was full of speakeasies and had acquired a slightly unsavoury reputation. In bridge circles, his plan was to set himself up as a sort of *éminence grise*, with a view to building up a behind-the-scenes reputation. It was a long-term strategy that, if it worked well, could provide them with financial security. He collaborated with George Reith, Chairman of the Card Committee of the Knickerbocker Whist Club, on his book *The Art of Successful Bidding*. Reith was much taken with Culbertson's Approach System.

All this was beginning to have its effect. Rumours began to spread about the mysterious Culbertson who was responsible for new and promising developments in bridge. Close associates of his and Jo's pressed him to write a book himself, in order to capitalise on his growing reputation. But he wanted to wait. Putting out a book at that moment would simply make it one among many others, all competing for the same narrow market, whereas if he waited for the time when a bridge-confused public really needed a definitive text, he stood a greater chance of success.

Initially he had developed his system mostly for his and Jo's use in their own competitive bridge games. Now he thought of how to make it appeal to the average club or social player. A learner can only take in so much at a time, he realised. It needed clear step-by-step presentation and simplified rules. The next step was to establish Jo and himself as top tournament players. Without tournament success, no one was going to take his system seriously. Jo and he began to enter for pairs events, and even take on challenge matches, but the real test for both him and his system would be in a team-of-four tournament.

Culbertson versus Lenz

BRIDGE BATTLE OF THE CENTURY

The biggest test and most decisive moment of Culbertson's bridge career was the Lenz match. Here he took on the old guard of contract bridge, feeling convinced now that his success in the tournament field, using his Approach Forcing System as described in his best-selling *Blue Book*, would lead him to victory. Twelve eminent bridge authorities were ranged against him for the beginning of the 'War of the Systems' that was to dominate the bridge scene from July 1931 until February 1932.

Culbertson welcomed the challenge. Firstly he had enough evidence to show that the American bridge-playing public liked his system and would go on buying it – the survey he had carried out showed that eighty-four per cent of the public were now pro-Culbertson. His books were selling fast, and there seemed no reason why they should not go on doing so. A 'War of the Systems' was bound to engender a great deal of publicity and, handled right, it could work in his favour. Much depended on the way he presented his case. Culbertson had a gift for having his finger on the public pulse. It was the era of the 'New Deal' and the old order was being challenged, so the public was likely to side with him as the upstart raising his voice against entrenched authorities. He would depict himself as David challenging the Goliath of the bridge establishment, the lone fighter who pits himself against the mighty giants of authority and government.

His opponents were Bridge Headquarters, represented by Milton Work, Wilbur Whitehead, Sidney Lenz, George Reith, E. V. Shepard, Commander Liggett and Shepard Barclay from New York; Charles Adams from Chicago; Walter Wyman from Boston; and Edward Wolfe and Henry Jaeger from Cleveland. The twelve of them had banded together 'in the best interests of the American public' in order to standardise contract bridge on an 'official' basis and to promulgate a new system that would be understood by all. A printed version of their

Official System was issued. The Official System was really a hotchpotch of different systems, the main component being the one-two-three sequence of opening bids: 'If you have a small hand, bid one. For an intermediate hand, requiring help from partner, bid two. For a sure game, bid three.' It included a 4-3-2-1 point count (a contribution from Milton Work) and an artificial two club bid.

As he looked at a copy of the new system, Culbertson had to admit that it presented a bigger threat than he had at first anticipated. The public were bound to be impressed by it. It looked official and had an authoritative ring to it. 'We knew,' he later wrote, 'the time had come for the biggest fight of our lives. To all appearances we were on top of the world; only Jo and I realised how shaky our position really was. We were still ephemeral little bridge gods, playthings of public fancy to be pulled down tomorrow and forgotten the day after tomorrow. We had made our bid – and it was a forcing bid – but arrayed against us were the most formidable and most intelligent bridge authorities, who had been in the field for years. Even Jo's first teacher, Sidney Lenz, was in the enemy camp.'

But Culbertson was a fighter and his plan was to give his side the advantage. 'Always attack' had been his policy at the card table. Now was his chance to do so again. He had to act fast and decisively. His simple but audacious plan was to invite the other side to a challenge match with each side playing its own system. By doing this he was robbing them of the initiative, turning them into the hunted and making himself the hunter.

He quickly put an announcement to this effect in the *Herald Tribune* on 24 June:

BRIDGE EXPERT SUPPORTS CHALLENGE WITH $10,000

Culbertson Offers to Meet Group That Has New Bidding System

Ely Culbertson, bridge expert, pitted against twelve other masters of the game who have merged to found a uniform system of bidding, announced yesterday that he had placed $10,000 in a bank to cover a challenge made by him to the other group to play two hundred rubbers of bridge. He and Mrs Culbertson challenge any four members of the other group to a bridge match, the losings and winnings to go as a donation to the New York Infirmary.

Culbertson's $10,000 would be pitted against only $1,000 of the group, according to the terms. If only two members of the group wished to play, the odds will be only $5,000 to $1,000.

Now he could sit back and wait for their reply. He guessed it would catch them on the hop as they wouldn't have been expecting a move like this so soon. His 'challenge' was met by a deafening silence. Time now for his second line of attack, a specific challenge to Sidney Lenz, their leading player. He broadcast this on NBC's Station WJZ. Lenz, he said, could choose whoever he wanted as partner. Behind this seemingly open-handed and generous offer lay a well-thought-out stratagem. He knew that Lenz was likely to turn down the challenge if it stipulated that he had to play with another member of the Bridge Headquarters as his partner. By widening the choice to anyone, he was pre-empting this and making it very hard for him to refuse. He repeated the terms of the match, two hundred rubbers for a stake of his $5,000 to their $1,000, the winnings to go to the New York Infirmary for Women and Children.

Culbertson waited to see what sort of reply this would elicit. Meanwhile, having *The Bridge World* at his disposal, he thought he would indulge in a little gentle humour at Bridge Headquarters' expense. The July issue included a section entitled 'From the War Front' with these 'Decoded Telegrams from our Intelligence Department':

BROOKSVILLE, PENNA

BRIDGE HEADQUARTERS
NEW YORK, NY PAID

SHIP AT ONCE ONE GROSS BRIDGE PENCILS
EMBOSSED IN GOLD
OFFICIAL SYSTEM WON SIXTY-NINE DOLLARS VERSUS
CULBERTSON SYSTEM
(SIGNED) A. DUBB

BROOKSVILLE, PENNA

BRIDGE HEADQUARTERS
NEW YORK, NY COLLECT

PLAYED AGAIN – CANCEL ORDER
(SIGNED) A. DUBB

Culbertson used practically every opportunity to have a dig at the group. On the radio, Station WJZ again, where he had an estimated one million listeners, he compared the Official System to a cooking recipe as follows:

> Put five pages Work's common sense in a pan. Add thirty-five cents' worth advice to dubs and stir well. Add seventeen pages of Lenz' *ein, zwei, drei* after mixing with Reith's one-under-one forcing. Season with Shepard's mathematical formula. Boil down gently. When finished serve in small portions.

For all its corniness this method worked. It was all part of his plan to get the public on his side. By using his radio talks to confide in them, and depict the other side as old fogies, he could infiltrate himself into their homes.

> Being a bridge doctor (which incidentally is a dog's life) I am often awakened by long-distance calls from my suffering bridge patients who get a violent attack of slamitis or a vulnerable rash. Perhaps the Depression has something to do with it – for all my answers are free. The only thing I ask of my listeners or readers is please to limit their questions to bridge. Only the other day for instance I received a letter addressed 'Air Mail, Special Delivery, Urgent, Personal Attention Mr Ely Culbertson'. With some trepidation I opened the letter. I read the following: 'Dear Mr Culbertson, I am the fiancée of a young Prince Charming who is perfect in all respects except one. Yesterday, while playing bridge against him, I unfortunately revoked. He called a penalty for a revoke. Do you think that under the circumstances I should marry him?' A delicate problem ...

Just as the 'War of the Systems' seemed to be hotting up, Culbertson was forced to leave on a trip to Europe. He felt, though, that he had done enough for the moment. The ball was firmly in the other side's court. He and Jo went to Naples, Capri, Rome, Florence, Venice, Milan, and thence by train to Warsaw; from Warsaw to Kiev, then a change of train to Dnepropetrovsk in the Ukraine where they visited an old friend, Colonel Hugh Cooper, who was in charge of building the massive dam there, and finally on down to Sebastopol and to Yalta on the Black Sea before crossing to Novorossisk. Culbertson was back in his beloved Caucasus for the first time for twenty-five years, and what he saw shocked him. The people were downcast and depressed, ill-shod and poorly fed.

He had last left Russia as a youthful university student, his head full of radical ideas, to study in Europe. His father, an American from Titusville, Pennsylvania, had originally gone out to the Caucasus in the early 1880s after oil was discovered there. He had struck lucky, found oil and married a local Georgian. His family, including Ely, his second son, was brought up in affluent surroundings. The Russia Ely now saw was different. Back then, after the 1917 revolution, his family had lost most of its money as the Caucasian oilfields were quickly appropriated by the Bolsheviks, his father miscalculating in his belief that the Bolshevik uprising would not last. Ely was in Europe at the time and had to cut back on his expenditure. Once the First World War was over, he made use of his American passport to join the influx of new European immigrants arriving in America. In Europe he had played cards regularly and knew enough about them to earn his living from them once he had set foot in America at the beginning of the 1920s.

Now after the Crimea, the Culbertsons moved on to Moscow. At the Hotel Metropole they received noticeably better food and accommodation, and Jo enjoyed the sightseeing. They had one or two friends to visit in Moscow, among them the newspaper correspondent, Walter Duranty, author of several books on Russia. But Culbertson's main purpose in Moscow was to visit the Russian Card Trust. He had his own five-year plan for the Soviet government to consider. Why not, he told the Director, introduce contract bridge into Russia? It might take five years to get established, but it could run alongside the current five-year work-plan and it could prove an excellent means of psychological relaxation for the Soviet workers. Culbertson offered to translate his *Blue Book* free of charge, organise teachers where necessary and even do a little inconspicuous sales promotion. The net result for the Russian Card Trust would clearly be a tenfold increase in the sale of playing cards.

The Director of the Trust looked at him for a few moments and then quietly said, 'Mr Culbertson, you do not seem to understand the purpose of our Card Trust. Our aim is not to sell as many cards as possible, but as few as we can. Cards remind our workers of the old days of kings and queens and bourgeois society. All the people you see here in this office are trying to restrict the sale of playing cards not increase them.' Undaunted, he suggested that, since the Soviet government objected to kings and queens, the difficulty could be overcome by calling the ace of spades 'Lenin'. But by then the Director was gently ushering him out of the door.

By 18 September 1933 the Culbertsons were back in New York and back into the intricacies of the 'War of the Systems' with Bridge Headquarters. Asked by reporters on the quayside for his comments on the Official System, Ely categorised it as 'eighty per cent Culbertson, twelve per cent Work and Lenz, and eight per cent rubbish'.

Culbertson was itching to get back into the struggle. There had been no reply from Lenz to the challenge he had issued in the summer. He got one instead from Damon Runyon who chipped in and offered to play him with a team of Broadwayites for five dollars a point, but on closer inspection it looked like the outcome of a late night at Mindy's. To keep the ball rolling, Culbertson summoned newspaper reporters and told them, 'They call me a gigolo; they treat me like a suspicious Russian; but when I issue a challenge, for the benefit of a charity, no one says a word ... Moreover Mr Lenz probably will not accept the challenge, and if he does, the match will probably never take place. Mr Lenz's reputation is only based on tops in whist, and articles written by him in which he is the hero.'

The more pressure he put on Lenz, the harder it would be for him to back down. Culbertson knew that he had to 'get Lenz's goat', needle him to the point where it became a question of honour for him to accept. Lenz was a rich man who played cards for enjoyment and interest rather than monetary gain. He once turned down an offer of $1,000 for a single bridge lesson saying he did not have time. In fact, he had already made it widely known that he refused to play card games for high stakes. This was because of his special skill as a magician and his famed ability to deal seconds. He did not want the opposition to suspect he had an unfair advantage. He was the first amateur to be elected an honorary member of the American Society of Magicians. Houdini, a close friend, often stated how relieved he was that Lenz never turned professional.

Sidney Lenz was born in Chicago in 1873 but brought up in Vienna, from where his family originally came. Returning to the USA as a young man he entered the timber business in Michigan and was so successful in pulling off a series of spectacular coups that by the age of twenty-seven he was rich enough to retire. He decided to take a trip around the world and spent a year in India studying Hindu magic, oriental philosophy and, presumably, the Indian rope-trick. Back in the United States, he became a man of leisure and devoted himself mainly to sport, at which he excelled. He played tennis against 'Little Bill' Johnston to an almost equal standard, he was a scratch golfer who later 'shot his age' at sixty-nine. At bowls he once held the national record of an average of 244 points for twenty-one consecutive games. He was a table-tennis champion and he regularly played chess with José Capablanca.

But it was cards that really interested him and many considered him the finest auction bridge player of his era. By the mid-1930s he had won so many trophies, cups and medals that he had a special cabinet built to display them in his bachelor apartment at 240 West End Avenue in New York. He was a prolific writer, noted for his classic book *Lenz on Bridge* (1926). He was a wit and well-known raconteur, though this was not always apparent in his dealings with Culbertson. He introduced the term 'squeeze' into bridge, borrowing it from baseball, and many of the better-known plays at bridge, which have since become standard technique, were introduced by him, though none bears his name. In later years he became known as the 'Grand Old Man of Bridge' and was often asked to act as honorary referee at tournament matches. He lived, like so many other bridge 'greats', to a ripe old age, dying in 1960 at the age of eighty-seven.

The Culbertsons were well aware of his versatility. Lenz had been one of Jo's first teachers. Because he was such a skilled player the match was bound to be a true test of systems. Culbertson's confidence in their ability to win was greater than Jo's. She wondered whether they had not taken on too much. He sought to convince her by a 'scientific' argument based on his reading of the laws of probability. He brought out sheets of paper covered with his calculations. He had gone through a series of hands, scoring them according to the Official System and the Culbertson System. Supposing the average rubber was 1,000 points, his calculations showed that the Culbertson System was seven per cent better than the Official one. That was seventy points per rubber. Jo rightly pointed out that they might get a run of bad cards. But Culbertson had taken that into account as well. The variation of luck in cards worked out at about four per cent over a lengthy period, such as the 150 rubbers they were now intending to play. That still gave them a margin of three per cent in their favour – enough to be a winning one. In point of fact, when the match was played Culbertson's predictions on the run of the cards were right and both sides had more or less equal holdings of good cards.

A great deal depended on this match. It was make or break. Either they would be ruined and fade into obscurity, or they would triumph and be recognised as the number one team at contract bridge and be able to control the development of the game from then on.

On 19 October news came through that Lenz had at last accepted the challenge, 'with all the reluctance of a small boy whose parents have told him not to fight unless he has to', as one newspaperman put it. He hated being 'used' by Culbertson. He deposited a cheque for $1,000 with his publishers, Simon and Schuster, and nominated Oswald Jacoby as his playing partner. Here then were a trio of men and one woman, about to embark on the 'Battle of the Century'.

Oswald Jacoby was a relative newcomer. Then aged twenty-nine, a Brooklyner by birth, he had been to high school at Erasmus Hall in the old Flatbush part of Brooklyn. At the age of fifteen he was already showing signs of his prodigious memory for figures – he was captain of both the chess team and the maths club. After school he went to Columbia University but quit after two years to become an actuary. He joined Metropolitan Life and became, at twenty-two, the youngest actuary to qualify. Indeed, so well did he do out of his actuarial business that he was able to retire six years later in 1928, thinking he had enough money to last him for the rest of his life. But the Wall Street Crash put paid to that and he was forced back into work.

He first got into serious bridge in 1926 when he went to play at the Knickerbocker Whist Club with Dr William Lamb, the principal of Brooklyn High School, in the Thursday night duplicate game. It was the first time he had played duplicate, but despite the presence of some of the auction bridge 'greats', such as Whitehead, Lenz and so on, they won. He went back again the next week with a lawyer friend, Fred Payne. They found themselves playing in a different section, among unfamiliar faces. Jacoby asked the tournament director George Reith why they were not playing in the first section again since they had won last week. Reith told him this *was* the first section. At the tables were Culbertson, Sims, von Zedtwitz and so on. Jacoby recalled that Sims watched him play a series of hands in this tournament and, when a group of them went out to eat afterwards, told him that he was the best natural player he had ever seen. It was the beginning of a long friendship and Jacoby was indebted to Sims for the way he helped him to better his game in the early stages.

Jacoby first played contract in 1928 when he was in Palm Beach. He was invited to the house of Jules Bache, a well-known stockbroker, whose daughter insisted on playing the new game of contract. From that moment on Jacoby was taken by the possibilities of the game. His first introduction to tournament contract came in 1929 through George Reith, who rang him up and asked him to be his partner for the first Goldman Pairs event held at the Eastern Championships, of which Reith was in charge. They won and from then on Jacoby's reputation grew.

Lenz and Jacoby had never played in a tournament together but they had practised in private. When their partnership was announced, Culbertson immediately warned his *Bridge World* readers that Jacoby suffered from a 'chronic weakness for the so-called psychic bid'. It was an essential part of Jacoby's armoury, as he himself admitted. Culbertson called the psychic the 'boomerang' of bridge: 'Thrown accurately at the enemy, it produces havoc in their ranks, but, should it go wide of the mark, it returns, frequently causing even more damage to one's own side.' Lenz was to understand the full import of this remark during the match in which Jacoby made thirteen psychic bids in all, one or two leading to severe partnership misunderstanding at crucial points. The term 'psychic' had been invented by Dorothy Sims back in 1923 to indicate a bid that was short on playing strength but might confuse the opposition.

The terms of the agreement for the match were drawn up and signed by Culbertson and Lenz on 14 November with some of the razzmatazz normally reserved for champion boxers. Each of the main contestants must play at least seventy-five of the one hundred and fifty rubbers with their principal partner – Culbertson with Jo, Lenz with Jacoby. Play was to start on Monday, 7 December, and thereafter four sessions per week were to be played, preferably on Monday, Tuesday, Thursday and Saturday nights. Each session was of eight rubbers, starting at 8 p.m. and the last rubber had to be commenced before 12.30 a.m. The match would begin at the Chatham Hotel on 48th Street, where the Culbertsons had their apartment, and continue at the Waldorf-Astoria. Lenz nominated Fred Rogan as official referee, Culbertson nominated Ralph Liebenderfer as his, and Lieutenant Alfred Gruenther was agreed as the third official referee and was, in fact, to become the acting referee.

Gruenther was then aged thirty-two and on the teaching staff at West Point. He had to be on parade at 8 a.m. each morning following the bridge session, which seldom ended before 1 a.m. His wife drove him back while he slept on the back seat. He was a first-rate tournament director, his firmness and tact being qualities that underlay his subsequent distinguished career as a general during the Second World War. He became a close friend of General Eisenhower. Indeed, it was rumoured they played bridge together on the night of the North African landings. After the war, as Chief of Staff at NATO and then Supreme Allied Commander of SHAPE, Gruenther kept up his bridge interests via the ACBL and the Laws Commission. He was the author of several books on bridge, notably *Duplicate Bridge Simplified* (1931) and *Duplicate Bridge Complete* (1933).

As soon as the agreement was signed Culbertson posted his cheque for $5,000 destined, if he lost, for the Unemployment Relief Fund (Lenz's nominated charity). If he won, the New York Infirmary for Women and Children would be $1,000 the richer. He now started orchestrating his publicity campaign. The agreement had foreseen extensive coverage by the press and radio. Culbertson already had many contacts in this field, notably Deac Aylesworth, President of NBC, and he sought to capitalise on these. Through Aylesworth, he went to see Jack Wheeler, President of the Bell newspaper syndicate, to discuss their coverage of the match. Discovering that Wheeler himself was not a bridge player but might like to learn the game, Culbertson suggested that he got together with a group of his friends and associates and Culbertson would teach them himself. Flattered at this offer from the 'master', Wheeler rounded up a small group of extremely influential media personalities: Bruce Barton, of the Batten, Barton, Durstine and Osborne advertising agency; Frank Crowninshield, editor of *Vanity Fair*; Kent Cooper, general manager of Associated Press; Grantland Rice, newspaper columnist; Sumner Blossom, editor of *American Magazine*; and Deac Aylesworth. They played a regular weekly bridge game at different venues, usually at the home of one of the participants, with Culbertson there as mentor. Their various reporters and other representatives can hardly have failed to notice the boss's friendship with Culbertson.

His pre-match publicity campaign concentrated on the same themes as before – Jo and he were depicted as the young couple taking on the forces of parental oppression in the guise of the twelve jealous elders of Bridge Headquarters. It was, he claimed, a grudge match with the two giants of bridge locked in gladiatorial combat. Out of all this the public stood to gain by being able eventually to choose their 'winning' system.

Soon, the match was a topic of conversation at most bridge tables and many non-bridge dinner tables besides, long before it actually took place. An atmosphere of tense expectancy had been created. Three weeks before the date set, Culbertson knew the match had generated enough interest to be 'one of the biggest publicity tidal waves in the history of sport'.

Wires and cables for newspapers all over the world were laid right into their apartment. Associated Press assigned two of their first-rank men to the match, and prepared for a play-by-play coverage. Later Western Union and Postal Telegraph each took over one of the spare rooms for their exclusive use. They had six employees on practically twenty-four-hour duty whose function was to relay a blow-by-blow account of the match to the waiting world outside.

Culbertson took as much trouble over the arrangements within the Chatham Hotel as he did outside. The apartment, on the tenth floor, had ten rooms leading off a long central corridor. The décor was appropriately rose-coloured, and every room was to be used for the match with one exception – this was the bedroom where their two children, Nadya nearly four and Ely Bruce aged two and a half, slept. Their lives, too, had to fit in round their parents' busy bridge schedule. At night while the match was in progress a notice was hung on their door: 'Children Sleeping and Dreaming' – an unmistakably Culbertson touch.

The night before the match started, Jo suddenly became apprehensive. She wondered how Culbertson would stand up to the strain of playing the hardest match of his life as well as doing all the other things he had contracted to do – writing his article, annotating the hands after play and giving the stream of interviews and talks on the radio that were to go with it. 'Don't worry,' Culbertson told her. 'I'm at my best like this.' He was right. Like many whose temperament swings between elation and despondency, Culbertson, once he had set his mind to something, was unstoppable and thrived on bouts of intense activity.

Culbertson did not stint on his hospitality. At the best of times he was a lavish spender with little regard for money, as his creditors and most of his office employees discovered, and he was always punctilious about paying his gambling debts. Oswald Jacoby recalled how he had bet him in 1936 that Roosevelt would be returned with a landslide majority in the election and was surprised to find his cheque waiting for him the next morning. The Russian in Culbertson liked to display largesse and as a host he was effusive and flamboyant. He also knew that nothing sharpened the quills of visiting pressmen more than the sight of attractive food and drink. The press were given their own room by the entrance of the apartment.

Play was to take place in the main room of their apartment, the large drawing-room at the end of the corridor. Guarding the entrance, like Cerberus, as someone commented, was Lewis Copeland. Visitors were by invitation only and absolute silence had to be maintained in the playing area. About fifteen spectators at a time could enter the room and sit on chairs on one side. Then in turn they would get up to peek at the play. Culbertson had erected two large leather screens in the middle of the room with inch-wide cracks in them. Through these, spectators could get a glimpse of the actual play. Not much could be seen, but Culbertson knew exactly what he was doing. The fact that only four spectators could see through the screens at any one time and that no spectator could remain in the end room for longer than fifteen minutes only stimulated interest and the sense of exclusivity. The queues to get into the room were continuous, though people did pause briefly to sample the rival attractions of the corridor buffet table. Eminent visitors to the match included such dignitaries as Charles Schwab, Judges Freschi and Corrigan, Henry Taft, the Grand Duchess Marie of Russia, Chico Marx, Mr and Mrs Marshall Field III, Mrs Vincent Astor, Franklin P. Adams, as well as sundry presidents of banks, generals, bishops even, movie-stars and society figures. It became, to use Culbertson's term, 'the Greatest Peep-show in History'.

The preliminaries before the match on the Monday evening were hectic. Five hours before the first hand was dealt the Culbertson drawing-room was a seething mass of cameras, radio microphones, Kleig lights, sound-newsreel apparatus, photographers, reporters and the usual uninvited kibitzers. Cameramen were trying to photograph the players in groups and individually. Culbertson and Lenz were asked to pose under the glare of lights, first to smile at each other and then to scowl. Next a microphone was thrust in front of them. They had to wish each other the best of luck, and then to hope that the other would hold nothing but Yarboroughs throughout the match.

The match was to be preceded by a dinner. At 7 p.m. Culbertson finally made his appearance, having kept everyone waiting for an hour – not for the only time in the match. Lenz had meanwhile sat down to a game of cut-throat with Frank Crowninshield and Bruce Barton. The bidding over, it was Lenz's turn to play. He put down what seemed at first to be the ten of spades but it changed right in front of the players to the ace. Barton jumped up from the table, threw down a ten-dollar bill and said, 'That's enough for me.' Eventually the players, referees and about forty distinguished guests, all in formal attire, sat down to a sumptuous eight-course dinner, interrupted at regular intervals by radio interviews. During one of these, Culbertson recited a little doggerel he had made up about 'All the Lenz aces and all the Lenz kings'. Lenz, a vegetarian, looked on and took another swallow of spinach. The Culbertson babies, 'Fifi' Joyce and 'JumpBid' Bruce, emerged unexpectedly from their adjacent room clad in blue satin nighties and had to be led back to bed. Jo, wearing a blue taffeta evening gown with an elaborate corsage of orchids, then had her say on the radio. She felt her selection as her husband's partner was a 'direct compliment to the millions of women bridge players', and the many thousands of women listeners immediately took her side; Culbertson's central strategy in holding this match in his home was paying off. Other married couples would identify and side with his and Jo's progress.

Finally, two hours late at 10 p.m., the players withdrew to the playing area. A notice was hung up above the table proclaiming 'Absolute Silence'. The room was cleared of all extraneous persons and Alfred Gruenther, in his uniform of the United States Military Academy with its gold epaulettes and red stripes, broke out a new deck of cards, spread them on the specially made table with its inlaid ashtrays, and announced that Hand No. 1, Rubber No. 1, of the historic match was about to be played.

In the press room, reporters waited with bated breath. The *America Mercury* correspondent described the scene:

> After minutes of unbearable suspense, the first messenger burst forth, panting and breathless with the world-shaking communiqué: Mr Lenz wins the cut and sits down in the North seat. The first words of the match were spoken by Mrs Culbertson.

They are 'Where do you wish to sit, Ely?' Telegraph instruments start flashing this piece of news to the farthest outposts of civilisation. Copyists, scribbling frantically, distributed copies of the hands to the throngs milling about in the corridors and lobby. In the room set aside for the working press, reporters phoned in the news. Hot upon the heels of the first message came another: Mr Lenz and Mr Jacoby get the contract on the first hand at three no trumps. Pause. They are set one trick. Later the communiqué runs: Flash! Mr Lenz and Mr Jacoby win the first rubber amid some of the most terrible bridge ever played by experts.

It was true. The effects of the bibulous dinner undoubtedly influenced the first few hands of the contest. Take the fourth hand played:

North-South vulnerable
Dealer East, No score

Jacoby
♠ Q J
♥ K 2
♦ K 8 7
♣ K Q 7 6 5 3

Jo
♠ 10 7 2
♥ J 10 8 7 6 5
♦ J
♣ A J 2

Culbertson
♠ K 9 8 5 4 3
♥ 9 4 3
♦ 5 4
♣ 10 8

N / W E / S

Lenz
♠ A 6
♥ A Q
♦ A Q 10 9 6 3 2
♣ 9 4

The bidding:

South	*West*	*North*	*East*
			Pass
2♦	Pass	3♣	Pass
3NT	Pass	4NT	Pass
Pass	Pass		

As he looked at the dummy, Lenz could see there was an easy slam in diamonds so he began to play the hand as if that was the contract, leading out the side suits first. He was set two tricks by West's hearts.

'I'm sorry, Jo,' Lenz said. Then, blushing, he realised his error. 'I mean Ely,' he tried to correct himself. 'I wouldn't be surprised,' said his partner, 'if in the final analysis, when all is said and done, you mean me.'

Two days later, at a dinner reception for fellow members of the Knickerbocker Whist Club at their new club rooms at 47 East 47th Street, Lenz again referred to this hand and jokingly remarked that he had made a small slam in diamonds, but had been set two tricks at four no trumps. For Jacoby this was an early warning of the difficulties to come, showing Lenz's predilection for no trumps rather than suit bidding. Jacoby had no idea his four no trump bid was going to be left in by Lenz. It was one of the weaknesses of the Official System that a player was always fearful of the bidding stopping short of game, even after an original two bid, hence the quick exit into no trumps.

Due to the lateness of the start only three rubbers were played on the first night. Lenz and Jacoby, holding first-rate cards but missing a couple of slams, won all of them and were 1,715 points ahead. As the second session started, Culbertson discovered that Jacoby still had not placed any bets on the match. Odds of two to one were immediately offered and Jacoby snapped these up to the tune of $1,000 to $500. Culbertson was just about to repeat the offer when Lenz intervened testily, 'Let's get going.' Culbertson next hung a wishbone over the bridge-lamp. It made little difference. They still ended the session 2,075 points behind. The cards were clearly running Lenz and Jacoby's way.

The following day Culbertson tried another tack. In the midst of play, he ordered a rare broiled porterhouse steak to be brought to the table and began eating it. Jo let him get started, then said, 'Ely, we're playing cards, you know.' Culbertson had to acknowledge that was the case and took another mouthful. Jo now flashed him a last warning and a frown. Lenz joined in and asked him why he could not 'eat at the proper time like the rest of us'. But Culbertson was ready for that, 'My vast public won't let me, Sidney,' he replied. The cards still went with Lenz and Jacoby, and by the end of the fourth session on the Friday they were 5,650 points ahead.

Now it was Jacoby's turn to steal the limelight. He arrived with a finger heavily bandaged and decorated with mercurochrome. He had, it seemed, been behind on his rescue work and on his way to the

Chatham he had picked up a dog that had been knocked over by a car in Park Avenue. The dog, unimpressed by such gallantry, bit him.

But he wasn't the only one to arrive late. Culbertson was constantly behindhand. At the beginning of every session the others were kept waiting. Never once did an apology pass his lips, except for the one occasion when he actually arrived five minutes early. He apologised, then pointed out that his watch must be faulty. To Lenz, waiting impatiently and increasingly irked by these late arrivals, the same question was always addressed, 'Well, Sidney, have you changed your system yet?'

The newspapers seized upon all these details and played them up for all they were worth. As welcome was the news that now Jacoby was ordering venison steaks for himself and once munched a whole basket of strawberries while a hand was being dealt. The public reports lapped up how the experts had fluffed their play, Lenz's famous forgetting he was playing no trumps on hand four and, not long afterwards, Jo leading out of turn allowing Jacoby to choose a lead and make a small slam. By the sixth session the Culbertsons had begun to pull back. They won six rubbers in succession and that night were in the lead for the first time by a mere fifteen points. Once they had gained the lead they were never to relinquish it.

Jacques Curley, the wrestling impresario and promoter of Madison Square Gardens, put in an appearance on 15 December. He took one look at the assembled throngs, nearly wept when he realised that no admission charges were being made, and rushed up to Culbertson to ask him why he had not thought of putting on the whole show at Madison Square Gardens. Curley described how he would have put the players in a big glass enclosure and have had huge scoreboards for the estimated hundreds of paying customers. But Culbertson told him that he saw the match quite differently. His audience was locked away in the privacy of their own homes, listening to the radio, reading the newspapers and watching every move. They were the silent millions who were waiting to see the outcome of the match before committing themselves. What Culbertson stood to gain in this way potentially far exceeded anything he could get from putting on a short-lived spectacle at Madison Square Gardens.

At the end of the seventh session Jo retired to be with her children and to do her Christmas shopping. Her place was taken by Theodore Lightner who, with his 'angular frame and Michigan drawl', proceeded to hold a sequence of exceptional hands that put the Culbertson side even more firmly in the lead. What helped them was this hand, perhaps the most controversial of the whole match:

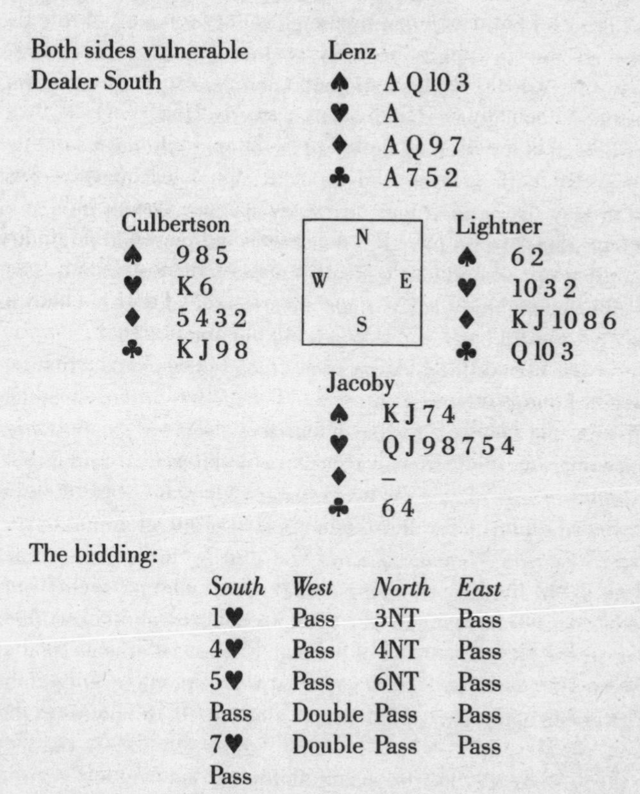

This bidding sequence was the subject of much subsequent comment. An extremely interesting and informative account of the whole contest, a 438-page book entitled *Famous Hands of the Culbertson–Lenz Match* (*Bridge World*, 1932), was published shortly after the match. All the important hands were analysed from three different viewpoints, those of Culbertson, Jacoby and Gruenther. This hand, for instance, merited special attention. Culbertson strongly criticised Lenz's obsessive no trump calls, particularly his three no trump call which looks like a shut-out bid. He praises himself for his shrewd, 'largely psychological', double of six no trumps, as this forced Jacoby into seven hearts, against which he had a defence.

Gruenther terms this 'one of the most grotesque hands of the match', criticising Jacoby for his vulnerable opening semi-psychic bid of one heart and Lenz for being blinded by the glitter of four aces. While the race between the two partners, one of them bidding no trumps ferociously, the other equally insistent upon hearts, was going on, neither noticed that a grand slam in spades was makable.

Jacoby defended his opening heart bid as follows: 'Although I did not hold two and a half or even two quick tricks, I was nevertheless prepared to play the hand at four hearts, even if my partner held very little. In fact, I might well have bid four hearts on this hand originally were it not that my second suit was spades, and I did not want to shut out a possible spade bid by my partner.' Hearts were clearly his 'port in the storm'. He found Lenz's six no trump bid the worst of all.

Whatever the blame, the bidding shows clearly the characteristic of each player – Lenz's lack of flexibility and his auction bridge obsession with no trumps and the honour value of four aces, Jacoby's propensity for psychic openings, and Culbertson's aggressive 'psychological doubling'.

After Lightner had played for two sessions, his place was taken by von Zedtwitz who played for one session before going off on holiday to his house in Florida. Remarkable too that during this session Lenz, affected no doubt by the prevailing climate, hazarded a psychic bid. Jacoby missed it! That resulted in five down doubled and vulnerable, 1,800 points, the highest penalty of the match. The last session held at the Chatham Hotel was on 22 December at which point seventy-eight rubbers had been completed and the score stood at 10,705 points in the Culbertsons' favour.

After the festive season, the scene shifted to the Waldorf-Astoria where Sidney Lenz was host. The lay-out there was more or less similar to that at the Chatham, with a twelve-room apartment set aside especially for the match. By now tempers were getting a little frayed.

Culbertson continued to turn up late and, just as unforgivably, took ages to play a card. Once, on lead in his own contract of four spades, he spent ten minutes making up his mind. Lenz dozed off. Finally awakened and told it was his turn to play, he put down the jack of spades. This only confused Culbertson more since this was the first round of trumps. 'Go back to sleep, Sid, I have another decision to make,' Culbertson told him. Lenz stormed off into the corridor, flinging back a taunt as he did so, 'Send me a telegram when you are ready!' Soon he was to refer to his opponent as 'That guy Ely'.

Whenever he was dummy, Culbertson never waited to see the hand played but used to leap from his chair and dash from the room, too nervous to watch. Often he would go into the press room to check on the newspapermen. Lenz would turn to Gruenther after the hand had been played and say, 'Get Ely!' (Lenz was later to remark that these words haunted his sleep in the last days of the match.) In his account, Gruenther nevertheless had high praise for Culbertson, admiring his tremendous energy and his ability to attend to five or six things at once while engaged in playing the most important bridge match of his career.

At times disputes arose about whether each side was sticking to its declared system. Lenz at one point accused Culbertson in a sharp tone of not doing so. Culbertson insisted he was, and quipped, 'Why don't you read my *Blue Book*? Every sucker in the country has read it except you.' 'I haven't,' piped up the kibitzing Chico Marx in the tense silence that followed, rapidly changing an awkward incident into a light-hearted one.

When the match was resumed, Culbertson presented each of his opponents with a copy of the self-same *Blue Book* as a Christmas gift. Jacoby thanked him and told him he now needed only two more to make a table in his study stand level. Culbertson asked him if he had seen the inscription inside. It read 'To Ossiebuco'. 'That's stew in Italian,' Culbertson reminded him.

Culbertson kept up his frequent excursions to the press room, usually to hand in his communiqué or bulletin on the hand just played (usually a factual 'Down one' but once or twice more enigmatic such as 'Ah *Mein Gott*, Teddy' referring to a particular act of treachery by his partner). On 30 December, just before play started, he got into an altercation there with Sir Derrick Wernher. Wernher, an Englishman with an Eton and Oxford background, was a well-known figure in bridge circles, unmistakably so because of his massive build (he was over six foot three inches tall and weighed over 250 pounds). After a misspent youth, Wernher went, partly voluntarily, partly at his father's instigation, to live in the USA, where his main interest was bridge. He became a playing partner and close associate of Hal Sims, spending much of his time at Deal, New Jersey. Later he helped introduce the Master Point System. On this occasion, Wernher was sitting in the press room analysing the play with, among others, George Reith and the author Louis Vance, when Culbertson walked in. Wernher, choosing an inopportune moment, asked Culbertson what had happened to the challenge he had issued the previous summer. Culbertson, clearly out of sorts, dismissed Wernher in an offhand way, saying he had no time for 'minor shots', and started to walk away. Wernher resented this and called after him, 'You're yellow.' There was a brief scuffle and Culbertson was about to leave when he spotted Lenz who had come in to see what all the fuss was about. Culbertson immediately challenged him: 'Why do you bring your friends in here to insult me? They call me yellow and a coward. Don't you think that's an insult?' Lenz pondered for a few moments and then responded, 'Well, it's certainly not a compliment.' Jo came in and pulled Culbertson away to the playing room, but Culbertson refused to start play until Wernher had left the hotel.

The assembled pressmen drank all of this in and, as the words became more heated, they rushed to their typewriters. One young cub reporter watched the whole proceedings with awe and edged over to where Thomas H. O'Neill, the Associated Press representative, was feverishly dictating to an operator. 'You're not going to send anything about this fight to the newspapers surely?' he stammered. 'No, sonny,' replied O'Neill. 'I'm just writing a letter to mother. Run away and play with your blocks!' Some of the *Bridge World* staff at the match feared the effect of such unfavourable publicity, but Culbertson himself was not put out. 'They'll print what they want to print, and it's a good thing for bridge,' he declared. 'I hope they tell the whole story.' With his keen news sense, Culbertson could already visualise the story of the 'fight' across the front page – along, that is, with the figures showing the Culbertson lead had now mounted to 14,525 points.

As the match progressed, visitors became more numerous. Friends of friends of the players and others descended on the Waldorf. A Boston businessman said he had come all the way from the Bay State simply to look at Mr Lenz and Mr Culbertson. A middle-aged couple from Kentucky pleaded for admittance on the grounds that they came from the sticks and wanted to tell their neighbours about the sights of New York.

Now the rift in the partnership between Lenz and Jacoby became more accentuated. There had been occasional 'petty squabbles' and the break finally came after the 103rd rubber. Jacoby subsequently claimed that Lenz's public criticism of his bidding at various stages of the match often had little justification. Their mismatch as partners had become apparent to Jacoby after the fourth hand of the match (when Lenz had misplayed the four no trump contract). Matters finally came to a head in the 102nd rubber when Jacoby interposed a couple of 'psychic' bids, while the Culbertsons, ignoring Jacoby's interventions, bid up to an easily made game. While the hand was being played, Lenz kept muttering about Jacoby, and afterwards challenged him with, 'Why do you make such rotten bids?' Jacoby countered this by asking Lenz why he made such stupid defensive plays, particularly the one he had made in the second rubber that same evening which had allowed Jo to make a contract of one no trump when she should have been set a trick. Jacoby felt once again the criticism was unjustified and said he was resigning. Gruenther came up to the table and reminded them that, according to the match agreement, they were still due to play another rubber (it was not yet midnight). Jacoby replied, 'Not with me in it,' and rose to leave. He was persuaded to play out the rest of the session, but the next day he announced he was withdrawing from the match and issued the following statement:

> Due to last night's misunderstanding quite natural to many bridge matches, I have been unfortunately misquoted in regard to both my partner, Mr Lenz, and my opponent, Mr Culbertson. I consider Mr Culbertson one of the truly great practical and analytical players in the world, and no list of the first five players of the world can reasonably be made up without including his name. While we all make mistakes, I have learned during this match to respect, even more than before, his subtle and most imaginative game.
>
> As for Mr Lenz, it would be, to say the least, presumptuous on my part not to hold him in highest regard, both as a gentleman and as the Grand Old Man of Bridge, to whom we all owe so much. Our differences are of ideas and methods of treating bridge, not of personal friendship. However, I have now become convinced that these ideas are so radically distinct that it would be unfair to him for me to re-enter the match. I will always remember the high honour that Mr Lenz has done me by selecting me as his partner, and only regret that I could not have done better.

The good-tempered nature of these comments and Jacoby's sportsmanlike decision to retire when he felt the situation between himself and his partner was irreparable gained him many friends. His place was taken by Commander Winfield Liggett Jr, an old friend of Lenz and a former First World War naval commander. Jacoby had played for 103 out of the 150 rubbers and most experts agreed his skill had been fully in evidence during the match. It was he who contracted for all the eight slams bid and made by his side, and four times he selected the only lead to defeat a Culbertson slam contract.

When he left, some of the sparkle went from the game. But the fact remains that, as a partnership, Lenz and Jacoby were incompatible. What Lenz probably had in mind when inviting Jacoby to be his partner was the latter's brilliance as a card player. Lenz was hoping to prove that the combination of two outstanding card players would triumph over any 'system'. But partnership requires more than individual brilliance – they were more like, as *Bridge World* put it, 'an express-train and a hansom-cab' harnessed together. Jacoby belonged to the younger generation that welcomed the advent of contract for the aggressive and imaginative bidding it allowed. He was a strong opening bidder, whereas Lenz was the opposite, favouring light openings as befitted the auction bridge player that he still remained underneath. Jacoby remained as a friendly observer until the end of the match and can be seen in the post-match photographs. Shortly afterwards he joined the Culbertson camp as secretary of the United States Bridge Association and went on a lecture tour on Culbertson's behalf.

By now it was 29 December and the fifteenth session was due to start. Soon the Culbertson side reached its high-water mark of 20,535 points in the lead. Jo absented herself for the eighteenth and nineteenth sessions, being replaced for the first by Michael Gottlieb and the next by Howard Schenken, both promising players of the young school. But Lenz and Liggett held phenomenally good cards for these sessions, leading Culbertson to comment, 'We weren't playing. We were kibitzing.' His side dropped 8,065 points, and Schenken earned the dubious distinction of losing more points during his session than were lost at any other time during the match.

Jo returned to play for the final and twentieth session on 8 January. As the cards were dealt for the final rubber, Culbertson, with his unassailable lead, refused to pick them up. 'I can't lose now, so I'm not going to bid.' Jo was not going to stand for this. 'Pick them up, Ely.' As it happened they had good cards and even managed to win the rubber. Culbertson played the final hand of the match in a five diamond (his favourite suit) contract and made six. The winning margin was 8,980 points.

The match had truly become the subject of breakfast-table conversation in several million American homes. Listeners to the midnight broadcast of the results of the day's play were estimated at five million. Much of the credit, or the explanation, for this phenomenon must go to Jo. Here was a woman and mother participating in the most important bridge match ever played, competing with ranking bridge players of the opposite sex. The American public longed to see how she fared. Edwin Hill of the *New York Sun* described her thus:

> There in the East seat, eyes veiled by drooping lids – motionless except for a flicker of white fingers as the cards drop or a jeweled cigarette holder cuts an arc – she seems detached, immeasurably removed from bickering and back-biting – gentle, tolerant, forbearing, slightly superior.

Her successful partnership with her husband was probably the decisive factor in the match. Just as Lenz and Jacoby 'lost' the match through their ill-suited partnership, so it was the practised, harmonious partnership of the Culbertsons that won the day. A glance at the penalties incurred by either side emphasises the crucial importance of partnership understanding in this match. The Culbertsons incurred seven penalties of 600 points or more, totalling 5,900 points. Lenz and his partners incurred fourteen, for an aggregate of 11,500 points. Thus, since the winning margin was 8,980 points, well over half, some 5,600 points, came from penalties and indicated the Culbertsons' superior accuracy in bidding. The statistics of the match make interesting reading and bear this point out. They also confirm Culbertson's earlier prediction that the distribution of luck in cards was more or less even.

The show was over. Culbertson's comment was, 'We had won millions of new friends. We were world famous. But we were broke.' It had been an expensive undertaking, feeding the endless lines of spectators and the newspapermen. While the match was in progress, the public had stopped buying his books, preferring to wait for its outcome first. Now at least they would start buying again. The bets on the match had gone to charity, as arranged, but the biggest bet of all was for the future control of the bridge industry and Culbertson had won that one.

Predictably the match had taken its toll on Culbertson's health. Jo and he decided that they needed a short break and went off to Havana for a week's holiday. Between a little bridge at the American Club, they relaxed at their hotel and sunned themselves on the beach. Culbertson needed this time to reflect and plan his future and work out his priorities. Foremost in his mind was the overriding need to provide for his family. He was haunted by the spectre of his father whose failure to think ahead had caused them all such uncertainty. He decided what he needed was a slogan for himself, 'First consolidate, then expand'. Consolidate his system, make his name impregnable and expansion was bound to follow.

Back in New York he found things had got off to a flying start. The *Blue Book* and the recently issued *Summary (Contract Bridge at a Glance)* were selling at a phenomenal rate. On one day alone orders had come into the *Bridge World* offices for over 5,000 copies of the *Blue Book* and 11,000 copies of the *Summary.*

History of Bridge

All I said was 'I know you started to learn to play bridge this morning, Reggie, but what time this morning?' – but he didn't like it.

P. G. Wodehouse, *Do Butlers Burgle Banks?* 1968

The precise origin of bridge, and where it was first played, remains a mystery. As a card game, bridge first became known towards the end of the second half of the nineteenth century. The best evidence supports the theory that bridge was first played in diplomatic circles in the Middle East in the 1880s, and in Constantinople and Cairo, in particular. A letter that appeared in the 1904 issue of *Notes and Queries*, written by A. M. Keiley, stated that, in 1886, he was a member of the Khedival Club in Cairo and that bridge was the principal card game there. Other members told him that had been the case for some time. In the south of France, where well-off winter residents gathered at Monte Carlo and elsewhere, bridge was known as *khedive*, presumably because of its Cairo connection.

Further evidence for its Middle Eastern origin comes from an article that appeared in the London *Daily Telegraph* in November 1932. This was by O. H. van Millingen who stated that he had lived in Constantinople in the 1880s and remembered 'a very interesting game called *biritch*', which took over from whist in card clubs there. Millingen cited another letter, dated 7 January 1922, from a friend of his, Edouard Graziani, who had worked in Constantinople at the same time as a translator for the Italian Embassy, and used to play bridge regularly at the *Cercle d'Orient*. Graziani said he first played bridge in August 1873 at the home of Mr Georges Coronio, manager of the Bank of Constantinople, whose house was in Buyukdere along the banks of the Upper Bosphorus. The other players on that occasion were Mr Eustache Eugenidi and Mr Serghiadi, a Romanian financier. Graziani claimed in his letter that 'after Constantinople, bridge came first to

Cairo, from where it conquered the Riviera, Paris, to London and then New York'. A later book entitled *Modern Bridge* by 'Slam', published in London in 1901, has this to say, 'Bridge, known in Turkey as 'Biritch,'. . . has been played in South-Eastern Europe ... ever since the early sixties.'

Millingen's letter uses the word *biritch*, and this links it with a pamphlet in the British Museum, dated 1886, entitled '*Biritch*, or Russian Whist'. In this anonymous four-page pamphlet a new game based on short whist is described, the main difference being that no card was turned up for trumps. Instead, the dealer, after the cards had been looked at, had the option of declaring the trump suit or – another innovation – no trumps. If declarer decided on no trumps, he called '*Biritch*'. A novel word for a novel idea. Hitherto, every form of whist had a trump suit. There was no competitive bidding in the new game, but doubling and redoubling were allowed. Declarer's partner exposed his hand after the opening lead.

Biritch is phonetically similar to the word we now use and the link looks compelling. Card playing was certainly popular in Russia during the second half of the nineteenth century. Culbertson himself first learnt to play cards in a Russian prison in 1907. There are some Russian words somewhat like *biritch*, and the actual word appears in several etymological dictionaries of Russian. The word, with its accent on the second syllable, meant a herald, bailiff or town crier, whose job it was to make public announcements. In French, *annoncer* is the word used for 'to bid', which suggests a similar derivation, and one of the major innovations of the new game of bridge was to give the dealer the right to announce, or declare, the trump suit. The four-page pamphlet in the British Museum no longer exists as it was destroyed in the Second World War. The British Museum had only one copy. Two other Russian card games, *vint* and *yeralash*, included the no-trump feature, so the Russian link is persuasive.

Another theory is that the name bridge is derived from bridge-whist. In other words it ignores the above theories. This takes the view that since in bridge-whist the dealer can either name the trump suit or 'bridge' it to his partner, i.e. leave the choice of trump suit to his partner opposite, the name could have come from that. Bridge-whist first appeared almost simultaneously in New York (1893) and London (1894), according to two contemporary writers, J. B. Elwell and R. F. Foster, and combined elements of both games. In London, the Portland

Club began to play bridge itself in 1894, mainly because one of its leading members, Lord Brougham, had already played it in Cairo, probably en route to, or back from, India via the Suez Canal. The story goes that, on his return to London, Brougham was dealing the cards at the Portland Club in a game of whist and forgot to turn up the last card as trumps. He explained he had got into this habit from playing bridge in Cairo. He explained the new game to his fellow players and hence bridge had its first introduction in London. A year later the first Laws of Bridge were drawn up by the Portland Club, which has retained that role in this country – and in a large part of the rest of the world – ever since.

Another writer claims that the first English game of bridge was played in 1892 at the St George's Club, Hanover Square, introduced by a Colonel Studdy, who said that he had learned it in the trenches at Plevna during the Russo-Turkish War of 1877–8.

In 1904, the auction principle was introduced. Tradition has it that this was started in India among army officers with time on their hands. Snooker also originated in India with Indian army officers at an out-station who, again for much the same reasons, made up a variation of billiards. Auction bridge grew steadily in popularity. It introduced competitive bidding and doubling. Declarer, if successful, was still credited with the full value of the tricks whether he had bid for them or not. For instance, a bid of two spades making six would still be credited with the value of a small slam.

The next major change was Plafond, which was developed in France from 1918 onwards. A similar game, S.A.C.C., was described by Sir Hugh Clayton as having been 'invented' in India in 1912, and similar games had been tried in the United States before 1915. In all such games each side had to bid to its 'plafond' or ceiling, and only tricks bid and made counted toward game. This variation rapidly became the standard French game but did not succeed elsewhere in spite of occasional experiments.

Auction reached its peak just after the First World War when demand for home-based entertainment reached its zenith. Mah-jongg was then in its heyday. Indeed, in 1922 and 1923 mah-jongg sets outsold radios. But auction bridge continued to gain in popularity and by 1926 when contract was introduced, its ascendancy over mah-jongg was absolute.

Contract came about as follows. In 1925 Harold S. Vanderbilt perfected a new form of the game, embodying the Plafond principle but including the element of vulnerability and producing a scoring table that corrected the major faults in Plafond. He succeeded so well that his game of contract bridge became the staple diet of card players everywhere.

Afterwards, Vanderbilt wrote his own account of its discovery:

> Many years of experience playing games of the Whist family were, I think, a necessary prelude to acquiring the background and knowledge needed to evolve the game of Contract Bridge. Starting as a young boy about 70 years ago, I have played successively over the years Whist, Bridge, Auction Bridge, and Plafond. I compiled in the autumn of 1925 a scoring table for my new game. I called it Contract Bridge and incorporated in it, not only the best features of Auction and Plafond, but also a number of new and exciting features; premiums for slams bid and made, vulnerability, and the decimal system of scoring which by increasing both trick and game values and all premiums and penalties was destined to add enormously to the popularity of Contract Bridge. An ideal opportunity to try out my new game presented itself while I was voyaging shortly after completing my scoring table with three Auction Bridge playing friends on board the steamship *Finland* from Los Angeles to Havana via the Panama Canal, a nine-day trip. At first, we were at a loss for a term, other than 'game in' to describe the status of being subject to higher penalties because of having won a game. Fortunately for us, a young lady on board the *Finland* solved that problem by suggesting the word 'vulnerable.' We enjoyed playing my new game on board the *Finland* so much that, on my return to New York, I gave typed copies of my scoring table to several of my Auction Bridge playing friends. I made no other effort to popularize or publicize Contract Bridge. Thanks apparently to its excellence, it popularized itself and spread like wildfire.

Contract bridge, therefore, can pinpoint its conception and the first time it was ever played with accuracy. The *Finland* reached Balboa on 31 October 1925, too late to proceed through the Canal or for passengers to go ashore. Francis Bacon III, one of Vanderbilt's friends on board, recalled that the lady who suggested the word 'vulnerable' was allowed to join their game of Plafond and attempted to suggest some exotic and impractical changes based on a game she said she had played in China. This so irritated Vanderbilt that, while the *Finland* passed through the Canal the next day, he worked out the scoring table for contract which, except for no-trump tricks then being valued at 35 points each, remained virtually unchanged half a century later. On that night, 1 November, the game became contract bridge, scored under Vanderbilt's new rules.

By 1927 three codes of laws had been produced for the new game. Those of Robert F. Foster and the Knickerbocker Whist Club (both 1927) were withdrawn in favour of the more authoritative code issued by the Whist Club of New York. In 1928 the game was adopted in the major New York clubs, and late that year the first national championship was held, with the Vanderbilt Cup as the prize. In 1929 the American Auction Bridge League dropped the word 'auction' from its title and it became clear that contract had supplanted auction. The established auction authorities struggled to achieve expertise in the field of contract, but for the most part unsuccessfully.

Leadership in the new game went to Ely Culbertson, who founded the first contract magazine, *The Bridge World*, in 1929 and wrote his celebrated *Blue Book* in 1930. This revolutionary work set out the principles of approach-forcing bidding which became the nucleus of all modern standard systems. Thanks to a thriving organisation which exploited every phase of bridge activity and to his natural flair for publicity exhibited notably in the Culbertson–Lenz match, Culbertson retained his leadership throughout the 1930s. But his interest and enthusiasm declined, and in the 1940s the leadership passed to Charles Goren, who achieved great success by adapting Culbertson's methods to point-count valuation.

The Culbertson System

—♠♥♦—
♣

The Culbertson System was first published in the *Blue Book* in 1930. It was to undergo various modifications over the years, sometimes as a result of the Culbertsons' own suggested improvements (for example, strong no trump in 1933, asking bids in 1936) and sometimes in response to changes being introduced elsewhere (for example, point-count bidding after Goren had popularised this in 1949), but fundamentally the system remained much the same throughout the 1930s and 1940s. The standard text and reference book was the *Gold Book* of 1936. Rather than list all these modifications, here is an outline of the system as it was first introduced in the *Blue Book.*

The Approach Forcing system was based on two principles:

APPROACH PRINCIPLE
'When there is a choice between a suit bid and a no-trump bid, the suit should be preferred with few exceptions, regardless of distribution or whether the suit be a four-carder, a major, or a minor.'

FORCING PRINCIPLE
'A forcing bid shows great honour strength and indicates that a game, or slam, is probable, provided the most satisfactory bid is selected. Partner of forcing bidder must keep the bidding open until a game contract is reached.'

HAND VALUATION
Culbertson introduced his Table of Honour Tricks:

Holding	*Count*
A K	2 honour tricks
A Q	1½
A	1

Holding	Count
K Q in the same suit	1
K J 10	1
K x	½
Q J x	½
Q x and J x	½

Plus values: King by itself or Q-x or J-x when unable to combine with another honour in hand. Two such plus values equal about a half honour trick. To give honour trick value to unsupported lower honours was an innovation.

OPENING BIDS

Culbertson emphasised the importance of valuing the hand in more ways than one. Opening bids were based on honour strength; attacking bids on distributional values; defensive bids on these same values were reconsidered in the light of a different trump situation. It was a 'natural' system where bids announced information about the general strength and shape of the hand with the initial call.

A. Requirements for opening suit bid of one

2½ honour tricks, and a biddable four- or five-card suit.

B. Requirements for opening bid of one no trump

2½ honour tricks distributed in at least three suits, and no biddable suit.

(Both the above require an extra value when vulnerable.)

C. Requirements for opening bids of two in a suit (forcing)

From four and a half to six honour tricks, depending on strength and length of trump suit and distribution of the hand. To justify an opening bid of two a hand should be (1) so strong in playing tricks that a game is assured with only slight distributional support from partner; and (2) so strong in high cards that a bid of only one would run substantial risk of a pass by all other three players.

D. Requirements for opening two no trump bid (not forcing)

Usually about five (or a shade less) honour tricks distributed in all four suits.

E. Opening bids of three
These are strength-showing bids indicating powerful trump suits.

F. Opening bids of four
These are pre-emptive bids and are purely defensive overbids.

BIDS BY THE RESPONDING HAND
Responses by partner may be divided into three categories:

Minimum responses
These suggest that unless opening bidder holds values in excess of a minimum bid, there is no game in the hand, and the bidding should be allowed to die (introduction of two no trump response to a forcing two bid – this was devised by Waldemar von Zedtwitz).

Strong responses – multiple raises and no trump takeouts of more than one
These indicate that game should be made if opener has slight added values.

Forcing bids – jump takeouts in a new suit
These bids announce an almost certain game even though partner has a minimum opening bid.

The last section of the *Blue Book* was devoted to bridge psychology and emphasised the importance of distributional values and the 'language of inference' as the basis for partnership understanding.

Culbertson's innovations were introduced when auction bridge still dominated the thinking of most bridge players. Albert Morehead wrote in 1954: 'Only a handful of the millions of bridge players have any idea of the extent to which they are following "Culbertson law" each time they play bridge – even when they think they are playing some other system.' When it came out the *Blue Book* had immense influence and went through sixty-five consecutive printings between 1930 and 1933.

Harold Vanderbilt

♠♥♦
♣

Harold Stirling Vanderbilt was born in 1884, part of the famous and immensely wealthy railroad family. His father died in 1920 leaving an estate of over fifty million dollars. The Vanderbilts were part of New York's upper echelon, the Four Hundred, a select group of families so named after the annual ball given by Mrs Willa Astor in her home at 350 Fifth Avenue – she could accommodate only four hundred people in her ballroom.

Growing up in a privileged background, Vanderbilt went to Harvard where he gained a high-level law degree. He then joined the family companies, notably the New York Central Railroad and its subsidiaries. Despite many outside interests, he participated in his business life with diligence and care. He took up flying, still in its early days, and owned a six-passenger Lockheed Electra Monoplane equipped with a full buffet and, another essential for him, a card table.

Aside from cards, sailing was Vanderbilt's great love. He took up ocean yacht racing in earnest in the 1920s. His 109-foot steel-hulled schooner *Vagrant* was famous for the numerous races it won off Newport, Rhode Island, and he became Commodore of the New York Yacht Club. His lasting fame in the yachting world came from his defences of the America's Cup, the most prestigious prize in yacht racing, his main challenger being the British tea merchant Sir Thomas Lipton. The race was limited to sloops of at least sixty-five-foot waterline, or schooners of at least eighty-foot waterline. In 1930 a historic race featured his J-type schooner *Enterprise*, with several innovations in nautical design, against Lipton's *Shamrock V*. Lipton lost again – he had already been defeated in four previous contests. Vanderbilt's book *On the Wind's Highway* relates the story of this.

But it is as the inventor of contract bridge that his fame lies. He first took up card play seriously in his early twenties when he started playing auction bridge, as he describes here:

My experience as a player of games of the Whist family – first Bridge, then Auction Bridge, and finally Contract Bridge – dates from the turn of the century when my mother persuaded Joe Elwell to give us some Bridge lessons in Newport, Rhode Island. I played Bridge until Auction appeared in 1907. Elwell became a few years later my favorite Auction Bridge partner, and remained so until his still unsolved murder in June, 1920.

In the early Twenties I played Plafond occasionally. I liked Plafond's main virtue: namely, that you could not score a game unless you bid it. I disliked slam bonuses at Auction, even though they were necessarily modest. They irked me because they were awarded for unbid slams. But their very existence put ideas into my head. And so – influenced perhaps by this like and dislike – I began to think about devising a new game of the Whist family. I had seen Whist go, Bridge come and go, Auction come. Was it time for Auction to go? I thought so and christened my game Contract Bridge after its principal divergence from Auction Bridge: having to contract for a game in order to make one. In view of this drastic change I foresaw, as I dreamed up my new game, that slam premiums would have to be vastly increased in order to make it worth while to risk the loss of an otherwise certain game. The increases in trick and game values and in rubber premiums and penalties followed more or less automatically in the wake of the higher slam premiums, and, for simplicity's sake, I adopted the decimal system – round figures – in scoring.

I did not foresee a rather obvious result of all these increases in points scored; nor did I realise what was happening until years later when, as we were revising the International Contract Bridge Code in London, the Portland Club representative said, 'You know the thing that has made your game so very popular is those big figures: Mrs. Smith just loves to say proudly to Mrs Jones: "My dear, you know I set Mrs. Snooks 1,400 points."'

The first chance I had to test my new game was on a ten-day cruise on board the steamship *Finland* en route from California to Havana via the Panama Canal in November 1925. I was travelling in company with three friends, Frederic S. Allen, Francis M. Bacon III, and Dudley L. Pickman, Jr., who agreed to try the game. So I produced my scoring table, which we changed slightly during the voyage, but by the time we reached Havana it was very similar to the one in use today. It differed principally in that no-trumps counted 35 points per trick, and doubled penalties increased in an ascending scale as the number of tricks increased. Today there is only one increase – from the first to each subsequent doubled undertrick, a change adopted more, I think, in the interests of simplicity than of equity.[1]

My scoring table provided at the outset for lower penalties for a side that had not won a game, to enable it to 'fly the flag' at not too great a cost and to add variety, singularly lacking in Auction, to the new game. But we were at a loss for a word to describe a side that is subject to higher penalties. A young lady we met on the boat – none of us can recall her name – who had played some strange game in California that called for higher penalties under certain conditions, gave us the word used in that game, and 'vulnerable' – what a perfect description – it has been ever since.

After we got back to our respective homes in New York and Boston we made no particular effort to popularise our newborn game. It never occurred to me that it was destined to sweep the world, or that its eventual promoters were to make millions. I explained the scoring to a number of my friends. I may even have supplied them with typewritten scoring tables. Without exception, they all instantly gave up Auction. Like the flu, the new game spread by itself, despite the attempts of the old Auction addicts – too old to change – to devise a vaccine to stop it.

In 1927 the Whist Club published its first laws of Contract Bridge, after making me a member of the Card Committee to assist in devising them; and the first important Contract Bridge tournament was held in Cleveland, Ohio, in the fall of 1928, for the cup then newly presented by me and still competed for annually.

Such, in brief, is the story of the origin and childhood of Contract Bridge.

As a player, Vanderbilt was notoriously methodical and slow. Dorothy

[1] In 1987 the scoring table was changed, so that the penalty for losing a fourth (and subsequent) doubled non-vulnerable undertrick was increased to 300 points per trick.

Sims often watched him play with his favourite partner Baron Waldemar von Zedtwitz and wrote up her account of it:

> 'May I introduce Mr. Vanderbilt?' said my hostess. No hypocritical pleasure lit Mr. V's grave countenance. His interest was focused on the card table with the intentness of a dog gazing at a bone.
>
> We cut. I drew the ace of spades, he, the deuce of clubs and the Baron von Zedtwitz.
>
> With well-bred relief, he sank into his chair, courteously allowing me the choice of cards.
>
> I dealt – bid one club.
>
> Mr. Vanderbilt took off his glasses, wiped them abstractedly – and thought the matter over. I studied him with interest. When Mr. V. thinks, you have time both for study and recreation.
>
> Eventually, he passed. We bought the contract for three no trumps, which was made.
>
> On the next hand, I again bid a club. I like to bid clubs – I almost always bid clubs. I laughed; my partner laughed. Even the Baron wanted to laugh, but the Skipper merely swung his nautical eye to a latitude of about twenty-two-and-a-half degrees of my position, lowered his head, and began a marathon of thinking.
>
> We waited patiently, and were in due time rewarded, on straining our ears, to hear a suppressed, 'Double.'
>
> The Baron who, though never surprised, is always unprepared, now shouldered his responsibilities and, with a solemnity fitting the occasion, went into a huddle before bidding a diamond.
>
> Mr. V. now supplied with food for thought, re-crossed his legs, settled back in his chair and after fifteen minutes, impulsively said, 'One heart.'
>
> The Baron grabbed his ear, twisted it, snapped it, lit a cigarette, snuffed it out, consulted the ceiling, and essayed, 'One no trump.'
>
> Two were eventually made.
>
> Mr. V. pushed back his chair, took off his glasses, wiped them, and asked the Baron whether he had read the inference of his double. The Baron's hand flew to his ear as he replied that, of course, he had guessed it, but considered it illogical under the circumstances.
>
> Mr. V. demanded to know under what circumstances the Baron

would consider it logical. The Baron said it would take too much time to explain it offhand. Mr. V. answered that he did not care about time, as there was a fundamental at stake ...

Not in any way intending to be rude or to hurry the debate, I passed Mr. V. the cards to cut.

He looked at them vaguely – cut them dead – and, turning to the Baron, inquired whether he (the Baron) didn't think that his (Mr. V's) heart bid was the killer. The Baron meditated before pronouncing it 'not bad, but hardly a killer.' Mr. V. asked what improvement he could suggest.

The answer will always remain a secret to me, for, unnoticed, I had slipped away and was speeding towards home to finish reading a thriller called 'A Treatise on Philosophical Introspection of the Aztecs.'

Vanderbilt was the first to devise an artificial one club bid to show a strong hand. He donated a cup named after himself, the Vanderbilt Cup, for teams of four, to be competed for annually. He paid for proper replicas of this trophy each year out of his own pocket and shortly before he died in 1970 set aside a trust fund of $100,000 to ensure that these replicas would be made in perpetuity. He held Bridge Laws Commission meetings in the boardroom of his New York Central Railroad company, around a table that could seat thirty people, and Vanderbilt never missed a meeting. But losing, despite his wealth, always troubled him. Once, Vanderbilt was playing in a high-stake game at a New York club and after some hours' play was down several dollars. He was due to take a midnight train to Chicago but was irritated at his losses. He looked at his watch. It was time to leave and there was no time to start a new rubber. But he insisted on a final rubber. They played, the train due to leave any moment. His office called, the club attendant reminded him of the train's imminent departure. Yet Vanderbilt was determined to win back his losses. His office called again, telling him that Grand Central Station had been asking where he was as the train should have left three minutes ago. Eventually Vanderbilt won his rubber, and dashed off in his waiting car. The train pulled out half an hour late. But then he was Chairman of New York Central and a director of thirty-seven railroad corporations besides.

Dorothy Sims

Most things that are good for the brain are bad for the disposition. Bridge is an exception. Its addicts are inclined to get what is called 'run-down'.

Dorothy Sims, *Curiouser and Curiouser*, 1939

Jo may have been the first female player of note on the contract bridge scene but women of every sort soon moved into contract bridge in a big way right across the United States and then in Europe. In many senses it was women who 'started' contract bridge. They were the first to take it up on a widespread social scale. Culbertson sensed this. When he came to develop his hold on bridge and started spreading his system, he was shrewd enough to appoint women as his front-line troops, as teachers of his system. In his student years while still in Europe he had read and been much influenced by Gustav Le Bon's *Psychology of the Crowd*. Now he had his chance to put such ideas into practice. His teachers, drawn from all walks of life, would enact this psychology of the crowd. They would be all women, with group leaders in charge, and given extra status by being entitled to earn national and regional certificates at specially organised Teachers Conventions. Soon husbands began to envy their wives' new status and prowess at, and knowledge of, the game. Women, meanwhile, had organised social functions, an afternoon or evening bridge four, which dispensed with men. This was threatening and made husbands even keener to learn the game. Culbertson's psychology of the crowd was right. Soon it became for men as much as for women a social requirement to learn bridge, and the way to learn the game was, as Culbertson had predicted, to learn the best-known system, his Culbertson System. The publicity generated by his Lenz match was aimed at this. He wanted people to say, 'Culbertson is standard, we play Culbertson,' or, if four strangers met up on a train and wanted to play bridge, they could say to each other, 'Do you play Culbertson?'

which would become their *lingua franca*. His best-selling *Blue Book* became the ready-made passport to the game. It described his system in a comprehensive but manageable way – 'two and a half quick tricks to open ...' The success of the *Blue Book* had been phenomenal, the first edition selling out within twenty-four hours and the second and third printings pre-sold even before they appeared. This first edition went through sixty-five consecutive printings within two years, so much so that the hardened steel and nickel printing plates became worn out and had to be renewed.

Jo had set the pace but she was not alone. Dorothy Sims was another woman who played at the top level, though she kept a certain feminine wilfulness to her game. Helen Sobel was to follow her and become in the late 1930s and 1940s the queen of bridge, sweeping all before her through her successful partnership with Goren. In Europe at this time the Austrian Ladies team were winning their events, the young Rixi Markus among them. Coincidentally, in 1937 this trio of women – Jo Culbertson, Helen Sobel and Rixi Markus – played against each other in the World Championship staged in Budapest that year.

Dorothy Sims was a spectacular and unusual woman. Born in 1889, she was one of three talented and eccentric daughters of Isaac L. Rice, a lawyer, chess player and inventor. He had been involved in the manufacture of the first submarine. Dorothy grew up at Asbury Park, New Jersey. Even at an early age, she was something of a rebel. At twelve, after a rather uneventful childhood, she, as she later wrote, 'retired' from school. 'The school took this in its stride. I was not a bad student, I was not a student at all. I saw no point to clogging my mind with things that everyone knew.' At first her parents were pleased to have her home. 'Father knew so much that ignorance fascinated him. He saw charm in it that stupid people overlooked. He called my spelling "original" and "phonetic". I was delighted to have it appreciated. Only father could have made it sound so classical.' Her spelling never improved. Indeed, her good friend George S. Kaufman, the playwright, used to joke about her spelling by telling her that there was only one 'z' in 'is', Dorothy's comment being: 'I thought this funny – till I thought it over.'

As a teenager she was known locally as the 'Red Devil' because of her prowess on the motorbike. Aged twenty-two, she became the USA Women's Motorcycle Speed Champion. Once, had up for speeding and appearing before the local judge, she told him that in modern traffic it was safer to be reckless than careful. She followed much the same creed at the bridge table. She was the first woman in the USA to hold a pilot's licence; it was through this that she met Hal Sims. At the outbreak of the First World War she joined Air Transport and came across Hal who was serving in the US Army Air Corps. They got married and eventually set up home at Deal, New Jersey, not far from where she had been brought up. In later years her devotion to speed mellowed and she founded the Anti-Noise Society.

Their estate was on Roosevelt Avenue, overlooking the ocean, with ten bedrooms and an enormous hundred-foot combination living and dining room. In the early 1930s, the Simses were famous for their bridge weekends, managing at times to sleep as many as forty people in a state of 'modified chaos'. This created, as Dorothy noted, slight trouble with servants. 'They came down in gangs from New York (we exhausted the New Jersey supply early). We had Chinese, Filipinos, Swedes, and combinations; but when we found one that suited us, we didn't suit him. I suppose they felt like the butler Mother had on East 87th Street. He wanted to leave. Mother said, "Why?" He said, "This place is peculiar." Mother said, "But all places are peculiar." He said he knew but ours was very peculiar.'

Invitations to these weekends or bridge weeks were much sought after. Regulars there included Oswald Jacoby, Willard Karn, Walter Malowan, David Burnstine, Michael Gottlieb, Howard Schenken, Waldemar von Zedtwitz, Theodore Lightner, Sam Fry, Derrick Wernher, Dick Simon and many others. To quote their hostess again: 'All day and all night the games went on. Occasionally someone caught a train or went to bed, but there were always others getting up out of bed to replace them. The conversation was entirely devoted to "hands" – the narrator's good ones and his partner's horrible plays, who chucked who, when and how. There was generally a courteous understanding that if you listened to someone, he must listen to you. There was talk for a while of hiring the unemployed for an audience.'

The games varied in stakes from two-cent tables to ten- and twenty-cents games, and there were tournaments every so often. So popular were these events that the Simses, to cater for the overflow and because they were 'sick of running a hotel', started up the Deal Club nearby, a wooden-frame building on the ocean front, designed by Stanford White, with a private pier and thirty bedrooms, each elaborately furnished. Guests had to pay for their own accommodation and meals. Sims hired a chef and staff to look after them, but many found it too expensive and sought cheaper lodgings.

In 1935 she partnered her husband Hal Sims in the famous match they played against the Culbertsons over 150 rubbers, which the Culbertsons won after some exciting and exotic bridge.

Hal Sims had been one of Culbertson's earliest friends in his auction bridge days at the Knickerbocker Whist Club in the early 1920s. They had taken to each other immediately, in spite of their many physical dissimilarities – Sims was big-boned and muscular, six foot four inches tall and weighed over 300 pounds. They had much in common in other respects. They both liked to 'outsmart the other guy', using whatever form of subterfuge or psychological advantage they could to achieve this. Culbertson remembered that when he first met Sims he could usually tell when Sims had a bad hand. If he had been dealt poor cards, Sims, like a true Southerner, would play possum and lapse into a dreamy silence. Someone would then have to nudge him and say, 'Come on, Hal, your bid. Wake up.' Then his big grey eyes would open sleepily, and he would mumble 'What's that? What? My bid?' and it wouldn't be hard to guess the state of his hand.

Many a new partner trembled at the prospect of playing with Sims though. On hot days he had a disconcerting habit of chewing ice throughout the afternoon. His technique, as his wife related, would be to fix his new partner 'with a hungry glare, then let out a couple of roars, like a wounded lion in anticipation of the wrong that will shortly be done him and, in a tense silence, await results to prove his judgement correct'.

Sims was a naturally gifted bridge player, with a remarkable memory and an incredibly sharp eye. He could summon up the laws of percentages at will. Once, playing in a tournament, he called out every card in both opponents' hands. Then he explained to the director of the tournament that the same board had been played several days before and not been reshuffled. At bridge, Sims was a masterful handler of dummy and a shrewd analyst of defence. Like his wife, Dorothy, he used psychics daringly and was always keen to outmanoeuvre an opponent in the bidding. Dorothy was less effective as a player, only passable as a declarer and fairish on defence, but she had flair and occasionally pulled off some stupendous contracts. If luck was running against her during a tournament or a match at Deal, she liked to put all the opposing women's hats on a bed to bring them bad luck.

The 1935 Culbertson–Sims match came out of a challenge from Hal Sims himself, which stated:

> For years, you have been subtly instilling into the minds of a more or less unsuspecting public the idea that you and Mrs Culbertson are the leading pair in the world. After listening to your most recent boastful claims in the press and over the radio it occurred to me that you might be in a frame of mind to accept a challenge from Mrs Sims and myself. Contract is really a fascinating game, and I am sure that if you found the time to take it up, you would derive tremendous enjoyment from it.

Culbertson could not wait to reply:

> Your challenge is accepted with pleasure. All these years I have been itching to lay my bridge hands on you. At last you have emerged from your hiding-place to meet your master. Though I consider you one of the world's finest card players even your brilliancy cannot overcome the handicaps of your atrocious system. Let it be a real tough but clean fight to the finish.

Culbertson hoped to demonstrate that two sets of married couples could play a long-drawn-out match harmoniously and with little cause for argument. Such a triumph of domestic bridge would reinforce the appeal of bridge to the ordinary player who, presumably, if the Culbertsons won, would go out and buy his books.

Culbertson drew up a contract for the match but had some trouble getting Sims to sign it. He did not despair. Dorothy noted, 'Ely never despairs. While you have life, he has hope.' Eventually Culbertson ran into Sims in a restaurant off Fifth Avenue and asked him to sign the agreement there and then. Sims was not keen to sign any form of contract away from a lawyer's office. Important documents, he reminded Culbertson, needed witnesses. Culbertson was not to be put off. He jumped up, surveyed the restaurant and spotted a man and a woman he knew dressed in evening clothes. Before Sims could stop him he was across the room and returned with the two in tow. He had got his witnesses and Sims, admiring his nerve, had to sign.

The conditions of the match were as follows: 150 rubbers to be played over twenty-one days, starting on 25 March 1935. The referee was to be the familiar figure of Lieutenant Alfred Gruenther. A large side bet, reputed to be nearly $10,000, was involved. The Simses, with typical flamboyance, set up a training camp at the Molly Pitcher Hotel at Red Bank, New Jersey – following in the footsteps of the recent heavyweight champion boxer, Max Baer, who had trained at their oceanside home the previous spring in preparation for his title fight with Primo Carnera. Someone said at the time that if Baer could handle the Sims group, he could handle Carnera. Their schedule involved getting up at 9 a.m. (anathema to Sims) to go road jogging, followed by setting-up exercises. The whole Sims entourage, including the Great Dane, Duke, wore white turtle-necked sweaters with a large scarlet 'S' on the front. They kept to a strictly controlled diet, had dry toast for dinner and then steeled themselves for some 'shadow bidding' with their sparring partners, Derrick Wernher, George Unger and others. Curfew was strictly enforced at 11 p.m. Sims for all his bulk was a remarkably fit man; he had always been an all-round sportsman, a near-scratch golfer and skilled tennis player. Culbertson, for his part, was forced to confine his training and roadwork to one-night stands on his prearranged lecture tour of the Middle West and Texas. For nearly a month, in early 1935, he lectured twice a day, except when travelling from one town to the next.

The match was to take place at Culbertson's Crockford's Club in New York and the whole of the second floor was given over to it. Special bridge furniture of modernistic tubular stainless aluminium was commissioned and the score-keepers were given a block-rubber grip on each arm-rest to help them write the score on, or, it was suggested, for holding on to in moments of convulsive excitement. The bridge table was larger than normal in deference to Sims's giant frame. Size became an issue at a later stage of the contest when Culbertson, as part of his relentless jockeying for position, insisted on a chalk demarcation line beneath the table to mark where the legs of each of the contestants were allowed to be. Sims, squeezed for room, was not at all amused.

Play got under way on the evening of Monday, 25 March 1935, following a dinner at Crockford's. By the time they had finished their eight-course meal, it was 9.45 p.m. Champagne had flowed liberally throughout the meal and compliments had flown almost as fast across the table between Ely and Hal. Culbertson managed to 'lose' a card on the first hand. A hurried search revealed that it had fallen under his chair. As the evening progressed the good-natured murmur from the spectators increased to such an extent that Culbertson complained that he could not hear the bidding and insisted that the kibitzers keep quiet and 'just look significant'. By the end of the first session the Simses had taken a lead of 2,200 points, thanks partly to a small slam which Dorothy freely admitted she had bid up to make sure that Hal played the hand.

The second day started badly for the Culbertsons and in mid-afternoon Culbertson ordered his Crockford's house flag, bearing the apposite Latin motto 'Fair Play and Good Fortune', to be lowered to half-mast. There it fluttered mournfully in the wind, awaiting better times. And sure enough, in the evening session, Culbertson rose from his table and signalled to an attendant for the flag to be hoisted to the end of its pole. The Culbertsons were now in the lead by 130 points; a short while later they captured the rubber, eventually ending the day with a plus score of 1,750 points. They never lost the lead again.

The match was conducted mostly with good humour. Communications between partners were always a rich source of entertainment to spectators. Once, when the Simses went off three tricks in a three no trump contract, Hal reminded Dorothy, 'Darling, must I tell you every time you have a king and one in a suit that I have bid, you must raise?' 'But Hal I thought ...' 'Thought,' thundered her husband. 'How many times have I told you not to think. Just do what I tell you!' There was constant badinage and repartee between players. Each had his or her way of addressing the other. Sims called Culbertson 'Professor' and was himself called 'Maestro' or 'Petronius' by Culbertson. Dorothy's husband called her 'My sweet' or 'My angel', while Culbertson addressed Jo as 'Darling' or 'Sweetka' (Russian for the same thing, as he quickly explained). Culbertson was rather proud of his appellation for Sir Derrick Wernher, one of the main referees, or umpires – he kept calling him 'the British Empire'. Name-calling reached its peak and bordered on adulation after this hand:

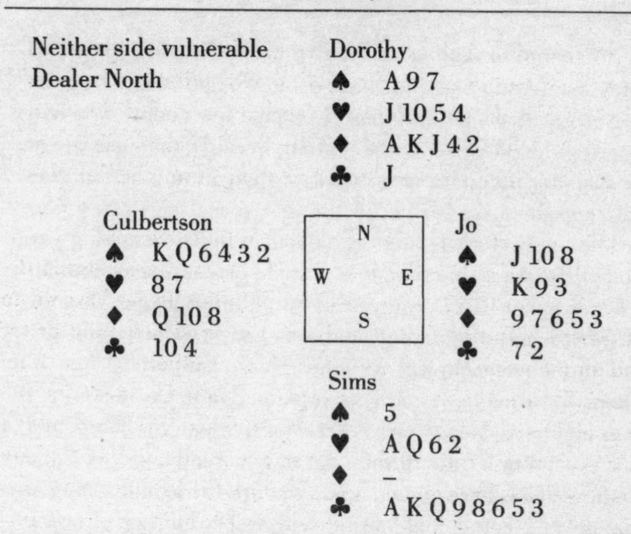

Dorothy dealt and made a characteristic 'psychic' opening bid of one club on the North hand. Sims bid seven clubs straight off and the contract was made. As the last trick was played, Sims, in a husky voice charged with emotion, declared 'My angel!' Then, after a moment's thought, he added (fearing his first declaration had been inadequate) 'My sweet!'

In the end the Culbertsons won the match by a margin of 16,130 points. Of the 150 rubbers played, the Culbertsons had won eighty-two and the Simses sixty-eight. The match achieved what it set out to do. It proved that two sets of married couples could play a long match together, and it proved to the public at large that the Culbertsons still seemed to be as good as ever at bridge.

From 1940 onwards Dorothy and Hal spent their winters in Havana, Cuba, and it was there while bidding in a bridge game at the Havana Country Club that Hal died of a heart attack in 1949. After her husband's death Dorothy toured the world for some years, acting as a political correspondent for various newspapers. She died in 1960, aged sixty-one. She wrote three books, *Psychic Bidding* (1932), *Curiouser and Curiouser* (1940) and *How to Live on a Hunch* (1944). George Kaufman, the humorist and playwright, wrote this Foreword to *Curiouser and Curiouser*, which gives a flavour of her personality:

> Being a fascinating and a brilliant person, Dorothy Sims has written a fascinating and a brilliant book. No one who knows her will be surprised at that, but there may be a few people who will be surprised that she ever wrote it at all, because the mere act of writing calls for a certain orderliness of thought and action. You have to send for a typewriter, in the first place, and put a new ribbon in once in a while, and when you've finished writing you have to put the pages in order. It is a whole process, somehow, for which a free spirit like Dorothy seems unfitted. Because Dorothy is slightly brushed with genius, and somehow you don't associate genius with the commonplace activities.
>
> Perhaps I should let it go by saying that she is Quite a Girl. I have run into her several times a week for five years or more, and she has never yet let me down. One day last summer, with the temperature somewhere around a hundred, the air conditioning at the Regency Club was suddenly discovered to be out of order. (The Regency, I should explain, is a bridge club in which I lose money to the experts.) In desperation we opened a window, but that only made matters worse. So, having no alternative, we simply perspired. All but one of us, that is. Dorothy Sims smiled happily, bundled up to the ears in a mink coat. Beneath the coat I caught a glimpse of two sweaters. It then developed that Dorothy had personally put the air conditioning out of order, by the simple expedient of stuffing her muff into the machinery. This left her hands rather chilly, but she made the best of it. Dorothy, as you may have gathered from all this, does not like the cold.

Kaufman's summary of *Curiouser and Curiouser* was: 'Like Dorothy herself, it has never a dull moment.'

Dorothy Sims belonged to the first generation of bridge players and she became disillusioned about changes to bridge. Not long before she died she wrote in an article for *The Bridge World* in May 1956:

> In the old days contract bridge was a game. A delightful stimulating game. You pitted your wits against the cards, and tried by strategy and psychology to make aces out of spaces; to make booms from busts. Those were the days of freedom for enterprise. Win or lose, you got action for your money. Then, suddenly, it was discovered that there was money in contract bridge. Big money. It

> is now Big Business. Big Business needs conformity. Books are being written, articles syndicated, all advocating one or another point-count system guaranteed to take all the thought out of thinking. Individuality is out. Reasoning is out. There is a formula for every situation. Before the conversion (to point count) days, concealing your holdings from the opponents was a recognised art.

Concealing was the essence of psychic bidding which Dorothy Sims invented. The origin of her use of the word 'psychic' was as follows: 'I was writing an article for the old Auction Bridge Magazine. My spelling is notoriously bad. I was trying to spell "psychological" but stuck. "Sycic" was as far as I could go. Good psychological bids have since been called "psychics" and bad ones "sycics".' She went on: 'The first psychic I ever bid was at the Knickerbocker Whist Club about ten years ago. I was playing Auction Duplicate. I, as dealer, picked up five spades with the ace, king, and five hearts with the ace, king. Not knowing which to bid, as in Auction Duplicate the combined honors are a very important factor, I bid a club. My partner bid a heart, which gave us top on the board. She had five hearts to the queen, jack, and four spades to the queen. Had I bid a spade, she would have passed. After this, I saw possibilities of carrying on strategic research along these lines.' It became her trademark and it paid off at times, though there were disasters en route, mostly with psychic doubles: 'I have had amazing results at times with psychic doubles overcalling with voids and singletons – but these are only gambling bids and often as disastrous as profitable.'

She sums up the attraction of psychics: 'The psychic is a mental cocaine that gives the addict the delusions of brilliancy. Cocaine instills fear; so do psychics. Every hand to the addict presents problems. You have a weak hand – fear. The opponents must have game. You bid to stop them from bidding. You have a good hand – fear – you must conceal its count and veil its honors. You are afraid of one suit – fear again – so you blindly bid your weakness: forcing bids from your partner, frantic denials by you, and you are swallowed under in a sea of doubles. So it goes. Big hands – you bid to conceal weakness. Weak hands – you bid in a camouflage of strength. Important hands – unimportant hands – all reach gigantic proportions in the hysterical reaching out for the star of brilliancy.' It's a dangerous game plan, and, as subsequent players have learned, sometimes to their cost, to be used sparingly. Dorothy Sims recognises these dangers: 'Psychics are to Bridge what futurism is to art – a camouflage for lack of knowledge. Some years ago, at the Independent Exhibition in Paris, a group of artists tied a paint brush to a mule's tail, backed him up to a canvas, and "A Winter Sunset" was conceived. Nature took its course, and this painting was pronounced the masterpiece of the year. Similarly, the psychic in unskilled hands is as aimless as the brush at the end of the tail. A stab in the dark – the wheel of chance spins round and the player anxiously watches the little ball to discover whether he is a genius or a fool.' She concludes: 'Psychics are the fourth dimension of Bridge – making aces out of spaces.'

Psychics gained prominence in the 1930s and for a time were all the rage. Oswald Jacoby was another notorious user. Culbertson, a keen strategist and psychologist, was not above making an occasional psychic bid himself, but didn't want to recommend them to the masses. His reasoning was that the techniques of the Culbertson system were designed to create partnership harmony and confidence. Psychic bidding, being one-sided and individualistic, would destroy this harmony. An expert once asked Culbertson why he was so opposed to this type of bidding, since theoretically there was a higher percentage chance of success with the deceiver having two opponents to trick and only one partner. Culbertson's answer was, 'Mathematically, you are right. Two to one is good odds. But, unfortunately, the opponents may not believe my bid and my partner will believe my bid. If he doesn't, regardless of the result on any one hand, our partnership, at that moment, will have begun to disintegrate.'

However, Culbertson wasn't averse to including psychics in his books. This one from *The Culbertson Webster Contract System* shows a hand played by Richard Frey as South. The comments are Culbertson's.

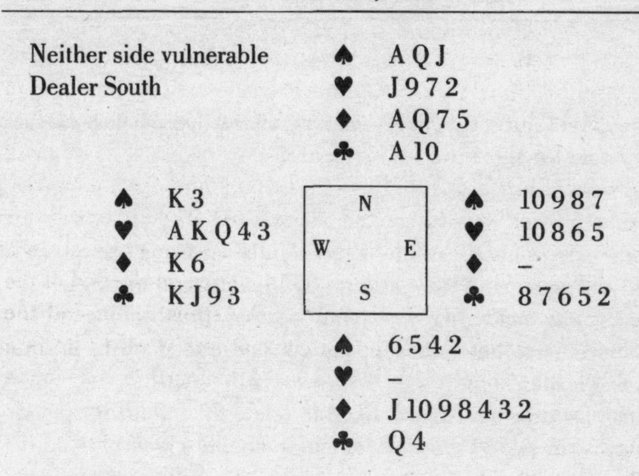

The bidding:

South	*West*	*North*	*East*
1♦(1)	2♥(2)	3♥(3)	Pass
4♥(4)	Double	7♦(5)	Pass
Pass(6)	Double	Redouble	Pass
Pass(7)	Ha-Ha(8)		

(1) A psychic opening bid, fearing an adverse game or slam.

(2) A sounder bid than a double on this particular hand, because one or two honours are required in East's hand to operate a hand of this type successfully.

(3) Suspecting that West's non-vulnerable jump overcall is psychic, and lying about the heart situation in order to give partner an idea of the enormous high-card values in his hand.

(4) Faced with the horrible necessity of making another bid, South bid four hearts, because:

(a) showing a duplication of values, it might serve to slow up North.

(b) realising that a rebid of diamonds – the only other possible bid – would almost certainly result in a slam by North.

(c) Determined that whether North's next bid was clubs, spades or diamonds, South would now pass, and rather hoping that North would bid four spades.

(5) So far West's bids might still be intended to intimidate (West might make the same bids on seven hearts to the king-queen and a bust); South's attempts to show duplication of values has merely reassured North concerning the one weakness of his hand. Hence, the grand slam.

(6) Sinking!
(7) Sunk!
(8) This was West's reaction to North's redouble, and assisted a little in planning the play of the hand.

West led the ace of hearts and by successfully finessing the queen of diamonds, and squeezing West eventually in clubs and his high heart, the contract was made. Frey, having opened the bidding with a worthless psychic to deter the opposition, had ended up in a grand slam, bid and made.

Hal Sims, Dorothy's husband, liked to relate the following episode. He was playing in a 1931 tournament and the bidding went:

South	*West*	*North*	*East*
2♣	Pass	Pass	?

Sims as East turned to South and asked, 'Madam, what system do you use?' 'The forcing,' she replied. 'My partner *must* keep my two bids open.' Sims hurriedly passed. But when the hand was over, and the declarer had struggled with a minimum hand to barely make two clubs, she turned to Sims, who would otherwise have bid and made a game with his hand. Seeing the look of anguish on his face, she queried softly: 'You bid psychics too, don't you, Mr Sims?'

Psychic bids are aimed at creating an illusion of strength or length in a particular suit, or at concealing weaknesses. A psychic bid can be defined as 'any bid made primarily with the purpose of interfering with the opponent's bidding or play rather than with the idea of aiding the bidding and play of one's own side'. S. J. Simon, as always, came up with a worthwhile definition. 'I am concerned here only with legitimate dishonesty, or, if you prefer, psychics.'

Around 1952, psychic openings re-emerged in a more disciplined form as parts of the Roth–Stone, Stayman, Kaplan–Sheinwold and Bulldog systems. The aim again was to force opponents out of their familiar bidding patterns and put them into strange and uncomfortable situations. Yet psychic bids were never fully effective against skilled opponents, who would go ahead and bid positively on good cards in spite of any psychic interventions. By 1964, the Roth–Stone system had cut out the opening psychic because the complications it created outweighed the benefits it might produce. Nowadays, psychics are used sparingly. Their main function can still be to disrupt communication between opponents, but they run the risk of deluding partner as much as the opponents, and are usually kept only for emergencies. Strong pass systems are played nowadays by a few international sides with the same aim in mind as psychic bids, namely to interfere with the opponents' bidding. In such systems a pass shows opening values and all other bids deny (though there is a certain amount of variation). While they are not psychics in that the meaning of the bidding is disclosed to everyone, they are designed to disrupt (though a few of their followers argue otherwise).

Kibitzers

—— ♠♥♦ ——
♣

The word *kibitzer* itself derives from the German word for a green plover, a highly inquisitive bird which likes watching other birds build their nests. The modern dictionary defines a kibitzer as someone who likes meddling in the affairs of others. Bridge is fertile territory for kibitzers watching on the sidelines and sometimes meddling with their comments. Many stories, true and apocryphal, have been told about them. They even appear in the Laws of Bridge under Proprieties. A kibitzer may be removed at a player's request without cause.

A classic story, and a true one, took place at a well-known New York club. The contract was five diamonds doubled, and, with the opponents on lead to the tenth trick, declarer spread his hand, claiming the balance, and just making his contract. The opposition agreed, and the cards were just about to be thrown in, when the only kibitzer watching pointed out a defensive lead which would have defeated the contract at that point. Bitter harangue and confusion then ensued and the matter was at length referred to the card committee. The final decision was that declarer be credited with making five diamonds doubled, the defence be credited with defeating the contract one trick, and the kibitzer be ordered to pay the difference.

A stranger case of kibitzing, also true, was the following. Many years ago, John Crawford, a top American player in the pre-war era, was declarer in seven spades on the deal below:

North-South vulnerable
Dealer South

♠ 3
♥ K Q 7 6
♦ J 9 8 2
♣ A K 4 2

♠ A K Q 10 8 7 6 5
♥ A 2
♦ A K
♣ 3

Crawford, always a lively, charismatic figure, was surrounded, as often happened, by an array of spectators. West had led the club queen and Crawford won in dummy. He was about to lay down his top trumps and claim his contract, when he noticed that the kibitzers were not moving and were sitting on the edge of their chairs. Surely, he reasoned, if trumps were about to divide normally there could be no problem. So why, he went on to ask himself, had the spectators not all moved away? Why were they staying? Crawford thought about it, and the only conclusion was that he would have to finesse the ten of spades, a line that gains only if East holds all the outstanding trumps. Crawford used his judgement, table presence and intuition to take just that line. The kibitzers had helped him. He finessed the ten. East indeed held all four outstanding spades and was predictably not amused to find the contract being made this way.

Helen Sobel

—♠♥♦—
♣

Helen Sobel dominated the world of women's bridge after the Culbertson and Sims era. In fact, she has been thought by many to be the greatest woman player of all time and an outstanding candidate for 'the bridge player you'd like most to have as a partner in a tough match'. Her first victory was in the Eastern Mixed Teams-of-Four Championship in 1934. The triumph signalled the beginning of a spectacular bridge career.

Helen Sobel was born in 1910 in Philadelphia and started her career as a chorus girl in *Animal Crackers*, a Marx Brothers show of 1926. Her maiden name was Helen Martin, and she had joined the show when it opened in her native Philadelphia. Her ambition at the time was to be a Broadway dancer. Cards, aside from pinochle, were not part of her life. When the show closed, Helen, struggling to find the work, gave up dancing and got married instead, but this lasted only a short time and by 1930 she was single again, not quite sure of her next step. Meanwhile, she had become intrigued by bridge. A broken pinochle date, as she told the story, was responsible for her conversion. 'It was a wet day, and two of our four hands hadn't shown up, so the other girl took me to a bridge club. You get to know something about trumps in pinochle so that part was easy to pick up.'

It didn't take her long to get going on bridge. Before long she was playing in New York bridge clubs where, at the Contract Bridge Club, she met Al Sobel, an industrial engineer turned bridge expert. They struck up a partnership and went in for duplicate tournaments. It was her first taste of competitive bridge, and she loved it. Then, in 1934, she and Al Sobel went across to Los Angeles at the invitation of Tom Stoddard, a Pacific-coast promoter of bridge. Al was hired to conduct and score duplicate matches while Helen taught bridge and helped Stoddard run his clubs. Hearing of their work, Ely Culbertson made them an offer to return East and become part of his expanding Culbertson enterprises – Helen as hostess at Culbertson's Crockford's

Club and Al as an editor of *The Bridge World.* They could hardly refuse and accepted, but got married on the way, just across the Mexican border on 28 March 1937.

Travelling back by car and crossing a state border they were stopped by an agricultural inspector checking their car for pest-infected fruit. Tired and dusty, they submitted to the search. In the first suitcase, the inspector came across a bridge cup won by Helen, and his eyes lit up when he saw that it was for bridge. He told them all about a bridge hand his wife had played the night before that had caused a sharp argument. He launched into the familiar exhaustive description of the bidding and play heard so often by experts, once cornered by lesser players. Some time later, the Sobels managed to drive away, even more exhausted.

In New York, Helen was soon carried off by Culbertson to the 1937 International Championships in Budapest, with the Culbertsons and Charles Vogelhofer as team-mates. There she played against the Austrians, including the young Rixi Markus. When she returned, Al and she organised their bridge life together. He would do the directing and administrative end of tournament bridge, while she did the playing. At the *Bridge World* office where Al worked, the key figures were Albert Morehead as editor, and Alphonse Moyse and Alfred Sheinwold as technical editors. When Al Sobel joined them, a cry of 'Al' from the editor-in-chief, Culbertson, brought four Als running.

Partnered with Sally Young, Helen soon won the Women's Pairs Championship, in 1938 and 1939. They were so far ahead of their field that Oswald Jacoby commented they could have come over into the men's section and walked off with that too. Helen's name began to appear on other major trophies, usually bracketed from now on with Charles Goren, soon to be her favourite and long-standing partner. In 1941, and again in 1942, she was ranked, on the basis of master points and tournaments won, as the number one bridge player in the country.

Yet at the time bridge was still male-dominated. Many men, seeing her as a cute blonde, fussed over her and gave her presents without realising what a skilful player she was. Others, men again, begrudged her success by commenting that her major triumphs were won while the competition had been thinned out by the war. Envy, as always, was part of the bridge scene. 'It's a lonesome feeling,' Helen said. 'You realise there's nobody among all those bridge players who is pulling for you and nobody you can discuss hands with or compare notes. And there's just no security. Anything is liable to happen to you.' Fed up with this stereotyping and the 'dumb-blonde' approach, Helen soon gave up her dark, Hollywood-style, tinted glasses, which she actually wore to disguise a severe myopia caused by long hours at the bridge table, for ordinary clear-lensed spectacles. But her determination never wavered, and her record soon spoke for itself.

Helen was not a keen bridge theorist. Asked the secrets of her success, she usually told people to go and ask the people who played with her. She never liked psychics, claiming they were more suited to a seance than a bridge table. She preferred natural bids and was not particularly in favour of conventions, particularly slam ones. She would rather cue-bid aces. She liked to feel free to come up with a bid or play that made the most sense to her in a particular situation, regardless of what the 'rules' called for. This playing 'by ear' was part of her feminine intuition. She readily admitted that an inspired play or bid or killing lead might come from a hunch, or be 'just one of those things I know'. Quizzed as to why she had made a certain successful bid or play, she would invariably raise her eyebrows and say, 'It worked, didn't it?'

One of her regular partners commented, 'You really appreciate how fantastically good she is. She has an artistic approach and an elegant style that is beautiful to watch. She plays for all possibilities with a cold and well-directed determination. I'd say she is a keen psychologist as regards both sexes. She can be the least bit stubborn at times, but all she expects of you, her partner, is dependability. In return for which you get perfect co-operation.'

Another said: 'Don't let anybody tell you that Helen Sobel is not a first-rate technician. I've never seen her make the wrong percentage play for a situation, and that despite the fact that she may pretend she's a lousy mathematician. She's an absolutely natural psychologist, the greatest little trick stealer you ever saw and commits her larceny in a bland manner. And her temperament, you won't find any better in tournament bridge. Nearly all women have some characteristic that betrays them under strain. Not Helen. When the long tournament grind is over and the rest of us feel like something the cat dragged in, there sits Helen Sobel as fresh as you please ... Good Lord, what stamina.'

Contemporary men players paid her what was then, to them, the supreme compliment by saying she played a 'man's game'. She admitted that she thought like a man at the bridge table, chiefly because years of competition against male opponents had made her familiar with their point of view. Rixi Markus felt the same about her when she first met her at the Budapest tournament in 1937. But Sobel felt that the essential differences between what might be called a woman's game and a man's was that men showed more aggressiveness, assertiveness and drive. But in certain other and equally important respects, she considered women to be naturally superior. They were, she firmly believed, more perceptive, subtler, 'more flexible, and more responsive to partner's intentions'. She wrote in her book, *Winning Bridge*: 'One of the minor hazards a woman has to combat when she plays bridge with a man is that her thinking tends to be geared to the theory of The Dominant Male. In everyday life we may be right to respect this quaint old notion and to take the trouble to employ sufficient subtlety to seem guiltless of back-seat driving. But there are many defense situations where such refinement can be costly. Quite often you do not merely have to brave the charge of back-seat driving – you have to lean over and grab the steering wheel with both hands.'

She was never in favour of husband and wife partnerships, and spoke against it. 'Play with anybody else and you can at least make believe a bonehead play doesn't matter. But with your own husband or wife familiarity breeds a little too much contempt, and it's hard to resist letting fly.' She gave as proof the fact that she and Al never did well together in tournaments, even though Al was a high-standard player.

At the table a characteristic she had was the twisting a strand of hair in her fingers while pondering a bid or play. After a while observers noted she gave that up and switched to twisting her mouth instead and pursing her lips. But decisions at the table never took long. Indeed, she was one of the fastest among top-level players. If a plan went wrong, she would sometimes pout in chagrin and might even burst out into a high-pitched laugh, expecting others to join in.

Her bridge theory was picked up in the hard school of tournament experience. She had little interest in teaching the game and did so only occasionally. Away from tournaments she played bridge mostly at New York's Cavendish Club, which, as time wore on, became more and more the pivot of her life, particularly after her divorce from Al Sobel. She always managed to gather a crowd of expectant kibitzers around her while she played.

Her fame, in historical terms, rests mostly on her partnership with Charles Goren. In 1940 they won their first tournament, the National Open Pairs title, the first of many championships for what was to become one of the most enduring and successful bridge partnerships ever. They played together for nineteen years altogether. Temperamentally they were well suited, both calm and methodical, with enough flair to keep their game alive. Goren once referred to her 'incomparable co-operative temperament, the peer of which I have never observed in any field of sport', and he went on, 'Then there is another quality ... I don't know how to describe it. I only know that Providence sees fit to bestow it but once in a generation. She has it.'

She wrote of her partnership with Goren: 'A perfect partner, Charlie will generously sugar-coat any pills that he has to hand out, and the only reason he ever raps his partners' knuckles is to make sure they stay awake for the next deal. Yet in the days when we regularly haunted the tournament trail, the traffic in ideas between us was very much a two way affair. Charlie was well aware that half the world's bridge players are women, and he profited from the experience of feminine psychology that he got from our numerous post mortems, which usually took place in transit from one tournament to the next one. Which brings me to my first precept on how to play with a man: Charlie and I seldom post-mortemed deals while actually at the card table – except when our opponents initiated a discussion – and I feel that such a policy is a judicious one for mixed partnerships. Men usually abound in sweet reasonableness when they are handing out advice, but they have a tendency to be slightly less rational when it comes to taking it themselves; and since in quite a number of mixed partnerships the female of the species is defter than the male, the best way to preserve masculine self esteem is to save the inquests until after the game.'

She went on regarding men players: 'Men are my favorite partners. They are also my favorite opponents. I like a tough game and, at the top level of competition, I think men as a class play better than women. If this be treason, make the most of it. First, let's see why I think this. Well, men have greater physical stamina, for one thing. That's important in tournaments, where play runs nine days and world championship battles go on for close to two weeks.

'Men appear to have greater powers of concentration. I say "appear to have" because I don't really believe that they can concentrate any better; it's just that they do. Few women are willing to stop thinking of family, clothes, beauty, appearance, men and other interests in order to bend every effort toward excelling at a game. A man is quite willing to partner a fellow he doesn't even like; he'll return your lead even if you just burned his house down – provided he is satisfied that this is the best percentage play he can make. But he will not return his best friend's lead or his boss's lead or his sweetheart's lead if he thinks he has figured out a better plan. And he expects his partner to do likewise, even when his partner is a woman.

'But a woman – let's face it – may refuse to return partner's lead if she happens to be annoyed with her partner. Or she may return his lead out of love and loyalty even when she knows darn well there's a better play available. Men don't expect this and don't understand it. So if you are going to play with a man, you will do well to try to adopt his single-minded pursuit of the best percentage chance and accommodate yourself to his way of thinking.'

Another bridge partner, the theatrical impresario Howard Deitz, wrote: 'Helen is always self-assured, and I suspect knows how to handle a forcing pass even in a taxicab. She has no dogmatic attitudes, no rigid systems, no counts. She believes bridge is a game of judgement. Her system is all human, all logic; her playing follows from the inferences of the bidding, and she has an instinctive interpretation of the percentage chances of a finesse or a squeeze or a break in a suit.'

Her last two major championship wins with Goren were the Life Master Pairs in Miami Beach in 1958 and the Master Knockout Teams (Spingold) in Los Angeles in 1960. Her last national championship – thirty-four years after her first – came in 1968 when she won the Mixed Teams in Minneapolis with Oswald and Jim Jacoby and Minda Brachman. She died in 1969.

She wrote her book *Winning Bridge* in 1950. Here are some extracts:

> The important point I want to make here is that a winning player must learn to recognise his partner's style and act accordingly. If you know your partner to be aggressive and fancy, for the sake of your own pocket-book give him leeway during the bidding. On the other hand, if you know your partner to be a steady player who is consistently on the conservative side, you in turn can be more aggressive.
>
> More points are lost at the contract bridge table through bad or pointless overcalls than in any other way. An overcall, by definition, is a bid made in the face of declared strength by the opponents. Consequently logic would dictate that to overcall, one needs more strength than one needs to open the bidding.

In general, playing bridge together seems to bring out the very worst in a married couple. How often have I arrived at a table during a tournament to find some normally pleasant, kind man slouched there in his chair, only half-facing the little woman across the table from him! And the three-quarter view of his face does little to conceal the scorn and sarcastic pity written on it. Needless to say, his bride does not take to this contemptuous attitude very kindly. She, too, is bristling with indignation. 'Whatever made me marry this impossible man?' is approximately what's going on in her mind. I'd like to think that their respective attitudes only make them play harder and better on the hands to come. But the opposite is true. Bad bids and plays are made partly out of the inability to think clearly any more and partly out of sheer temper and a desire to deliberately 'fix' each other. Their bad play is usually only exceeded by their bad manners to each other and sometimes to the opponents. All this seems to me rather sad, particularly since the participants in these feuds are normally very happily married and loving couples.

Charles Goren

—♠♥♦—
♣

Charles Goren first got into bridge as a result of a young woman's derisive laughter. She was his hostess at a bridge game in Montreal in 1923. Goren was then aged twenty-two and a beginner at the game. His gaucherie and lack of skill were soon painfully exposed. The young woman's laughter really got to him. He determined from then on to learn the game properly.

He came from Philadelphia originally, from a family of Russian-Jewish immigrants. Born in 1901, he grew up in a poor, tough section of the city, populated by Irish and Jews. His father was a cabinet-maker, and the two sons, Charles and Edward, had to contend with many a street battle. Edward Goren, later a successful Philadelphia businessman, recalled: 'Charlie had blond curly hair but he fought like a tiger. He was not afraid of anything in the world.' The young Charles Goren also manifested a remarkable indifference to pain, and an ability to concentrate on whatever interested him for hours on end. This endurance was a key factor in his later bridge life. His competitive spirit was sharpened at the same time. Charles Goren looked back on his childhood and recalled as the main lesson he learned from it: 'It was important in our community to do things better than the other fellow or you'd never be noticed.' His determination to succeed stemmed from this.

Poverty left its mark in a penny-pinching side as well. For example, years later, now well-off and successful, he decided to donate a bridge trophy in his name for the National Men's Teams Championship. He went out and bought a used horse-racing cup, had the old inscription chiselled off and a new one put on instead. At school he led his class, and used to earn extra pocket money by tutoring less able pupils in Latin and Greek. His first job was as a furniture salesman, where his prodigious memory was a distinct asset. A customer might not return for six months yet Goren would still be able to recall his name. Then a better-off, older cousin, living in Montreal, suggested that, with his academic ability, he should go to college. Goren enrolled at McGill

University Law School in Montreal, selecting law because, he said in his rather diffident manner, 'It had the easiest hours'.

It was there that he played the bridge game mentioned above. Just before graduation he had met a girl who invited him to play bridge. 'She said to me, "Do you play bridge?" and I knew that girls play bridge in the afternoon, so I said, "Sure," and I sat down to play and made a complete ass of myself. She laughed at me like nothing you ever saw. I liked this girl. For her to laugh at me was like putting a knife through me. So I took an oath then that I was never going to sit down at a card table again until I knew how to play bridge.' He went back home to Philadelphia and bought Milton Work's classic book *Auction Bridge*: 'If they had destroyed the plates, I could have reconstructed the book from memory.' He followed its dictates by dealing and laying out hands and analysing the play, card by card.

When he went back to McGill the following year to visit, the girl wouldn't play with him. 'But I wouldn't call the time wasted,' Goren later commented wryly. He was now on his pathway to bridge. Back in Pennsylvania for the bar exams, Goren found that Pennsylvania law bore little resemblance to Canadian law. 'I bluffed my way through the bar exam,' he recalled. 'I didn't really know enough to pass the bar. But I was able to sling the language around by that time. I bluffed it through by citing decisions. I'd say, "Well, in the case of Hotspur vs. Hotspur, the House of Lords decided so and so, from which we draw the following principles . . ." I spoke with such authority that the examiner thought, "Well, this fellow must know what he's talking about," and I passed.' Despite this verbal facility and early technique of bluffing, he was nowhere near as successful as a lawyer as he was later at the bridge table. 'I should say that the law gave me up, not that I gave up the law,' he said.

Initially bridge was a spare-time activity but soon he felt confident enough to enter a local bridge contest organised by his local paper. He won. Yet he was still smarting from his Montreal experience, and resolved to play publicly only once he felt he was good enough. He saw himself like a person who wasn't going to get into the water until he was an expert swimmer. Between 1923 and 1936 he still made his living as a lawyer in Philadelphia, but he never earned more than $5,000 a year. Bridge promised better money. He was a late starter in the tournament world, his first being in 1931 using the Culbertson System, but his success there soon attracted the notice of Milton Work himself, a fellow Philadelphian. Goren became his technical assistant – part-time, as he was still practising law – and helped with the preparation of his books, lectures, and newspaper columns – an important training ground for Goren whose own newspaper columns were later to be syndicated world-wide. Work was, with Wilbur Whitehead, one of the leading figures of bridge in the 1920s and Goren learned much from him. Work earned about $20,000 a year from his syndicated column, but paid Goren only $35 a week, a disparity that Goren resented for years. Goren, a talented writer, soon found his own distinctive writing style with a flair for gently whimsical humour, yet, as he recalled, Work would 'edit out the brightness'.

The next year, in 1932, Goren, trying to advance his bridge prospects, sent Culbertson his own analysis of ten bridge hands and was gratified to see the hands appear in Culbertson's syndicated column, with a cheque for $30 back in the post. Then Milton Work asked Goren to try a few analyses for him, and offered him $5 a hand. 'So Ely got no more of my business,' said Goren. Milton Work was then an old man and it wasn't long before Work was using seven columns a week from Goren. They were entertainingly written, in marked contrast to the typical bridge commentary of the day, and the newspaper syndicate began complimenting Work on his new, colourful style. Emboldened by these successes, Goren tried writing a book of his own: *Winning Bridge Made Easy*. The book appeared to have little chance of succeeding. Ely Culbertson ruled the bridge publishing world in the mid-1930s. 'If it isn't Culbertson, it isn't bridge' seemed to be the guiding principle. But Goren's book when it was published in 1936 did well simply because it was clear, helpful, and, most of all, simple.

Before long Goren began tinkering with the idea of developing his own system. Goren was already a bridge teacher, an ability he had retained from his schoolboy years, and his methodical and analytical approach, the lawyer in him this time, made him a natural as a writer. In this first book, Goren described variations from the Culbertson System. He felt the defects in the Culbertson System were its fractions which Culbertson followers had to use to calculate 'quick tricks' (i.e. two and a half quick tricks as an opening bid). People had a natural aversion to fractions, Goren felt, and he became convinced that a whole-number system would have a special appeal. Milton Work had devised a system for evaluating no-trump hands, based on a point count of four for aces, three for kings, two for queens and one for jacks. Goren liked the idea, and extended it to all suit bids.

The point-count method became the cornerstone of his method, based on the forty high-card points in a deck. An opening suit bid would require thirteen points, a bid was mandatory at fourteen points, a partnership with twenty-six points should go for game in a major suit (twenty-nine points being needed in a minor suit), partners with thirty-three points should aim for a small slam, and thirty-seven was the magic number for a grand slam.

On the day his first book was published, Goren gave up his law practice. The next few years were marked by his rivalry with Culbertson, who at one point issued a public challenge to 'all-comers', apparently never dreaming that Goren would risk his growing reputation against him. Goren grabbed the opportunity. Goren always treasured Culbertson's letter explaining that a sudden business trip to Europe had now made it necessary for him to call off the match. 'Ely was using good judgment,' commented Goren ironically. Then one night at a tournament in Atlantic City, New Jersey, he spotted a blonde ex-showgirl playing her cards 'with the guile of a fox and the aggressiveness of a wolverine'. Goren liked her style and asked her to become his partner. The new partnership flourished. She was Helen Sobel and it became a bridge union of the best male player and the best female player in the world.

Goren's first breakthrough in his rivalry with Culbertson came in the early 1940s. He was writing a bridge column in Philadelphia and, with Helen Sobel, winning every tournament in sight. Culbertson was writing a column for the Chicago *Tribune* Syndicate, and dabbling in international politics. When Marshall Field started the liberal-minded Chicago *Sun*, Culbertson left the conservative *Tribune* for what he thought would be greener pastures. Goren, by this time nationally known, took over for the *Tribune*. A year later Goren had more columns in more papers than Culbertson.

A remarkable string of victories during the war years put him at the very top of the masterpoint winners list, and he held that place continuously from 1944 to 1962. His famous parsimony came out in this war-time story, when just about everything was rationed, including soap. He ran into Harry Fishbein, the bridge player and inventor of the convention named after him, at a major tournament in Buffalo. Fishbein was on an 'also-ran' streak – he had finished second in a number of tournaments, and seemed unable to get first prize. When they met, Fishbein was standing disconsolately at the train depot after finishing second again. 'It shouldn't be a total loss,' he said to Goren, standing alongside of him. 'At least I've got this.' Whereupon he plunged his hand into a capacious coat pocket and drew out five small bars of soap purloined from the hotel. Goren dipped his hand into *his* pocket and produced six. 'Second again, Harry,' he said.

Goren cashed in on the bridge boom after the Second World War. In 1951 he published *Contract Bridge Complete* and overtook Culbertson as the decisive bridge authority. Goren's *New Contract Bridge Complete* was on the best-seller lists for months, and Goren soon had as much success with his books as Culbertson ever had in the 1930s. A comparison might be that Culbertson was a sprinter, but Goren was a marathon runner.

This book in particular gained him millions of adherents; indeed, his point-count valuation soon became known as part of Standard American. It was easy to learn and gave the game a lift it had not enjoyed since the early Culbertson years. Goren offered a more natural system, which average and expert players alike could follow. Soon the old fractional point count of Culbertson ('two and a half to open, one and a half to respond') was abandoned in favour of Goren. Goren's wry style appealed to readers.

> Suppose I told you that you could simplify your game immeasurably, and *at the same time improve it immeasurably*. Suppose I told you that the more bridge complexities, subtleties, and nuances you try to cram into your game, the worse your game is going to be. Suppose I had the colossal gall to charge you with spending too much of your bridge energy trying to perfect superduper devices that are not worth learning, and at the same time failing to learn basic techniques that make the difference between winners and losers. Suppose I told you all that. Would you be insulted? Would you read on?
>
> Okay, now that we're rid of the hotheads, let's be more specific. Here are the basic faults you and I are going to uncover in the average American bridge player:
>
> 1. He gives away thousands of points a year with stereotyped, predictable bidding and play.
> 2. He often doubles when he shouldn't and more often fails to double when he should.

3. He rigidly obeys rules that are nothing more than general guidelines intended for the rankest of beginners.
4. He engages in repetitious mannerisms, right down to such minor matters as the way he sorts his cards, thereby giving valuable information to experienced opponents.
5. He persists in attempting plays he doesn't understand, and the same time failing to try plays he does understand (and which have just as good a mathematical chance of success).
6. He treats his partner like a lackey, or allows his partner to treat him like one, in either case destroying the calm, warm rapport that spells points to any team on any level.
7. He considers only his own hand and tries to turn bridge into a singles event.
8. And there are many others.

Soon the name of Goren became synonymous with bridge to millions. He was known as Mr Bridge. He was recognised as a world figure by appearing on the front cover of *Time* magazine in 1958. Readers saw a medium-sized man, with dark, rumpled hair and short in build. He made the first series of bridge shows for television, 'Championship Bridge with Charles Goren', produced in the early 1960s. By 1963, it was estimated that his books had sold more than eight million copies. In addition to his daily newspaper column (which had a readership of over thirty-four million), he wrote a weekly column for *Sports Illustrated* and a monthly article for *McCall's Magazine*, plus regular contributions to *The Bridge World* and other bridge magazines throughout the world. His annual income and his total earnings from bridge in the 1960s far surpassed those of Culbertson.

For years he answered, with the help of his staff, ten thousand letters a year from bridge fans, and also headed Goren Enterprises, which licensed the manufacture of card-table covers, cocktail napkins with bridge hints, and all sorts of gadgets. He gave his name to Goren Cruises and went on the road as an ambassador of bridge to small towns as readily as large tournaments.

Goren liked to see himself as someone the average bridge player could identify with. Once playing in a tournament, a kibitzer commented to him, 'You know there wasn't anything you did that I feel I couldn't have done, too.' Goren told him, 'That is the main idea in expert bridge – to do it when it has to be done. It's really that simple.'

Simplicity was his hallmark. He was tolerant of kibitzers and would even banter with them between hands. When one commented that his bid had not strictly followed the teachings of his book, he quipped, 'Madam, you couldn't have read the book all the way through.'

An indication of his phenomenal memory was that he once won a bet by recalling all of the hands he had just played in a three-day tournament. He had the expert's passion for post-mortems and this once led to a curious incident. He was on a plane flying back from Brazil with Sidney Silodor, B. Jay Becker and Helen Sobel. The four Life Masters had just completed a series of exhibition matches there and were going over the hands. A fellow passenger, reading a newspaper in a nearby seat, became more and more intrigued. Finally, putting down his paper, he apologised for his eavesdropping and introduced himself as a United Nations representative. He was amazed that they could remember bridge hands in such detail. They assured him it was not unusual among top bridge players. In the discussion that followed the diplomat disclosed that he was interested in horse racing and proceeded to recall the past form of well-known horses as far back as twenty years ago. Noticing the smiles on the faces of the bridge players, he broke off, realising that a good memory is always sharpened by those things that interest one most.

Goren gave freely of his bridge ideas to anyone who wrote to him for information. He believed that bridge teachers could get too technical and evangelistic. His bridge lectures were spiced with analogies and anecdotes. He saw himself as eighty per cent entertainer and twenty per cent teacher. 'Take my column,' he commented once. 'It has to compete with the comic strips for reader interest.' Goren said of his own bridge playing: 'I am neither conservative nor spectacular. I aim for soundness. In sound play, you have to take certain calculated risks and I'm not averse to taking them but that doesn't make me a reckless player. You have to make decisions, sometimes unilateral decisions, and unless you're willing to make drastic decisions you're at a disadvantage. Now a drastic decision may be something that appears to be on the conservative side. You take that course of action which is more calculated to produce points. Sometimes this takes guts. It takes guts to bid seven, but sometimes it takes guts to pass.'

Goren was especially good with women players and many of his bridge titles were won seated opposite women, a record that won him the description 'the perfect woman's partner'. His partnership with

Helen Sobel was a case in point. For him, a smoothly adjusted partnership was the most efficient route to success. Goren respected women as bridge players, feeling that their lack of vanity, their receptiveness to instruction, made them at times more focused players than men. But he felt that in a match between top experts, men would win out, if only for their superior stamina. Goren himself put this theory to the test once by playing in a tournament entitled 'The female of the species is deadlier than the male at the bridge table'. Playing with Morrie Ells, a Life Master, against Helen Sobel and Sally Young, both outstanding women players, his side only just won a twenty-five-rubber match by 770 points.

Goren never married. Why has always been a conundrum. His view, when asked, was that he was 'too wrapped up in the job of establishing myself ... I suppose I'm too closely wedded to bridge'. A lifelong bachelor, his apartment in Spruce Street, Philadelphia, was stocked with an array of cups, plaques, and medals – plus the usual assortment of bridge tables, ash stands, lighters and assorted prize loot from lesser tournaments. He retired from active competition in 1966, having captured virtually every major bridge trophy in US tournament play, including a record eight McKenney 'Player of the Year' trophies. He and Helen Sobel last played together in 1960, having enjoyed nineteen years of partnership. After his retirement, he lived quietly at his home in Miami Beach and then in the 1970s he moved to live with his nephew Marvin in Encino, Southern California. His health and mental abilities declined in later years and he was rarely seen out of the home – indeed his columns were soon written by someone else. He died in 1991, aged ninety, of a heart attack.

Somerset Maugham

—♠♥♦—
♣

Maugham was a passionate bridge player and played whenever he found the opportunity. On his eightieth birthday the *New York Times* ran the headline 'Somerset Maugham, Britain's master storyteller, began his day with half an hour of bridge'. Maugham took the view that 'bridge is the most entertaining and intelligent card game the art of man has so far devised'. He played bridge nearly every day at the Villa Mauresque in the south of France where he lived and he introduced it into his writings, most notably in his short story *Three Fat Women of Antibes.*

In fact, the earliest mention of bridge in his writings came in 1909 in *Smith*, the first play in the history of the theatre to open with a game of bridge. In his later short story *Christmas Holiday*, bridge features again with these memorable lines:

> 'It only made the difference of a trick.'
> 'A trick? A trick? A trick can make all the difference in the world.'

Bridge appealed doubly to Maugham. There was the fascination of the game itself but it also provided him, as a writer and student of human nature, with a further school for the study of mankind. Maugham used to claim that he could tell the essential facts about a man after a few rubbers at the bridge table. Whenever he was in London he played bridge at the Garrick. Fellow players remember that he did not like to make conversation during his game and that he always took it seriously.

His short story *Three Fat Women of Antibes* was written in 1933. It brings out two themes close to his heart – his dislike of women and his passion for bridge. He knew the setting of the story well, as he had a villa near Antibes at Cap Ferrat. It's not too fanciful to think he might well have come across those main protagonists on one of his outings to nearby Antibes.

Maugham bought the Villa Mauresque in 1926. The estate had once belonged to Leopold II, King of Belgium, who built on extra houses for his mistresses, plus one for his private priest to be close at hand in case of a need for last-minute absolution. His priest had spent most of his life in Algeria, and so asked for a house that was Moorish in style – hence the Villa Mauresque. Maugham kept the same décor, keyhole windows, domes and minarets and Moorish decorations.

Maugham lived there for the rest of his life, with the exception of a five-year period during the Second World War. It was his fortress. Maugham liked a certain Edwardian formality and guests had to abide by his house rules. Anyone breaking these rules was swiftly banished. He had thirteen servants in all: a cook, two maids, a butler, a footman, a chauffeur, and seven gardeners. Dinner was always at eight, with Maugham wearing a double-breasted velvet jacket, a black tie, and black velvet slippers with his initials sewn in gold braid, a gift from Churchill. The meal was served by his butler Marius and a footman stood by, both wearing white jackets with silver buttons. Guests were expected to leave soon after dinner unless a game of bridge had been arranged.

Maugham depended greatly on his constant companion and lover, Gerald Haxton. The latter's amiability of disposition enabled them to make friends on their journeys with people in ships, clubs, bar rooms and hotels to provide material for his short stories. Gerald Haxton was dapper and lean, but a heavy drinker. He was a risk taker and once dived headlong into an empty swimming pool. Maugham always forgave Gerald his transgressions. In fact, he bought the Villa Mauresque when Haxton, an American by birth, was declared an undesirable alien in England and was forced to leave the country. Haxton died in New York in November 1944. Maugham was grief-stricken.

In 1913, aged thirty-nine, Maugham had married Syrie, the daughter of Dr Thomas Barnardo, the founder of Barnardo Homes. She was married at the time to Henry (later Sir Henry) Wellcome, of Burroughs & Wellcome, the chemists, but she left her husband for Maugham. A well-known interior decorator, she was smart, pretty, with radiant brown eyes and a beautiful skin. She was also high-spirited and vivacious. Maugham was flattered by her interest. He claimed he wanted to lead a normal sex life. In his autobiography, written when he was over eighty years old, he still felt the need to assert this, 'In the circles in which we moved it was an understood thing that I was Syrie's lover.' The marriage was an immediate failure because, even before he married Syrie, he had met his lover, the young Gerald Haxton. Yet he needed to keep up his heterosexual pretence in public, and found it hard to be open about his homosexuality. Staying at the Villa Mauresque, his nephew Robin was dining alone with him one evening when he noticed his uncle had been silent for a while. Robin looked up and saw tears flowing down his wrinkled cheeks. 'I've been such a fool,' he cried. 'And the awful thing is that if I had my life all over again I'd probably make exactly the same mistakes. My greatest one was that I tried to persuade myself that I was three-quarters normal and that only a quarter of me was queer – whereas really it was the other way round.' He did not really like women as can be seen in *Three Fat Women of Antibes*. Only one heroine in his earlier books, Rosie in *Cakes and Ale*, is likeable and even then he cannot resist bringing her back later as stout and over-made-up.

His rancour against his former wife Syrie never lessened. He blamed her for much that had gone wrong in his life. During the Second World War he ran across her at a party in London. She came up to greet him. 'I am crossing the Atlantic and I am terrified of torpedoes,' she said. 'And I can't swim, so what should I do if the boat were to sink, and I was floundering in the water?' 'Ser-swallow,' Maugham stammered. 'Just ser-swallow.' His stammer had developed soon after his mother died when he was eight. When Syrie died in July 1955, the news of her death was relayed to him at the Villa Mauresque. He was sitting playing patience at a card table. He put down the pack of cards immediately and began to drum on the table with his fingers in a triumphant tattoo. 'Tra-la-la-la,' he sang. 'No more alimony. Tra-la, tra-la.'

Towards the end of his life, his face became almost the colour of parchment. His eyesight started to fail and at times his mind wandered, but he moved with dignity and his gestures were still of authority. He looked like a Chinese mandarin – ancient, fragile, wise, and benign, detached from the problems of the world.

Nearing ninety he kept himself alive by taking supposed life-prolonging injections of Niehan goat glands at a clinic in Switzerland. This obsession with health, with appearance and rejuvenation, comes out in the story that follows. Maugham died on 16 December 1965, aged ninety, enigmatic to the last. Few people ever really got to know him well or pierced the layers of morbid shyness to catch a glimpse of his real character. Much was always on the surface as this story, summarised below, bears out.

THREE FAT WOMEN OF ANTIBES

Three women are gathered at a house they have rented in Antibes in the south of France – Mrs Richman, a widow, Mrs Sutcliffe, twice divorced, Miss Hickson, unmarried. They were dedicated slimmers and dedicated bridge players, still in their forties and well off.

Antibes provided swimming, the slimmer's friend. But they still needed a reliable fourth at bridge which they played fiercely and enthusiastically. Mrs Sutcliffe, or Arrow as she was called, played the best of the three, a hard, brilliant game. Beatrice Richman was solid and reliable while Frank Hickson was dashing, a great theorist, referring constantly to the rival systems of Culbertson and Sims.

But the elusive fourth was still needed. 'This person played like a foot, the other was so slow that it drove you frantic, one was quarrelsome, another was a bad loser, a third was next door to a crook.' Then Frank remembered her cousin by marriage, Lena Finch, whose husband had died recently. Bridge might help her get over the shock. She was invited to stay. Frank met her at the station and introduced her to the others in the Monkey House at Eden Roc Hotel. This was an enclosure covered with glass overlooking the sea, with a bar at the back, where people gathered for drinks. As the waiter came up, Frank asked Lena what she would like to drink. Lena ordered a dry Martini to the shock of the other three for whom alcohol was not allowed.

They strolled back to the villa for lunch. Within each napkin lay two little antifat rusks. Lena smiled and put hers aside by her plate. 'May I have some bread?' she asked. The three women were shocked again. Not one of them had eaten bread for ten years. Even Beatrice, greedy as she was, drew the line there. Frank recovered herself first. 'Of course, darling,' she said, and asked the butler to bring some. 'And some butter,' said Lena pleasantly. There was a moment's embarrassed silence. 'I don't know if there's any in the house,' said Frank, 'but I'll enquire. There may be some in the kitchen.' 'I adore bread and butter, don't you?' said Lena, turning to Beatrice. Beatrice smiled weakly and gave an evasive reply. The butler brought a long crisp roll of French bread. Lena slit it in two and plastered it with the butter.

As they ate their grilled sole, Lena took more butter and spread it over her fish. 'As long as I can have bread and butter and potatoes and cream, I'm quite happy.' The three friends exchanged further glances. The rest of lunch consisted of lamb cutlets with the fat carefully removed and spinach boiled in water, with stewed pears to finish with. Lena tasted her pears and gave the butler a look of enquiry. The 'resourceful man' understood at once, and handed her a bowl of sugar. She helped herself liberally. The other three pretended not to notice.

Coffee followed, and Lena took three lumps of sugar. Beatrice's mouth drooped at the corners, and she gave the sugar a yearning look. 'Beatrice!' boomed Frank sternly.

Bridge was a relief after this. For the first rubber Arrow cut with the newcomer. 'Do you play Vanderbilt or Culbertson?' she asked her. 'I have no conventions,' Lena answered in her happy-go-lucky way, 'I play by the light of nature.' 'I play strict Culbertson,' said Arrow acidly. The three women braced themselves. No conventions indeed! They'd soon teach her. When it came to bridge Frank's family friendliness was soon forgotten. She settled down with the same determination as the others to put the stranger in her place. But the 'light of nature' served Lena well. She had a natural gift for the game and great experience. She played with imagination and assurance. The other players were gradually mollified. This was real bridge. They all enjoyed themselves. Arrow and Beatrice began to feel more kindly towards Lena, and Frank, noticing this, heaved a sigh of relief. Her idea was going to be a success.

After a couple of hours they stopped. Lena went down to Juan-les-Pins and came back to tell them she had discovered a 'dear little teashop where they've got the most beautiful thick fresh cream' of which she had ordered half a pint to be sent up every day as her 'little contribution to the household'. The others sat looking sullen and spiteful.

The next day Lena reminded them that her doctor had recommended her to drink burgundy at lunchtime and champagne at dinner and the butler disclosed that he could make half a dozen kinds of cocktail. The three fat women did their best, Maugham describing their reactions as 'gay, chatty and even hilarious (such is the natural gift that women have for deception)'.

It was when they played bridge that the strain showed itself. They had always been fond of talking while playing and their discussions had up till then been friendly. Now a distinct bitterness crept in. Mistakes were pointed out with 'quite unnecessary frankness'. Discussion moved from argument to altercation. Sometimes the session ended in angry silence. Once Frank accused Arrow of deliberately letting her down. Two or three times Beatrice, the softest of the three, was reduced to tears. On another occasion Arrow flung down her cards and swept out of the room in a fury. Their tempers were getting frayed.

Lena tried to keep the peace. 'I think it's such a pity to quarrel over bridge,' she said. 'After all, it's only a game.' It was all very well for her, they thought. She had had a square meal and half a bottle of champagne, and, worse still, she was winning all their money. There seemed to be no justice in the world.

Their affection turned to hate. Yet, even though they each hated Lena, they couldn't help confiding in her. Each went to her separately and told her how detestable the others were. Arrow complained about spending so much time with women older than herself. Frank let her know that, with her masculine mind, it was too much to expect her to be satisfied with anyone 'so frivolous as Arrow and so frankly stupid as Beatrice'.

By the time Lena's fortnight drew to a close, the three fat women were barely on speaking terms. They kept up appearances in front of Lena, but, when she was not there, they ignored each other with 'icy politeness'. Lena planned to leave to stay with friends on the Italian Riviera. Frank saw her off on the train. Back at the house, Frank changed quickly into her one-piece bathing suit, put on her espadrilles, her man's dressing gown – no nonsense about that – and went down to Eden Roc for a bathe before lunch. She went through the Monkey House, feeling peaceful at last, and stopped dead in her tracks. She could not believe her eyes. Maugham takes up the story:

> Beatrice was sitting at one of the tables, all by herself, still in pyjamas, a string of pearls around her neck, munching away at a plate of *croissants* and butter, with strawberry jam, coffee and cream by the side. She was spreading the butter thickly on the hot bread, covering it with jam, and then pouring thick cream over it all. 'You'll kill yourself,' said Frank. 'I don't care,' mumbled Beatrice, her mouth full. 'You'll put on pounds and pounds.' 'Go to hell!' She laughed in Frank's face. 'I'm disappointed in you, Beatrice. I thought you had more character.' 'It's your fault. That blasted woman. You would have her down. For a fortnight I've watched her gorge like a hog. It's more than flesh and blood can stand. I'm going to have one square meal if I bust.' Tears welled up in Frank's eyes. Suddenly she felt unusually weak and

womanly. Speechless, she sank down on a chair by Beatrice's side. A waiter came up. With a pathetic gesture she waved towards the coffee and *croissants*. 'I'll have the same,' she sighed.

The waiter brought her *croissants*, butter, jam and coffee. 'Where's the cream, you fool?' she roared at him, like a lioness at bay. She began to eat. She ate gluttonously. Soon the place filled up with bathers coming up from the bathing area to enjoy a cocktail or two before lunch. Presently Arrow arrived and caught sight of Frank and Beatrice. She stopped in her tracks, too, hardly able to believe her eyes. 'My God!' she cried. 'You beasts. You hogs.' She seized a chair. 'Waiter. Bring me what these ladies are having.' Frank lifted her great heavy head from her plate. 'Bring me some *pâté de foie gras*,' she boomed. 'Frank!' cried Beatrice. 'Shut up.' 'All right. I'll have some too.'

The coffee was brought, and the hot rolls and cream and the *pâté de foie gras*, and they set to. They spread the cream on the *pâté* and they ate it. They devoured great spoonfuls of jam. They crunched the delicious crisp bread voluptuously. They did not speak. They ate with solemn, ecstatic fervour. 'I haven't eaten potatoes for twenty-five years,' said Frank in a far-off brooding tone. 'Waiter,' cried Beatrice, 'bring fried potatoes for three.' '*Très bien, madame.*'

The potatoes were brought and they ate them with their fingers. 'Bring me a dry Martini,' said Arrow. 'You can't have a dry Martini in the middle of a meal, Arrow,' said Frank. 'Can't I? You wait and see.' 'All right then. Bring me a double dry Martini,' said Frank. 'Bring three double dry Martinis,' said Beatrice. They were brought and drunk at a gulp. The women looked at one another and sighed. The misunderstandings of the last fortnight dissolved, and the sincere affection each had for the other welled up again in their hearts. They could hardly believe that they had ever contemplated the possibility of severing a friendship that had brought them so much solid satisfaction. They finished the potatoes. 'I wonder if they've got any chocolate *éclairs*,' said Beatrice. 'Of course they have.'

And of course they had. Frank thrust one whole into her huge mouth, swallowed it and seized another, but before she ate it she looked at the other two and plunged a vindictive dagger into the heart of the monstrous Lena. 'You can say what you like, but the truth is she played a damned rotten game of bridge, really.' 'Lousy,' agreed Arrow.

Maugham has depicted a world he knew especially well, the Riviera, playground of the rich and spoiled. Bridge had always been played there – indeed, as we saw in the 'History of Bridge', the earliest forms of the game were tried out there when it was still known as *khedive*. Bridge was important to the three women in this story but not as much as it was to Maugham. It really mattered to him. The piece that follows bears this out. In March 1946, Maugham had agreed to write an introduction for Charles Goren's *Standard Book of Bidding*. His terms were that Goren would be his guest at dinner and bridge, but secretly he was both flattered and honoured to be writing it. Goren's *Better Bridge for Better Players* had been Maugham's bible up to that point. Maugham frequently played with Goren as his partner either in the USA or in Europe when Goren was visiting. Writing this introduction, Maugham said, made him feel 'as proud as a lieutenant bidden by his admiral to lead the flagship into battle'.

Once when they were playing together, Goren made a mistake which Maugham never forgot and he always liked re-telling the story of the hand where Goren had trumped his winning ace. Goren led his singleton heart against declarer's four spade contract. Maugham, who had bid hearts, won with the king and then led the ace. But Goren trumped this instead of waiting to trump a small heart on the next round.

Goren's view of Maugham's ability as a player was charitable. 'By expert standards,' Goren said of him, 'he was not to be feared as a player, yet he had the ability and the wisdom to bring something quite special to the game.'

On a later visit to the USA Maugham played in a game with Eisenhower. By the end of the evening Maugham had lost twelve dollars to Eisenhower. He was a bad loser, and in the taxi home to the Plaza Hotel with Alexander Frere of Heinemann, his publishers, Maugham said, 'Eisenhower is probably a very great general, but he's a bloody bad bridge player and a very stupid man.' His irritation later wore off and he wrote a letter to Frere stating that Eisenhower was 'very nice, absolutely simple, no frills or pose or anything, and we had a very agreeable game'. Maugham, as so often, was irked by losing and his habitual crossness came out.

In his Introduction to Goren's book, Maugham rates himself 'an indifferent player', though, since he never thought of himself as anything else, this might have been his chief asset as a partner. As he saw it, much in bridge depended on 'horse sense' more than 'cluttering up your brain with any great number of precepts'. The moral was clear. 'If you have a cool head, the ability to put two and two together and get the right answer, and if you will tell the exact truth about your hand, you will be a useful partner and a formidable opponent.'

Bridge, in his view, was not an idle pastime. 'That is stuff and nonsense.' Non-bridge players might claim conversation was more important, but Maugham was adamant about his preferences. 'No, let the carping carp, they don't know what they miss. If I had my way, I would have children taught bridge as a matter of course, just as they are taught dancing. In the end it will be more useful to them, for you cannot with seemliness continue to dance when you are bald and potbellied; nor, for the matter of that, can you with satisfaction to yourself or pleasure to your partners continue to play tennis or golf when you are past middle age; but you can play bridge as long as you can sit up at a table and tell one card from another. In fact, when all else fails – sport, love, ambition – bridge remains a solace and an entertainment.'

He went on:

> Bridge is the most entertaining and intelligent card game the wit of man has so far devised, and I deplore the fact that so many people go out of their way to make it a bore. There are the people who, after a hand has been played, will tell you all the thirteen cards they held. Well, you'd seen them played, so you know; but even if you didn't, why should they suppose you care? Then there are the people who during the deal or when you're sorting your cards start to tell you about Aunt Annie's operation or the trouble they're having with decorators in their new apartment. There is no stopping them.
>
> 'One heart,' you say.
>
> They take no notice.
>
> 'My dear, I've had three cooks in the last two weeks and not

one of them could boil an egg.'

'One heart,' you repeat.

'Well, I'll tell you what happened to me,' says your partner. 'I got a couple. They drove up in their car, looked at the house, and didn't even come in. They just drove away, and I was expecting eight people to lunch on Sunday.'

'One heart,' you say.

'You know that Betty's got a new beau?' the player on your right puts in.

'Oh, you mean Harry,' replies the player on your left. 'I've known that for months. She always has liked heels.'

Just to get a little attention, you have a mind to say, 'Seven no trumps,' but of course it might be expensive and your partner wouldn't be sympathetic, so you meekly repeat, 'One heart.'

Bridge has to make its way around the other preoccupations in people's lives, as his short story shows. A further recrimination was against the woeful partner: 'There is one player whom I have never learned how to cope with and that is the player who never stops to consider that you also hold thirteen cards; he will ignore your bids, he will pay no attention to your warnings, come hell or high water he will take command of the hand, and when he has been doubled and gone down several tricks, he'll ascribe it to nothing but bad luck. You are fortunate if he doesn't smile blandly and say, 'Well, I think it was worth it, partner.' I am still looking for the book that will show me how to deal with him. Shooting is too quick and too painless, and besides, there might not be another fourth available.' Again, the theme of his story.

In conclusion, he feels that, 'The essentials for playing a good game of bridge are to be truthful, clearheaded, and considerate, prudent but not averse to taking a risk, and not to cry over spilt milk. And incidentally those are perhaps also the essentials for playing the more important game of life.'

Rixi Markus

—— ♠♥♦ ——
♣

As a young member of the victorious Austrian Ladies team, Rixi Markus played against Jo Culbertson and Helen Sobel in 1937 in Budapest. She remembers that Jo caused quite a stir in Vienna with her short hair and boyish figure. There was something manly about her, she felt, from the way she smoked and the way she drank. Helen Sobel, too, she felt had a man's mind while playing bridge.

Rixi Markus was born in Vienna, Austria, in 1910, and came from a card-playing background. 'As long ago as I can remember – and I claim that my memory goes back to the time when I was four years old – my parents and their friends and relations played cards.' It was a game called preference, a distant relation to bridge, with only thirty-two cards but with an auction and a trump suit. As she watched them play, she noted the concentration on her father's face. Indeed, so great was their concentration that none of them noticed the little girl, just tall enough to peek over the table top, watching them with such intense curiosity.

An aunt of hers who lived in the same building played poker on Saturday nights. The youthful Rixi was allowed to watch and participate briefly, though her parents never knew. Her interest in cards increased and at the age of thirteen she got her break. One evening at home she was sewing and watching her family play bridge when her uncle said teasingly, 'Pity you can't play, it would break the monotony of this regular foursome.' She looked up at him and said, 'Of course I can play.' Her uncle insisted the game was too difficult for her, but she persisted, 'Let me try.' She joined in and turned out to be a winner that evening. She told them she had learned to play just by watching them.

At her finishing school in Dresden she tried to interest some other girls in bridge, but got little response. Back in Vienna, she found that contract had started and relations were taking lessons. Through a young married cousin of hers she became part of a bridge circle. Her talent quickly became clear and she was soon known as a bridge prodigy, flattered by the attentions of elderly gentlemen standing around watching her play. When tournaments were introduced, they were mostly pairs events. Her regular partner was a lawyer, Dr Hirschler, much older than her, who was an intelligent and talented player from whom she learned much. People were rather amused at first to see this young woman (she looked much younger than she was) lined up in partnership with a small, fat older man.

Then she met her husband. He tried to restrain her from bridge playing, jealous of the adulation she was receiving. But by now she had become a star performer and she wasn't going to stop. The marriage never really worked out. She referred to it as 'a disaster'. However, she was pregnant soon afterwards, and went ahead with the child, even though she felt the marriage would not last. Bridge playing soon compensated for the failure of her marriage. Vienna at that time was a stronghold of bridge with players such as Karl Schneider, Hans Jellinek and Elisabeth Klauber playing at the Vienna Bridge Club in the Grand Hotel. It was here that she met Dr Paul Stern, a prominent lawyer and a bridge enthusiast, who invited her to become a member of the Austrian Ladies team.

The Austrian Ladies team had an outstanding record. They won the European Ladies Championship in Brussels in 1935, won it again the next year in Stockholm; and in 1937 they won the World Championship in Budapest where Culbertson also played. This is how she described them: 'In the [pre-war] Austrian Ladies team there was real friendship. I don't recall any signs of bitchiness or jealousy. I think it was because we were such a harmonious team that we never found it difficult to win. We were nicknamed "the Goats" – in German, "*die Ziegen*" – by Dr Stern. He had goat-badges made for us, and although it seems funny today it was a great honour to be allowed to be a "goat" and wear the badge. We took it all very seriously; we had training sessions regularly and were taught that it was important to have the will to win. We were all friendly and pleasant creatures in ordinary life, but at the bridge table we were aggressive fighters and gave no quarter.'

They were in the midst of preparation for the next European Championship in Oslo in 1938 when Hitler invaded Austria. She admitted that up till then she and other Austrians had been deluded. 'Most of us did not notice the dangerous clouds darkening the horizon; we felt the Western powers would protect us from the Fascist menace.

How could we have been so blind?' Some Viennese still hankered after the splendour of the Austrian Empire and hoped, if Germany took over, that greatness could be restored again. 'One felt the growing fascination of the Hitler idea, particularly when one left Vienna and went into the beautiful countryside, high up to the Tirol and other provinces.' But she was Jewish and knew she had to be careful.

Soon after the *Anschluss* in March 1938, her father telephoned her anxiously from London, advising her to get out as soon as possible. The day after the *Anschluss*, Austrian passports were declared invalid. Jews were then given a German passport marked with a 'J', and were forbidden to leave the country without special permission. 'What are you waiting for?' he asked impatiently. She set about finding a suitable escape route for her daughter and herself. Her bridge mind provided a solution. People were being arrested when they tried to run to the nearby Hungarian and other frontiers. So she went to Hapag – the Hamburg–American shipping line – and daringly asked if she could travel through Germany to England. She was told, 'You must go to the *SS Oberkommando* in Brauenerstrasse.' She looked at the young man pleadingly, 'Could you telephone? I would rather not go there.' He telephoned for her and she got the tickets for herself and her daughter. She was told she needed a Belgian transit visa which she obtained from the Belgian Consul and the next morning went to the Westbahnhof. At the very same moment Hitler was making his triumphant entry into Vienna, her taxi was having to make a detour to get to the station.

The train was empty except for one English lady who asked her why she was going through Germany. She explained that as the Germans were busy entering Austria, she hoped to pass through Germany unnoticed. When the train arrived at Passau, the frontier between Austria and Germany, both a German and an Austrian passport officer entered the compartment and looked at her with surprise. They agreed to let her and her daughter go on and also to keep the two hundred Austrian schillings they had on them even though a ban had come into force that morning prohibiting travellers from taking more than twenty Deutschmarks out of the country. Feeling in need of a celebration she went to the dining-car on the train and ordered half a bottle of Rhine wine. When they arrived in Ostend, she cried unrestrainedly, her pent-up emotions at the strains and tensions of the past few days finally breaking through.

They boarded a cross-channel steamer which took them to Dover. On arrival she remembered that her father had told her always to tell the truth to British officials. When the immigration officer questioned her, she told him truthfully that she had fled from the Nazis as Jews were being beaten up and taken to camps and prison. Asked why she had no ready money, she said she had ample means in Vienna. 'What will you live on?' the immigration officer asked. She told him her parents were already in England. Then she was in for a shock. The officer said, 'I am sorry, you cannot land. And I must advise you not to attempt to try another frontier. You will never be allowed to enter Britain.' He stamped her passport and then crossed it. She nearly fainted. She went to a phone box to telephone her father and was pressing the button with trembling hands when a policeman put his hand on her shoulder. 'You must go back on the same ship,' he said. 'Your boat is about to leave.'

She had no choice. There were about twenty others on board like her, Austrians who had been turned away. She went to see the Belgian captain of the boat and, in tears, told him her story. He said that she would probably get back in because her parents were there and advised her to go straight to the passport officer in Ostend. At Ostend the passport officer told her, 'Don't go to Brussels. Stay here. It might be more difficult there. I can give you a visitor's visa until you can get into England.' She had very little money left and went with her daughter to stay in a hotel near the Gare Maritime. Typically she booked a suite and then telephoned her father. He asked her why she hadn't let him know she was coming. She explained that she had gambled on getting to Dover safely and didn't want him to suffer any anxiety beforehand. Within two hours of her phone call to her father, she received money from Antwerp by cable. Three days later her father telephoned again and said, 'Take the next boat, you can now come to England.' He had gone to the Home Office where they had shown him a typed copy of the interview she had had with the immigration officer at Dover. Her father had somehow persuaded them to let her in. When she got back to Dover the same immigration officer met her, this time with great courtesy, and told her that her father was expecting her.

She settled in London. When war broke out, she worked as a fire-watcher and for the British Red Cross. Bridge activities during the war were inevitably restricted. During the long nights waiting for air attacks opportunities for bridge sometimes turned up. She joined the Hamilton Club, which had been started prior to the war by Colonel Beasley, whose team had played against Culbertson in the 1930s. She and he became great friends. It was at the Hamilton Club that she met Lady Rhodes who was to become her regular partner in the immediate post-war era until her famous partnership with Fritzi Gordon began in 1955. Meanwhile, she had become a British citizen in 1950, and had divorced her husband.

Fritzi Gordon was a fellow Viennese who had also escaped to London. Born in pre-war Austria, like Rixi she was born into a card-playing family. From the age of six she played cards with her father, who insisted they played for real money and, when she lost, made her pay out of her savings, a powerful incentive to learn properly. She came across bridge by chance. As a young woman, on a train journey to a romantic tryst, some grit blew in her eye. Her swollen eyelids made her hasten to an oculist. Waiting for her disfigurement to abate, she went for the night to a small hotel where she happened to find, in the lounge, three strangers looking for a fourth to play bridge. She agreed to play. It really was her first experience of bridge. From then on, Fritzi took the shortest route to learning the game properly. She played against professionals in Viennese cafés. Even when losing, she knew she was gaining in knowledge and experience. Paul Stern, also in England post-war, suggested she should pair up with Rixi Markus, which she did when Rixi's partnership with Lady Rhodes was over. They soon became one of the strongest women's pairs in the world, winning a whole series of tournaments: five European Teams Championships, the World Women's Team Olympiad in 1964 and the World Women's Pairs Championships in 1962 and 1974, on the latter occasion by such a huge margin that it was almost unnecessary for them to play the last session.

> Few men play as well as Fritzi Gordon. No woman plays better. But it is with men, rather than with the women, that she should be compared for Fritzi's bridge is intensely masculine and he-man stuff, at that. Where Rixi Markus is fiery, Fritzi Gordon is icy cold. Where Rixi takes her contracts by storm, Fritzi makes hers through merciless efficiency – merciless towards the slightest lapse on the part of her opponents.

So wrote Victor Mollo in *Bridge Immortals*. Of Rixi Markus, Mollo commented: 'People love her and hate her, but no one is, no one could be, indifferent to her.' Her flair was undeniable and she had an almost feverish intensity about both her game and her manner. She was like a tigress at the table, known to have reduced strong men to the verge of tears. It was hardly surprising therefore that her partnership with Fritzi Gordon was tempestuous. Rixi Markus described their partnership as follows:

> As far as bridge is concerned, I have not a word of complaint about Fritzi Gordon, for she was a wonderful player and an excellent partner, who contributed greatly to my own success. As players we were in a rather similar mould, both aggressive players with a well-developed killer instinct. She may even have had a slight advantage over me in that she was more controlled, less impetuous. My flashes of unorthodoxy sometimes paid dividends, but sometimes they did not. Fritzi seldom took that kind of risk, and in competitive bridge it is sometimes necessary to restrain instinct and intuition in favour of sound judgement. When she was playing a hand I could relax in perfect comfort, never worried that she might make a mess of it.

But, as Rixi Markus said, their personal relationship was something of a stop–go affair and their tiffs away from the table soon got in the way of their partnership.

Predictably it reached the stage when they had little contact outside bridge and their partnership continued only until, as Rixi Markus put it: 'I felt I could stand her hostility no longer. We frequently broke off our partnership, to resume again a year or two later, although resumption would be difficult, since we had not spoken to each other in the intervening period. Sympathetic tournament organisers used to arrange things so that we should not meet. But in spite of interruptions, our partnership was not damaged: we were always able to take up where we left off.' An amusing side-effect of one of their victories together was that the prize for the Gold Cup was a pair of men's hair brushes, the organisers not having anticipated female winners. Rixi Markus kept hers until the end of her life, in mint condition.

Aside from bridge, Rixi Markus always enjoyed music and skiing and built these into her yearly calendar, spending time every year at the Salzburg Music Festival, and skiing twice a year, in December and January at St Moritz and in March at Crans-sur-Sierre. In her sixties she fractured a leg skiing but in the ambulance taking her away from the *piste* booked the same instructor for the following year. She wrote a famous column for the *Guardian* for more than thirty-five years and organised the House of Lords versus House of Commons matches, partly through her relationship with Harold (later Lord) Lever. Her books included *Common Sense Bridge* (1972), *More Deadly than the Male* (1984) and the autobiographical *A Vulnerable Game* (1988) in which she interspersed some choice pieces of advice:

> You cannot become a really good bridge player without a great deal of practice, plus some competitive experience. Each individual will develop differently – it depends partly on talent, and partly on character and temperament. You must not underrate the difficulties of the game. You must approach it in a humble way, however clever you may be in other fields. You must accept the fact that there is a lot to learn and a lot to know. You may soon find out that some people of much inferior intellectual prowess may easily overtake you, and you may look inept in comparison with them. Forget your pride and vanity, accept the fact that they have more card-sense than you and that what seems difficult to you comes naturally to them. Once you have acknowledged these facts you will also overcome most of your own difficulties.
>
> There are several ways to improve your game. One is to play with players who are better than you are, another to watch a first-class table, and a third to play for stakes so high that it hurts you to lose.
>
> To be a good bridge player you must have both courage and discipline. Show courage but don't overdo it, and use your self-restraint whenever it is called for. Here are the essential ingredients for success at the top: talent, humility, self-restraint, self-confidence, courage, respect for both your partner and your opponents, and, above all, excellent judgement and sound psychology. Logic helps a great deal too: I maintain that most women players lack logic but find in their intuition a useful substitute. Some players have some of these qualities, but very few have them all.

One of her favourite slogans was, 'Hope for the best but provide for the worst.'

Rixi Markus was as forceful as ever in her later years. I came across her while writing my Culbertson biography for which she gave me invaluable help, recalling her post-war meetings with Culbertson in the Russian Tea Rooms in New York – two displaced persons acknowledging their latter-day achievements. She died in 1992, aged eighty-two.

Cheating at Bridge

Man: How would you like to make a few honest dollars?
W. C. Fields: Do they have to be honest?

Cheating gains little at bridge. Bridge, being primarily a game of skill as opposed to a game of chance, provides little opportunity and incentive to cheat. But some people still do try. This has been the case since the earliest days. At the turn of the century a player was thought to have signalled for leads by humming particular hymns. For spades, the player would sing 'The Grave as Little as My Bed', for hearts 'As Pants the Hart for Cooling Streams'. Or with a Yarborough, he would hum 'Nothing in My Hand I Bring'. Once a player was permanently barred from a money game because he sang hymns in Latin whenever he was dummy. A Latin expert was called in and, posing as a spectator, confirmed that the man was indeed spotting honours on behalf of his partner.

Signalling at cards has always existed. Mechanical devices to convey signals appear in the sixteenth-century book by the mathematician and physician Girolamo Cardano *Liber de Lude Aleae* (*The Book of Games of Chance*) in which he described the *organum*, or organ, a loose floorboard with a string attached, which the cheat operated by sitting with one foot on the loose board while his accomplice made appropriate tugs on the concealed string on the other side to signal his card holding. Caravaggio's and La Tour's paintings, both entitled *The Cheaters*, attest the frequency of cheating in earlier times.

Thackeray wrote about professional gamblers and card cheats in his novel *Barry Lyndon Esq*. In the book his eponymous hero acts as accomplice to his wealthy uncle while playing écarté. Disguised as a valet, Barry signalled the situation as follows: 'If, for instance, I wiped the dust off the chair with my napkin, it was to show that the enemy was strong in diamonds; if I pushed it, he had ace, king; if I said "Punch or wine, my lord?" hearts was meant; if "Wine or punch?" clubs. If I blew my nose, it was to indicate that there was another confederate employed by the adversary; and then, I warrant you, some pretty trials of skill would take place.'

Cheating and signalling often go hand in hand. Methods used have included holding the cards at a predetermined angle, or by well-timed yawns or coughs, or by foot-taps, or by recognisable verbal quips, or by simply looking into opponents' hands. This last infringement, peeking as it is known, is hard to deal with. The unwritten law at bridge is that it is each player's responsibility to hold his cards so as not to be seen by other players. If another player sees your cards, it's your fault. Helen Sobel tried for years to convince her long-term partner Charles Goren of this. Goren used to hold his cards way out in front of him. Sobel held hers so close to her chest that she was sometimes accused of leaving a tournament with a card clinging to her *décolletage*.

There's a story about Hal Sims and his wife Dorothy making a bet with his next-door neighbours at his mansion in Deal, New Jersey, offering them a handicap system. 'Your handicap,' said Sims, 'is that you and your partner may cheat. I don't bar anything. You may have foot signals. You may bid spades when you mean hearts, and diamonds when you mean clubs. You can even signal for leads.' The bet was made. At the time, in the mid-1930s, Sims was a top player in the country. Charles Goren recalls the game. 'The Simses clobbered 'em. Sims knew that any cheating ingenuity they possessed couldn't produce a good enough game to win.'

Ely Culbertson, playing in a game in London, once began to smell a cheat. Experts usually have a nose for such things and can detect when the rhythm of the game is false. For a while, Culbertson couldn't work out how his opponents were cheating. Finally he realised that they were using a timing system. A certain number of seconds elapsed between bids, or plays, to signal a particular message. Culbertson figured out their timing, then finished one of the counts aloud: 'Eight, nine, ten, that knocks me out, gentlemen. Goodbye!'

Cheating at cards is often called 'coffee-housing', the name deriving from eighteenth-century English coffee houses where games of whist were usually in progress, and cheating seemed to be regularly practised. Coffee-housing has worked itself into the language and has come to mean any comment or mannerism or action aimed at assisting one's partner and deceiving one's opponents. It can range from the lifting of an eyebrow to the deliberate banging down of a card on the table.

Coffee-housing occurs at all levels. Once Helen Sobel was playing in a major tournament with Goren. She had played all her spades and eagerly awaited the chance to trump the next spade lead. Goren led a diamond instead, and Helen Sobel wriggled uncomfortably. Goren continued with another diamond, and her wriggling increased visibly. 'Helen,' said Goren, 'you've got to stop that. It makes for a bad partnership. And besides, I have no more spades.'

Verbal communication can be just as effective. The 1930s writer Morton Wild gave a list of verbal nuances used at the table: the hesitating pass, the hopeless pass, the brisk pass, the disgusted pass, the vacillating declaration, the firm declaration, the uncertain double, the belligerent double, the ominous redouble, the vindictive redouble, and the angry rescue bid. In this context Goren once played with a woman who was renowned for her coffee-housing. Even his legendary patience was tried by her exaggerated bidding. At the end of one hand, Goren remarked drily, 'Madam, that second hesitation certainly was an overbid.'

Albert Morehead told the story of a player who was desperate that his partner should not continue hearts. In his own hand, the player's lowest heart card was the eight, and he knew that if he played it, his partner would read it as an encouragement to continue the suit. So, instead, he dropped his entire hand on the floor. As Morehead related, 'As he stooped to pick it up, he said, "Don't wait for me. I'm playing a low heart."'

Another story concerns a woman player who wanted to signal to her partner to continue a suit in which her holding was K-Q-2. If she played the two on his ace lead, he would interpret it as a request to switch to another suit. On the other hand, she could not bear to part with one of her high honours for signalling purposes. So she started shaking her head sadly, taking the queen out and putting it back again, still shaking her head. Then she took out the king and put the king back, finally she pulled out the two, shook her head in despair and thumped it down on the table with a resounding slap. Her partner got the message.

Even seemingly offhand remarks at the table such as 'Unlucky at cards, lucky at love' can be construed as information-giving comments. The remark 'I really don't know what to do' can be a clear indication that you are holding good cards but have no clear suit preference. Another well-known tactic for imparting information is to bid out of turn and then apologise profusely for it.

In bridge, ethics, hitherto mostly unwritten, have been incorporated more and more into the laws. A player must not hesitate unduly before bidding, nor pause before playing a singleton, nor vary the inflection of voice, nor use body signals. Nor should a player make use of his partner's facial expressions or mannerisms. George Kaufman's jesting remark, 'Let's have a review of the bidding again, with all inflections', is an apt comment on this.

In tournament bridge, ethics are usually adhered to rigorously, but improprieties occasionally creep in. A classic moment occurred during the final round of the 1934 Men's Pairs Championship at New York's Hotel Commodore. Most of the other pairs had finished and stood around the remaining half-dozen games still in progress in the centre of the smoke-filled grand ballroom. Culbertson was in partnership with Ted Lightner and they were playing against David Burnstine and Oswald Jacoby. The result of the tournament depended on the outcome of this hand. Lightner had bid six spades. The lead, as all the other players spectating knew, was going to be all important. Burnstine was on lead. There was never much love lost between Burnstine and Culbertson. So Burnstine prepared to use a little psychology or subterfuge. He knew that Culbertson was always nervous and fidgety before putting his hand down as dummy, waiting impatiently for the opening card to be led before spreading his hand and hurrying away, often without arranging the suits. Burnstine made full use of this. He took his time. Then, very deliberately and slowly, he reached into his pocket and took out a piece of chewing gum. Even more slowly he unwrapped it, put it into his mouth and gave it a tentative chew. By this time both Lightner and Culbertson were losing patience. But still Burnstine delayed before leading. Suddenly he threw something down on the table. Like a flash, Culbertson put down the dummy. A second later he realised his mistake and scooped up his cards again, but it was too late. It had been the chewing-gum wrapper. Ethical or not, Burnstine had taken a peek and decided his lead accordingly and the contract was defeated.

A curious ethical dilemma occurred in a 1958 tournament. Ira Rubin, then a young USA player, reached a point of difficult decision in playing a hand. He walked out of the room to think about it. While cogitating, he ran into the British player Adam Meredith, and discussed the hand with him. Meredith told Rubin what he would do under the circumstances, Rubin returned to the table and announced that he had consulted with another player, 'but I'm not sure he gave me the right advice'. His opponents argued that the consultation was an impropriety. The four players finally decided that a flip of the coin should decide Rubin's play. He won and went ahead and made his contract.

Cheating allegations have occasionally accompanied World Championships. In Como, Italy, in 1958 one of the USA team, Tobias Stone, accused the Italian side of cheating. The Italians, well ahead at the time, had followed the usual habit of holding their hands over their heads so that spectators could see them before bidding. Stone claimed that the Italians held their hands up high when they were powerful, and low when they were weak. Following the Americans' complaint, the tournament director ordered all players to hold their cards below the level of the tabletop during the bidding. The Italians, infuriated that their honesty was being questioned, conjured up a humorous moment. One of their team, Giorgio Belladonna, mocked the decision by looking down at his hand below the table and commenting: 'But I can see my partner's feet!'

The USA team lost the tournament by a large margin and returned home. There, Stone put the word about that the Italians had cheated. Accusations and counter-accusations flowed to and fro. An Italian player, Walter Avarelli, threatened to sue, another felt the accusations were poor sportsmanship. The American Contract Bridge League intervened by censuring Stone and barring him from international tournaments for a year. They issued the following announcement:

> The Board of Directors of the American Contract Bridge League has voted official censure of Tobias Stone and has declared him ineligible to represent the American Contract Bridge League in the 1959 international matches. The charge upon which this action was based is conduct unbecoming a representative of the American Contract Bridge League. Our team played poorly in Como last January. They admitted it. The Italians played well. We were soundly beaten and we do not care to have the intemperate alibis of an ungracious loser damage our international relations or tarnish in the slightest the Italian team's victory. Charles H. Goren, who headed the 1957 team which was defeated by an even wider margin by the identical Italian team, has said: 'The Italians are fine sportsmen and magnificent players. They are great champions.' The American Contract Bridge League echoes that statement.

They hoped that would be the end of it. But Stone hadn't finished yet:

> You can ask every member of the board to state specifically what I did that was unbecoming, and not one of them can tell you. I was tried and convicted without any specifications. The directors voted eleven to nine against trying me on the charge of accusing the Italians of cheating, and came up instead with this vague accusation of unbecoming conduct. I have heard that I am supposed to have told Siniscalco directly to lower his hand. That is not true. Siniscalco was raising his hand at the beginning of play, and I complained to our captain, who went to the referee and protested that he was violating the rules. The referee instructed all players to hold their hands beneath the level of the table while bidding. When Siniscalco again began raising his hand, I protested to the referee, who instructed him that he was in violation of the rules. I said nothing to Siniscalco. Siniscalco also was staring at his partner, Forquet. I told the referee it made me nervous, and Forquet said: 'Are you accusing us of cheating?' I replied, 'No, it simply makes me uncomfortable.'

Stone took the matter to court. He asked the New York Supreme Court to award him $250,000 damages from the ACBL for defamation, and also for the court to set aside his year-long ban on international play. A hundred or so nationally known American players signed a petition in support of Stone's reinstatement. The ACBL eventually dropped the ban and Stone dropped his legal actions.

Cheating in international matches, however, almost certainly does take place. Once an Austrian team was accused of using hand signals. To indicate a strong hand, the Austrians were said to put a clenched fist on the table. Placing the hand flat on the table meant a flat, or weak, hand. Possession of the ace of clubs was indicated by holding the cards vertically in the right hand, the ace of spades by resting the hand on the table at a forty-five-degree angle, and the aces of diamonds and hearts by resting the cards on the table horizontally in either the right or left hand. Other codes used by the Austrians involved the positioning of cigarettes and the placement of a pencil on the table. Yet these accusations were never proved conclusively.

A strange and disturbing case of cheating was the Willard Karn case. In the early 1930s Willard Karn was among the select band of top contract bridge players. Indeed, the bridge expert Shepard Barclay in his ranking of the top players of 1932/3 put him at the head of his list. He had been Hal Sims's regular partner and was one of the original members of the very successful Four Horsemen team, which captured the Vanderbilt Cup in 1931 and 1932. He had even presented his own cup for pairs competition in 1932, and won it first time round with Waldemar von Zedtwitz. In 1931 he had published his own book on bridge, a loose-leaf publication entitled *Karn's Bridge Service*. In fact, his record was quite outstanding and he looked all set for a long and distinguished career in the game.

Then, quite suddenly, Karn disappeared from the bridge scene. In the middle of 1933, Culbertson had called him into his office at Crockford's, his bridge club on East 62nd Street in New York, and in the presence of two other witnesses, Michael Gottlieb and Walter Beinecke, had told him he had good reason to believe that Karn had been cheating at bridge. For a near-professional card player like Karn, with an established reputation, there could be no more serious allegation. Culbertson told Karn that they had been suspicious of him for some time. Furthermore, his winnings at Crockford's seemed disproportionately large. Rather than confront him outright, Culbertson had arranged for a well-known card detective, Mickey MacDougall, to come to the club and observe him. MacDougall had disguised himself as a waiter and watched Karn play. With a good 'mechanic' it was almost impossible to tell if he was cheating but MacDougall knew almost immediately from the way Karn held the cards that he was doing so and, as he watched him more closely, he could see that the technique he was using was to interleave the high and low cards whenever he took in a trick on a hand before he was due to shuffle. Then he would use a high speed, pull-through shuffle that none but the most experienced observer could detect was wrong. Technically, a pull-through shuffle is meant to divide the pack into two, but Karn did it in such a way that the cards did not change position. Then he would crimp them before they were passed across to be cut. Thus, in one hand out of every four, namely when it was his turn to shuffle and the player on his right was the next dealer, he could be certain where some of the cards were placed. It was even suggested he might at times ring in a cold deck (a previously 'prepared' fresh deck of cards) on his own deal.

Culbertson presented these allegations to Karn backed up by MacDougall's testimony. As a result, Karn agreed to withdraw from high-stake and tournament bridge immediately. Why then did Karn choose to cheat, as was alleged? His background seemed impeccable. Born in Montgomery, Alabama, and educated at the Horace Mann School in New York, he went to Cornell University before becoming a First World War pilot. By 1933, Karn was Sales Director of the eastern half of the USA for National Distilleries. Socially, he was very highly placed, having married a Russian aristocrat, Princess Lilli Davidoff. Why then put all this at risk? One explanation was that he was living beyond his means. The main game at Crockford's had dropped its stake as a result of the Depression, and Karn's winnings had gone down accordingly. Financially, he needed to keep up to his former level of winnings and saw cheating as a means of doing so. A likelier explanation is a psychological one. Karn was one of those men who simply had to win. Winning, for him, was the basis of his self-esteem. He needed constantly to prove to himself that he was one of life's winners, that he had the Midas touch, that fortune smiled on him. Gambling for such individuals is a perpetual questioning of fate with an equally desperate need to get the right affirmation, or confirmation, afterwards. After a time, such a compulsion becomes almost obsessive, and a gambler will resort to any methods to achieve his goal. Karn's downfall may have been that he had chosen a game of skill to satisfy these egocentric demands, and sooner or later he was likely to be unmasked.

Karn was not heard of again until five years later in March 1938 when he decided to bring a lawsuit before the New York State Supreme Court alleging conspiracy and claiming $1,000,000 damages. He named as defendants in the action seven bridge experts – Culbertson, Josephine Culbertson, Oswald Jacoby, Waldemar von Zedtwitz, Walter Malowan, William Huske and Lee Langdon – and he alleged that they had 'unlawfully conspired to eliminate him from the bridge world' and had damaged his reputation. Why seven defendants? Karn, or his lawyer, had read their law books carefully and had realised that in a case of conspiracy, the claim, if successful, could be pursued against any one of the defendants. Hence the inclusion of von Zedtwitz, an acknowledged millionaire. Others were less happy about being included. Bill Huske, the former *Bridge World* editor, on receiving the writ of summons, walked out of his office, took his battered old hat off the hat-rack and threw it in the waste-paper basket. Someone asked him why he had done that. 'Nobody,' he replied, 'who has been sued for a million dollars can afford to wear a hat like that!'

None of the defendants was particularly keen to go to court as conspiracy cases were notoriously hard to disprove. Oswald Jacoby's lawyer advised him to settle and so Jacoby wrote Karn a letter saying that he had never been aware of his cheating whenever he had played as his partner. Culbertson, predictably, was not prepared to back down. He made it a matter of principle to defy any threat, whether of physical violence, blackmail or even financial disaster. As might be expected, when the case did come to court, it was simply not strong enough to stand up. Indeed, Justice Aaron Levy in dismissing it in June 1938 stated that the complaint 'violates every known pleading'. Karn tried to reinstate the case a year later but without success. There was an out-of-court settlement whereby Karn was allowed to participate in future ACBL tournaments with one or two respectable players, and he did so for the record, but that was all. Through the years, he kept his job with various liquor companies ending up as National Director of Sales for Schenley Distillers, but his marriage ended in divorce and he never attained any of his former bridge pre-eminence. He died in April 1945 of a heart attack in his suite at the Hotel Beverly on East 50th Street in New York, at the age of forty-seven.

John 'the Professor' Scarne, the author of several books on card play, always took the view that 'more cheating takes place at private or so-called friendly card games than at all other forms of gambling combined'. In big-time money games his view was that at least one card-shark will be present and 'working' in as many as two-thirds of these games, held mainly in anonymous hotel rooms and private homes. The more transient and ephemeral the setting, then the greater the likelihood of cheating. A conventioneers' hotel, a cruise ship, long-distance trains, all provide ideal circumstances for the gambling cheat. Here are the 'fish' that 'sharks' will prey on. 'Cheat 'em while the cheatin's good' has been the motto, and the shark hopes to be long gone before the sucker thinks to complain. His research was based on American examples, and Scarne reckoned that in most of the thousands of annual bridge tournaments in the United States, a rumour of cheating, usually by illegal signalling, is bound to occur. Formal, prolonged accusations of cheating were rare, however, because, he felt, most bridge players prefer to get on with the game and ignore the problem.

Illegal signalling is clearly not tolerated in bridge, but body language is harder to regulate. In other games such as rummy, poker and chess, verbal and body language are used to convey false impressions of strength or weakness, fatigue or alertness, knowledge or ignorance, luck or lack of it. These ruses have been developed into a fine art, although their ethical propriety is often questionable. Scarne takes the view that bluffing is the most sophisticated form of cheating. Bluffing in bridge comes under the heading of deception. Indeed, legal deception is part of the skill of the game and helps distinguish it from games of chance. A bluff does not necessarily change the chances of winning any particular hand, but it improves the chances of winning more often than the cards the bluffer holds deserve. In bridge, psychic bidding comes under this category.

The first card game involving bluff originated in Persia. This was *as-nas*, started in the fourteenth century and played with a deck of twenty cards divided equally among five values: lions, kings, ladies, soldiers, and dancing girls. In the early 1820s sailors brought this game from Persia to New Orleans. There it was adapted to local custom and the hybrid became poker.

In a classic work, *Theory of Games and Economic Behavior*, published in 1944, the mathematicians John von Neumann and Oskar Morgenstern wrote, 'Of the two possible motives for bluffing, the first is to give an impression of strength in weakness; the second is the desire to give an impression of weakness in strength. Both are instances of inverted signalling, i.e. of misleading the opposition.' Von Neumann and Morgenstern clearly saw the twofold nature of all deception, hiding and showing. In bridge, deception lies in the use, manipulation even, of the bidding and play. The borderline between honesty and dishonesty is challenged but not crossed. Legitimate deception, false-carding for example, is very much part of the game.

Deception spreads into many areas, none more so than in marked cards. Of the millions of decks of cards sold each year in America, Scarne reckoned that one per cent get marked at some point. Few players have any idea of how to detect these 'readers'. Many are deliberately planted in hotel lobby kiosks to be bought by unsuspecting 'punters' in anticipation of a rigged game. The invention of the radio was a boon to card cheats. The so-called Radio Cue Prompter allowed signals to be passed to a player by an accomplice peeking at the cards from a hole in the ceiling, or through a two-way mirror, or by just watching the game inside the room itself. The collaborator would strap a receiver to his body to receive a series of coded signals. The late Nick

'The Greek' Dandolos, America's most famous gambler in the mid-twentieth century, was once taken by a Radio Cue Prompter for a cool half million dollars in a supposedly private two-week poolside game of gin rummy at the Flamingo Hotel casino in Las Vegas.

It was the sort of incident that Roald Dahl would have relished and picked up on. As it was, he wrote his own short story about the deceptive side of bridge, *My Lady Love, My Dove* in 1952. Dahl's story is set in a country cottage in the Home Counties where an older couple, Arthur and Pamela, invite a younger couple, Henry and Sally Snape, for a weekend's bridge. It's clear that Pamela rules the roost – she is rich, comes from a titled family, and is always forthright in her views. She doesn't like the young couple – the husband is 'a dreadful man' who never stops telling jokes, his wife is 'pretty frightful, too'. In fact, Pamela says, 'They're absolutely the end,' and she has only invited them because 'they play an absolutely first-class game, and for a decent stake', and because she was 'sick and tired of playing with rabbits'. Still, the idea of having 'these awful people' in the house perturbs her and she comes up with the 'most marvellous idea'. She tells her biddable husband, Arthur, 'Let's have some fun – some real fun for once – tonight.' Her idea is to put a microphone in their guests' bedroom so as to listen to them commenting about their weekend stay. Arthur is initially horrified, 'That's about the nastiest trick I ever heard of. It's like listening at keyholes, or reading letters only far, far worse.' But Pamela won't be put off. Complicity is the glue of their relationship. 'Listen, Arthur. I'm a *nasty* person. And so are you – in a secret sort of way. That's why we get along together.' Arthur is drawn in, and he sets up a microphone in the spare room just before their guests arrive. The microphone has a wire leading along the corridor to the radio set in their own bedroom.

Their guests arrive. Although the wife seems attractive – 'had I met her fifteen years earlier I might well have got myself into some sort of trouble' – Arthur soon realises she is not, in fact, quite so merry and smiling as he had at first been led to believe. 'She seemed to be coiled in herself, as though with a secret she was jealously guarding. The deep-blue eyes moved too quickly about the room, never settling or resting on one thing for more than a moment.' Henry, her husband, was more predictable – 'an amiable simple young man with good manners whose main preoccupation, very properly, was Mrs Snape. He was handsome in a long-faced, horsy sort of way, with dark-brown eyes that seemed to be gentle and sympathetic.' He told them, as expected, one or two jokes, 'but they were on a high level and no one could have objected'.

All four were looking forward to their evening game of bridge. Sally Snape announced they played almost every night. 'We love it so.' Arthur asked them their secret. 'It's practice,' she said. 'That's all. Practice, practice, practice.' After dinner, at around nine thirty, feeling comfortable and well fed, they started playing bridge in the large living room – ten shillings a hundred, families playing together. It was serious, no one hardly speaking at all except to bid. The home team didn't do well, and the longer the evening went on, Pamela became more and more careless. Their opponents seemed to play exceptionally well, bidding expertly, and all through the evening they made only one mistake when Sally Snape badly overestimated her partner's hand and bid six spades. Arthur doubled and they went three down, vulnerable, which cost them eight hundred points. Arthur noticed that she was very put out by it, even though her husband forgave her at once, kissing her hand across the table and telling her not to worry. Soon Pamela announced that she was tired and wanted to go to bed. The evening's bridge ended.

Arthur and Pamela were hardly in their bedroom before she cried, 'Quick! Turn it on!' The little radio warmed up just in time to catch the noise of their guests' door opening and closing. Almost immediately the voice of Henry Snape came on the line, strong and clear. 'You're just a goddam little fool,' he was saying, in a voice now very different from the one he used downstairs, harsh and unpleasant. 'The whole bloody evening wasted! Eight hundred points – that's four pounds!'

'I got mixed up,' the girl answered. 'I won't do it again, I promise.'

Arthur and Pamela couldn't believe their ears. 'What's *this?* What's going on?' Pamela's mouth was wide open. They both leant closer to the radio to listen better.

'I promise, I promise I won't do it again,' the girl was saying.

'We're not taking any chances,' the man answered grimly. 'We're going to have another practice right now.'

'Oh no, please! I couldn't stand it!'

'Look,' the man said, 'all the way out here to take money off this rich bitch and you have to go and mess it up.' Pamela stirred at this mention of her name.

'The second time this week,' he went on.

'I promise I won't do it again.'

'Sit down. I'll sing them out and you answer.'

'No, Henry, *please!* Not all five hundred of them. It'll take three hours.'

'All right, then. We'll leave out the finger positions. I think you're sure of those. We'll just do the basic bids showing honour tricks.'

'Oh, Henry, must we? I'm so tired.'

'It's absolutely essential you get them perfect,' he said. 'We have a game every day next week, you know that. And we've got to eat.'

'Oh Henry, *please.*' She sounded very near to tears.

'Come on, Sally. Pull yourself together.'

Then he began the litany, now using the same voice as downstairs during the bridge game. '*One* club', emphasising the word 'one', drawing out the first part of the word.

'Ace queen of clubs,' the girl replied wearily. 'King jack of spades. No hearts, and ace jack of diamonds.'

'And how many cards to each suit? Watch my finger positions carefully.'

Arthur and Pamela suddenly realised it was a bidding code that conveyed every card in the hand. They were using the same routine as magicians use when they have an accomplice in the audience whose manner of phrasing is such that they immediately know what is being hidden from sight. They listened again, and Henry was making Sally repeat the formula.

'I'll go *one heart,*' he said.

'King queen ten of hearts. Ace jack of spades. No diamonds. Queen jack of clubs . . .'

It was clear he was telling her the number of cards he had in each suit by the position of his fingers. Pamela fetched a cigarette. She lit it and then swung round.

'Why, Arthur,' she said slowly, blowing out clouds of smoke. 'Why, this is a *mar-vellous* idea. D'you think *we* could learn to do it?'

'What!'

'Of course. Why not?'

'Here! No! Wait a minute, Pamela . . .' But she came swiftly across the room, close up to where he was standing, and looked at him – the old look of a smile that wasn't a smile. Her big, full grey eyes were staring at him hard. It was at moments like these that he felt he was drowning.

'Yes,' she said. 'Why not?'

'But Pamela . . . Good heavens . . . No . . . After all . . .'

'Arthur, I do wish you wouldn't *argue* with me all the time. That's exactly what we'll do. Now, go fetch a deck of cards; we'll start right away.'

Dahl got the idea for this story from the time he had been sent to Washington as Assistant Air Attaché in 1942 shortly after America came into the war after Pearl Harbor. Before that he had been an RAF fighter pilot in Libya, Greece and Syria before being injured. In Washington he was really part of an intelligence-gathering operation under the direction of Bill Stephenson, a Canadian millionaire and friend of Churchill, whose pre-war visits to Germany to buy steel had helped to alert Churchill to Germany's preparations for war. This intelligence-gathering was ostensibly linked to the British Embassy, but often seemed too wayward and free-wheeling for its superiors in Britain. It soon came under the scrutiny of Lord Beaverbrook who sent a man to Washington to find out exactly what Stephenson and his outfit was up to. Dahl connived with Stephenson to set a trap for the investigator. Dahl invited the newcomer to lunch at his home in Georgetown, and set up a concealed microphone to tape their conversation. As one drink followed another, Dahl began asking him leading questions about Beaverbrook. The investigator rashly proffered some disloyal remarks. The recording was then sent back to Beaverbrook, who rapidly lost confidence in any report the man had to make. Some of Dahl's colleagues were critical of this episode ('I thought it was a dirty thing to do against his own country'). But it had the desired result and their intelligence operation remained free from outside interference from then on. Dahl stored this memory of duplicity and entrapment away until he came to write this story.

Dahl, a six-foot-six, handsome, articulate young man, caused quite a stir in Washington. Towering half a foot over most people, with his keen eyes and his scratchy, smoker's voice, he was a performer always with a trick up his sleeve and people were never quite sure what to make of him. He soon acquired a reputation for practical joking. There was a famous incident when he made up a lengthy correspondence about English public schoolboys' sexual behaviour pretending it was coming from the august British ambassador, Lord Halifax, and he once painted the balls of the bison on Q Street Bridge in Washington. This rather boyish anti-authoritarianism eventually got channelled into his short-story writing, where his wry, ironic humour found an appropriate outlet. In time he became the English-speaking world's most successful writer of children's books. Famously, the initial print-run for *Charlie and the Chocolate Factory* in China was for two million copies, while in Britain it was calculated that, by the end of his life, every third British child bought at least one of his books each year. He always enjoyed stirring people up, whether with a book or at a dinner party or with a letter to *The Times*, and this is evident in this story too.

My Lady Love, My Dove was published in his first collection of short stories, *Someone Like You*, in 1953. Another story in the collection was also based on a true-life Washington occurrence. This was *Dip in the Pool*, which tells of a gambler travelling on an ocean liner who bets on the distance the boat has travelled that day, a daily occurrence on ocean liners. He has chosen too low a number and then tries to fix it by deliberately throwing himself overboard so as to hold up the boat and thus reduce the mileage in order to win his bet. He enlists the help of a woman he has met on board to raise the alarm. The idea for the story had been given to Dahl by his close friend Charles Marsh, another Washingtonian, who once had precisely that fantasy of scooping the pool when he was aboard a Cunard liner in mid-Atlantic. Dahl adds his own twist to the tale. In Dahl's story the gambler fails to realise that the woman whose help he has sought is mad. Once he is overboard, she lets him drown.

Cheating at bridge presents difficulties not found with other card games since it is essentially a partnership game. At poker, for instance, a player is on his own and can use various techniques to further his cause, such as marking cards, ringing in a cold deck or dealing seconds. Most people come to bridge to enjoy the finer points of the game, to test their skill, judgement, and discretion and to seek the enhancement of self-respect that the game can bring. Those who cheat, part-time or otherwise, are usually given short shrift. Indeed, much of the popularity of contract bridge is attributable to the high standards of etiquette required by players.

'The penalty of cheating is exclusion from society,' wrote Cavendish, the famous whist authority, in the nineteenth century. This has been the most effective deterrent throughout the years. Card playing depends on a code of honour, and the vast majority of card players are keen to protect this. So far as bridge is concerned, the laws of the game deliberately avoid any mention of cheating, the view being taken that it would be wrong to accord cheats a status by providing legal remedies against their activities. This is the policy of the main bridge organisations. Elsewhere the threat of exclusion from membership of a club or society is often enough to deter cheating.

Although the Laws do not recognise cheats, the section of the Laws called 'The Proprieties' defines two main types of improper conduct: breaches of ethics and breaches of etiquette. Breaches of ethics are unfair practices which just fall short of deliberate cheating, but the difference is often one of degree only. For example, a pair who take note of inflections in bidding would be considered unethical, while a pair who set out to impart similar information by secret signals would be considered cheats.

Breaches of etiquette at tournament play would include the following: discussion between two partners of a board just played when there is another board to play; looking at an opponent's hand after it has been placed in the board without asking permission; criticism of an opponent's bidding or any implication of bad faith on the part of the opponents without having previously called the director to the table. In tournament bridge, violations of proper etiquette are to be expected from inexperienced players, either through ignorance or inadvertence. A well-mannered opponent who is the victim of such a violation should try to make it clear that any comment he is making is intended to be helpful rather than admonitory.

Some infringements are not always easy to detect. An example was a player whose unethical practice was discovered when an observant tournament director noticed he seemed to score consistently better on even-numbered boards than on odd-numbered ones. Observation over a period of time showed that he made a practice of listening to conversations at adjoining tables once he had finished his own set of boards, and had then been making notes on his private scorecard.

Secret signalling has been the most often used form of cheating, in attempts to suggest an opening lead or to convey a hand pattern. Usually such methods are detected by the suspicions of other players.

An example of this was the Buenos Aires Incident of 1965 (see page 137).

Yet, on the whole, accusations of cheating are rare in serious tournament bridge, and recent improvements in the structure of the game have forestalled accusations of cheating, for instance the introduction of bidding boxes which first appeared in the World Championships in Sweden in 1970. These devices permit silent bidding. Each player has a box containing cards printed with all the bids from one club to seven no trumps, as well as various passes, doubles and redoubles. To make a bid, the player takes the appropriate card from the box and places it in front of him on the table. All the bidding cards remain on the table until the auction is concluded, thus avoiding the need for a review of the bidding. The possibility of mishearing or misunderstanding a bid is also eliminated. The consensus of those who have used bidding boxes is that they are a great improvement over verbal bidding, especially in international matches.

Screens were used for the first time by the ACBL during the Vanderbilt Knockout Teams in 1974. An opaque barrier is placed diagonally across the bridge table so that no player can see his partner. Each player can see only one opponent. The screen has an opening in the centre where the board in play is placed. Directly above the board is a curtain arrangement that can be lifted or pulled aside once the bidding is complete. This permits all players to see the cards being played, but the opening is shallow enough so that the players still cannot see their partner's face. The screen extends to the floor, blocking partners' feet from each other, the result of a foot-tapping incident in the 1975 Bermuda Bowl (see page 134). The bidding is done by a bidding box as above. Bids from one side of the table are revealed to the players on the opposite side either by monitors calling them aloud or by using some sort of rolling box. Both bids are relayed to the other side of the table simultaneously so that it is more difficult to discern who huddled.

The first appearance of screens at a World Championship took place at the 1975 Bermuda Bowl in Bermuda. At first there was a great deal of controversy about their use. Those who opposed them felt that screens would create in the public's mind the impression that cheating does take place at high-level bridge They also felt that screens would be distracting and dehumanising. Those in favour felt that screens would obviate most forms of cheating. Screens did receive almost unanimous acclaim from players once they had used them. Players felt it made the ethical side much easier. They no longer had to worry about making facial expressions, nor about a partner's huddle. Indeed, they no longer knew when partner huddled. Certain rule violations, such as leads out of turn or bids out of turn, became very rare because only one side of the table was involved at a time and such violations could be adjusted without any improper information being transmitted to partner.

Omar Sharif, for instance, has this to say about screens:

> Screens have made a big difference in bridge at the highest levels. Contrary to what many people around the world think, screens are a very good idea. You no longer have to worry about involuntary movements – your partner can't see them. Personally I feel more confident when I'm playing behind a screen. I don't have to sit like a statue. I don't have to worry about picking up my cigarette with my right hand. I can concentrate on the game.

BERMUDA INCIDENT

In 1975 the World Championships were played in Bermuda to celebrate the twenty-fifth anniversary of the founding of Bermuda Bowl as the World Championships are called. During the qualifying stages a member of the Italian team, Gianfranco Facchini, was accused of giving foot signals to his partner, Sergio Zucchelli. An American newspaper correspondent, Bruce Keidan, observed this and reported it to the North American non-playing captain, Alfred Sheinwold, and then to Edgar Kaplan, a member of the World Bridge Federation Appeals Committee. The World Bridge Federation, which was overseeing the championship, arranged for two observers to watch the Italian pair during their next match.

These observers claimed to see Facchini reach out with his feet on several occasions apparently to touch Zucchelli on the toes. Zucchelli's feet, meanwhile, remained completely immobile, and Facchini did not move his feet at other times. These foot movements happened only during the bidding and just before the opening lead. The World Bridge Federation decided to monitor Italy's next match, and bring in outside observers. But word of these allegations had got around and the North American team refused to play against Zucchelli and Facchini. Their scheduled match was postponed, and an official hearing was convened immediately.

Facchini claimed that he was moving his feet due to nervous tension, and Zucchelli testified that he was unaware of any foot movements by his partner. Having heard the evidence, the World Bridge Federation Committee was unable to find any specific correlation between the foot movements observed and the bidding or play of the hands and resolved that Facchini and Zucchelli '. . . be severely reprimanded for improper conduct with respect to the actions of Mr Facchini moving his feet unnaturally and touching his partner's feet during the auction and before the opening lead'. Small coffee tables were then placed underneath the card tables to prevent any possibility of further contact.

However, the Americans weren't satisfied and their non-playing captain, Alfred Sheinwold, issued his own statement: 'The North American team endorses the verdict of guilty but deplores the failure of the World Bridge Federation to bar this pair from further international competitions.' The postponed Italy–North America match was played later that evening and the suspect pair didn't play, their nerves, it was said, being 'frayed by the accusations'.

On the final day of the championships Sheinwold learned that Facchini and Zucchelli were scheduled to play again. Sheinwold announced that the North American team would not play against them unless instructed to do so by the ACBL. ACBL representatives in Bermuda met and unanimously ordered the North American team to play. Poetic justice seems to have been done, however, as the Italians did badly with the pair under suspicion in their line-up. It was only after two of their leading players, Benito Garozzo and Giorgio Belladonna, requested that the suspect pair be replaced that the Italian team recovered and staged a late rally to retain their world title.

HOUSTON AFFAIR

An earlier controversial incident occurred in January 1977 during the North American Team Trials when a team captained by John Gerber was forced to forfeit when two members of his five-player team, Larry Cohen and Richard Katz, resigned with thirty-two deals of the 128-board final still to be played.

After the ninety-sixth deal of the final, charges concerning irregularities involving Katz and Cohen were made. Closed-door conferences followed until an announcement was made by American Contract Bridge League President Louis Gurvich that Katz and Cohen had resigned from their team and from the ACBL. This reduced the Gerber team to three members, hence the team had to forfeit.

In the following days, there was much media speculation about the sudden unexpected resignations. Various newspaper articles quoted 'reliable sources' as saying that Katz and Cohen had been guilty of serious infractions against the proprieties of bridge. Soon after these accusations appeared in print, Katz and Cohen filed a $44 million lawsuit against the ACBL. The suit alleged defamation of character, interference with business interests, false accusations of cheating, coerced withdrawal from the Houston Trials, and forced resignation from the ACBL. The suit demanded that Katz and Cohen be reinstated as ACBL members and that the trials continue from the point where they were terminated.

The action finally was settled several years later on 23 February 1982. Katz and Cohen were readmitted to full membership of the ACBL but agreed not to play together as a partnership until such a request was submitted to the Board of the ACBL. Both parties to the lawsuit were compensated by Commercial Union Assurance Company, insurer of the ACBL, for costs and attorneys' fees. In an explanation of the settlement, the ACBL President stated in April 1982: 'This case was unique in that Katz-Cohen resigned from membership in the ACBL rather than face charges of improper communication and certain ejection from the ACBL should these charges be sustained. No matter how one may feel as to whether there was or was not improper communication, the fact remains that because of their resignations no evidentiary presentation of this charge was ever made.'

It was all rather mysterious. Much less mysterious, and very much an open drama, was the Buenos Aires incident of 1965.

The Buenos Aires Incident

♠♥♦
♣

Arguably the most sensational incident in the history of bridge took place in 1965. This was during the World Championships held in Argentina. A leading British pair, Terence Reese and Boris Schapiro, was accused by their American counterparts of cheating. It led to far-reaching repercussions. Two high-level international inquiries brought a guilty verdict in one country and a not-guilty one in another.

The background was as follows. Reese and Schapiro were playing for Great Britain, winners of the European Championship, in a four-sided World Championship. The other participants were the existing World Champions Italy, North America as winners of the latest Olympiad in 1964, and Argentina as host country. The allegations of cheating came to light only towards the end of the nine-day tournament.

Reese published his version of events in his book *Story of an Accusation*. It makes for fascinating reading. A second account, *The Great Bridge Scandal*, was written shortly afterwards by Alan Truscott. This challenged Reese's explanation and presented a differing view. Both these books are drawn upon here. Similarly a day-to-day account of the proceedings was written by the American pair involved, B. Jay Becker and Dorothy Hayden. These appeared in Alan Truscott's book. Becker's account sets the scene when they were playing against Reese and Schapiro on the first day of their match against Great Britain.

Not long after they had started playing, Becker happened to look over towards Reese on his right. It struck him that Reese was holding his cards in an odd and uncomfortable fashion, with two of his fingers spread in 'V' style in front of his cards. This seemed to Becker unusual since most players hold their cards with their thumb and four fingers. He then looked at Schapiro on his left and saw that he was also holding his cards with the same two fingers (the index and middle fingers) in a 'V' formation. It could be just a coincidence. After all, he had played against Reese and Schapiro on a number of occasions previously and had no reason to believe that their behaviour at the bridge table was anything but 'beyond reproach'. However, as the evening wore on, he kept looking and noticing that the number of fingers varied from hand to hand.

He began to get a 'gnawing feeling' that something improper was going on, and that finger signals of some kind were being exchanged between them. It was only after the session was over that he finally had a chance to speak to his partner, Mrs Hayden. She said she had seen nothing irregular and this made Becker wonder whether he had got it wrong. He offered to show her what he meant by demonstrating with a deck of cards the way he had seen Reese and Schapiro holding their cards. Mrs Hayden couldn't believe that Reese and Schapiro would go in for signalling in such a blatant and obvious manner. But she agreed to watch for herself the next time she played against them. Becker was anxious not to let the finger business upset Mrs Hayden's game. He also asked her to keep what he had said confidential for the time being.

Their next match against Reese and Schapiro was the opening session on Thursday. In the interval they hardly referred to the 'Reese–Schapiro problem' at all. Yet once back at the table again, as Becker saw it, the fingers went into operation and continued right through the fourteen-board session. He now felt sure that Mrs Hayden was seeing the same thing. Becker's frustration mounted as he was convinced that messages were going back and forth between Reese and Schapiro but he had no means of knowing what the messages meant. It gave him a feeling of 'eeriness and futility'. Mrs Hayden played badly during that session, and Becker feared that the march of the fingers had affected her game.

Their next session was on Bridgerama. This time Mrs Hayden played well and they did better, coming out on top. Even so, they both felt Reese and Schapiro were still using finger signals. They agreed they had to do something about it. They felt the best thing was to bring someone else into the picture and Mrs Hayden suggested Alan Truscott. Truscott was bridge editor of the *New York Times* and was known as a fair-minded person, and furthermore had lived nearly all his life in England. Also, he had been a member of the British international team in 1962 and knew Reese and Schapiro well. On all counts, therefore, he seemed to be the right person to go to, not only for advice but as a further witness to back up their suspicions. They found him in the press room and told him that they had an important matter to discuss with him. He was busy at the time, so they made a date with him later that same night when he expected to be free.

They met in the privacy of Becker's room, Becker closing the transom over his door so that they could not be overheard. Becker again asked Truscott to keep anything he said confidential and not to repeat it elsewhere. Truscott agreed, and Becker started to tell him that, in his opinion and Mrs Hayden's, Reese and Schapiro were unquestionably using a code of signals and were transmitting illegal information to each other. Truscott replied that he had heard such accusations against Reese and Schapiro in the past, but that no one had ever been able to prove anything. Becker explained what he had observed on Monday evening, and what both he and Mrs Hayden had seen in the two sessions they had played on Thursday afternoon. He also showed Truscott the various finger positions by using a pack of cards again. Much to Becker's surprise, Truscott did not think that Reese and Schapiro would engage in such a childish method of signalling. Such signals would be much too obvious. However, he agreed to watch Reese and Schapiro the next time they played, and see for himself whether the accusation was justified.

Becker felt, before going to sleep early that morning, that they needed one more witness, someone with prestige in the world of bridge, and thought of John Gerber, the American non-playing captain. Mrs Hayden agreed and Becker telephoned him to set up a time to talk later that day. Gerber was asked to keep everything confidential and Becker then proceeded to tell him everything that had transpired up to that moment. Gerber, impressed by what he said, also felt initially that he must be mistaken, but promised to watch Reese and Schapiro against Italy that afternoon when they were scheduled to play against Pietro Forquet and Benito Garozzo in the Open Room. Becker also went to watch, and met Mrs Hayden as he entered the Open Room. She said that Gerber had watched the first few hands and was now convinced that something was 'going on, all right'. He had seen the finger signals for himself and needed no further proof. Mrs Hayden had kept a record of the hands that afternoon by entering the board number and the number of fingers shown by Schapiro on each hand she had watched. She had done this on the back of a scorecard. Becker agreed to go to the opposite side and stand behind Schapiro so that he could see how many fingers Reese showed on each deal. In this way they hoped to compile a full record of all the hands they had both watched. However, at times, because of the height from which he was watching, Becker could not be sure whether Reese's little finger was holding the cards or was curled back out of sight, and in each of these cases, for the sake of accuracy, he asked Mrs Hayden to record the finger showing as '3d', that is, three fingers showing with a drooping fourth. By now he sensed that his data might be needed in the future and that it had better be accurate.

He also noticed that, soon after the bidding was over and play commenced, Reese and Schapiro both went back to the normal manner of holding cards, that is, with four fingers. This struck him at the time as highly significant. In addition, on one hand (Board No. 114) Reese held his cards in what seemed an extraordinary manner. He was using his thumb and all four fingers to hold the cards, but the four fingers were very widely spread, making three 'V's and, furthermore, extended almost the full length of the cards. This posture struck Becker as crude and awkward. Mrs Hayden was now beginning to think that the fingers referred to distribution rather than high-card strength. Truscott had taken his place, using his press privilege as a newspaperman, to sit right at the table between Reese and Forquet so as to have an even better view of the proceedings. However, he didn't take any notes, but saw what seemed to be changing fingers on each deal and was convinced that a code of some sort was being used by Reese and Schapiro, though he had little idea what the signals meant. When they all three met up, Hayden and Becker gave Truscott a copy of their notes and asked him to see if he could try to break the code. With the use of the official records of the hands played that afternoon, a comparison with their notes might yield results. He agreed to do this and to meet up with them again after the next session was over.

An unexpected development took place later that afternoon. Gerber came up to Becker and said that, having watched Reese and Schapiro in action and being convinced that they were transmitting illegal signals to each other, he had, therefore, felt obliged to inform both Robin MacNab, President of the American Contract Bridge League, and Waldemar von Zedtwitz, President Emeritus of the ACBL, of what he had seen. He apologised to Becker for breaking his promise of confidentiality but hoped he would see the point of his action.

Six people now knew what was going on and soon the matter was out of Becker's control. Later that night Hayden, Truscott and Becker met up again at an all-night restaurant some distance away from the Plaza

Hotel to try to solve the riddle of the code. Truscott brought the official record of hands that corresponded to the boards noted by Hayden that afternoon. He told them he had studied hands played by Reese and Schapiro against different opponents earlier in the week, and in some of those hands Reese and Schapiro appeared to have bid rather oddly, but he had made no real progress in trying to solve the finger code. Hayden then suggested they start with all one-finger signals and compare these against the corresponding hands. The only hand (No. 120) that afternoon which had a one-finger signal was examined and they found that Schapiro, who had held his cards with one finger, had a singleton heart. Mrs Hayden then recalled a hand (No. 51) they had played against Reese and Schapiro in which Reese had held the cards with one finger and it turned out he had the singleton ace of hearts. They had bid six spades and easily made it, and so both Becker and Hayden were able to remember the hand. Mrs Hayden felt they were near to solving the riddle and suggested that one finger meant one heart, two fingers two hearts, three fingers three hearts, and so on. They examined the hands in which two fingers had been shown, and it fitted – the same with three- and four-finger hands. They now felt in no doubt they had broken the code.

Then they hit a stumbling block. On the fourth board (No. 121) Mrs Hayden's notes showed that Schapiro held his cards with two fingers while the official hand record showed him to have had five hearts. They thought that two fingers might represent either two or five hearts, Becker comparing this to Roman Blackwood where a response of five clubs indicates either no aces or three aces and a response of five diamonds indicates one ace or four aces. Shortly after this, turning to four-finger hands, the theory seemed to be confirmed. On deal No. 114, the hand previously referred to in which Reese had shown four fingers very widely spread, Reese had had seven hearts. How, then, could these be signalled? With only four fingers available, there had to be another way, and they concluded that two fingers together meant two hearts and two fingers spread apart meant five hearts; that three fingers together meant three hearts and three fingers spread apart meant six hearts; that four fingers together meant four hearts and four fingers spread apart meant seven hearts. There had been no six-card heart suits held by Reese or Schapiro that afternoon, so they were unable to confirm the theory in full, but the two-finger signal with five hearts on No. 121 and the spread four-finger signal on No. 114 seemed to fit.

By the time they had finished it was close to 4 a.m., and, despite the hour, they felt they ought to notify Gerber at once of this newest development. Truscott tried to reach him by telephone at the Plaza Hotel, but his room did not answer. Truscott undertook to inform him later that morning.

Reese and Schapiro, meanwhile, had been oblivious of these goings-on. In his book, *Story of an Accusation*, Reese starts with a general survey of bridge, calling it 'a strange game', which engages certain emotions 'more powerfully than any other activity in life'. He cites, in particular, *amour-propre*, our self-worth or self-esteem. Reese goes on, 'At most games players find their own level and are roughly content with it.' But bridge was different. 'There is no reliable method of individual comparison . . . most players are extremely anxious to convince themselves and others that they play better than they do. It touches their *amour-propre.*' A famous story concerns a questionnaire submitted to top international players asking them to nominate 'the second best player in the world', the assumption being they would naturally fill first place.

If bridge reveals a person's character, Reese went on, then unexpected displays of emotion are likely to appear at the bridge table. 'A man who in ordinary life gets by as a sound and well-adjusted citizen may show himself at the bridge table to be stupid, vain, obstinate, greedy and dishonest. A couple who bill and coo at one another from dawn to dusk will storm and sulk when they play cards.' This is familiar territory to most bridge players, but has special relevance to the case being cited here. Reese called his opening chapter 'The Green Sickness', an unmistakable reference to jealousy, the 'green-eyed monster which doth mock The meat it feeds on' as Iago said. Competitive sport such as bridge, played under intense pressure, can be a hotbed of this. An item of medical research in the 1970s compared bridge players at the beginning and end of a tournament with surgeons before and after a difficult operation. Using indicators such as sweating, changes in heartbeat and blood pressure, the research concluded that bridge players were under greater strain.

Reese explains his side of the background to the 1965 World Championships in Buenos Aires. For many years he and Schapiro had been good friends and a successful partnership, considered among the world's best. But by the mid-1960s their relationship, on and off the table, had cooled. As Reese put it, 'The happiest of couples can have a rough patch after twenty years and in our case the Little Major was playing the part of the "other woman".' The Little Major was Reese's new system and Schapiro didn't like the system. Schapiro was an intuitive rather than an analytical player, and having tried the system, realised it didn't suit his talents. Reese, on his own admission full of impatience, had then played the system with Jeremy Flint. In the European Championship at Baden-Baden in 1964, Reese joined up mostly with Flint to play the Little Major. Schapiro played with Reese in the trials, which were on a pairs basis. 'It was a delicate situation and I managed it badly,' wrote Reese. 'My decision to play with Flint hurt and offended Boris in a way I had not foreseen. This interlude in my relationship with Boris makes an unedifying story, I know, but I have to relate it because it is relevant to what happened later.'

The rift with Schapiro still existed, but in the weeks before Buenos Aires tempers cooled and they became friends again. Reese still hoped to play the Little Major with Flint, especially in the critical match against Italy, but it was plain that the rest of the team, including Flint himself, wanted Schapiro and Reese to resume their partnership. The British team, with Ralph Swimer as non-playing captain, flew to Buenos Aires on Wednesday, 12 May 1965. They were staying and playing in the centre of Buenos Aires, at the Plaza Hotel, large and old-fashioned. The draw meant that they were due to play Italy in the first round on Saturday, Argentina on Sunday, North America on Monday. This sequence would be twice repeated, the championship lasting in all over nine days.

In their Monday match against the Americans, Reese played the first session with Flint on Bridgerama. Reese felt this was a critical moment, as Schapiro would be sitting out and watching the Little Major in action. 'It was not to be expected that he would be indulgent to any shortcomings.' That same evening Reese and Shapiro played their first match together against Becker and Hayden. Relationships between the two teams were strained from the start. 'As a small diversion' Reese made a formal complaint to the American deputy captain about the chewing of gum by the American players.

It was on Thursday that Reese and Schapiro next played against the Americans, against Becker and Hayden again, and then on Friday they played against the Italians, who beat them convincingly by 121 match points. Reese called it 'the biggest reverse of our career'.

Even so, the British team still had an outside chance of winning the championship. The match between America and Italy was still undecided; if America beat Italy, Great Britain might get into the lead on total match points. Thus it was important to win well against Argentina on the Saturday. Reese played the first session against Argentina with Flint and sat out for the next fourteen boards. Britain gained heavily on both occasions. Swimer made a point of playing Reese and Schapiro together for the final session. On their way to the Open Room they learned that America had fallen well behind Italy and therefore had no chance of winning their match. This meant that Britain's match against the Argentine no longer had any significance so far as winning the overall championship was concerned.

During this final match against Argentina, Reese noted the unexpected appearance of Geoffrey Butler in the 'captain's chair' at his elbow, making notes on a pad. This was the first time he had noticed him near their table during this championship. Reese remembers drawing Schapiro's attention to Butler's arrival with a quizzical glance, which Schapiro returned.

Reese went to bed late that night as was his custom during tournaments. At about half past ten the following morning he was just beginning to wake up when the phone rang in his room. It was his team colleague Albert Rose. 'Terence, there's something going on. Ralph Swimer has been closeted with the committee for nearly an hour. They want you and Boris. Can you come down?' It took him about twenty minutes to shave and get dressed. Downstairs as he approached the passage leading to the committee room he met Swimer coming out, looking white and strained. 'Oh, there you are,' Swimer said. Reese noticed Schapiro sitting in a public room nearby, puffing furiously at his pipe. Swimer took Reese into the committee room. The Appeals Committee of the World Bridge Federation was assembled: Geoffrey Butler, chairman, sitting in the centre of the room, Charles Solomon, President of the World Bridge Federation, Robin MacNab, President of the American Contract Bridge League, Baron Waldemar von Zedtwitz, also of the ACBL, and John Gerber, captain of the American team. Usually a player is asked to attend such a committee meeting when a protest has been made against him on a technical point, for instance making a bid or playing a card with undue emphasis, or taking advantage of partner's hesitation, or using a convention that has not been announced in advance. Worst might be accusations of a private understanding with partner which had deliberately been concealed.

Reese sat down. Butler informed him that he had the 'very

unpleasant task' of telling him that he and Boris Schapiro, whom they had already interviewed, had been under observation for several days, and that Becker and other witnesses would say that they had been using finger signals to indicate how many cards Reese and Schapiro held in the heart suit. Whenever they held a singleton heart, one finger was shown on the back of the cards, with two hearts, two fingers, and so on. He then asked Reese what he had to say. Reese's head, in his own words, 'whirled'. He immediately denied the allegations. 'I don't know what you are talking about. There's not a word of truth in it. I am tired of hearing this sort of accusation every time one plays against the Americans. It happened at Como, again at Turin, and now the same thing here. It is absolute nonsense.'

The Como and Turin incidents referred to earlier championships. At Lake Como in 1958 Reese had been there as a journalist while Italy played the United States for the World Championship. The Americans, particularly one 'very contentious' player, had accused Italy of using illegal signals (see previous chapter). The Turin incident referred to the 1960 Olympiad, won by France, with Britain second. An American spectator claimed that whenever Reese and Schapiro held their cards up before the bidding for spectators to see – this was normal practice – they held them in their right hand if they were strong, and in their left hand if they were weak. Again nothing had been proved. Becker, in the present American team, had also been in Como and Turin and so would have been well aware of both precedents. Reese had already noticed, in this tournament, how Becker frequently turned full face to look at his opponents during the bidding, not in itself an unusual procedure, but noticeable nevertheless.

Gerber, the American non-playing captain, was next to talk in the committee room. He gave his version of events, how Becker had told him his suspicions earlier in the week, how he saw Reese and Schapiro hold their cards differently at different times, making it seem as if signals were being exchanged. Gerber had informed the British captain, Ralph Swimer, of what he had seen. Swimer had then spoken to Butler. Hence the arrangement for Reese and Schapiro to play against Argentina in the Open Room so that Butler could observe them. Butler then recounted his evidence, namely that except for two hands where Reese held a void, and on one or two occasions when his vision was obstructed, the signals seemed to correspond with the code mentioned above.

Swimer spoke next and said that he had watched the first ten boards of the same session, and that on every deal the number of fingers shown by both players corresponded with their heart holding. Swimer's comments infuriated Reese who felt the British captain should at least be defending his players, not taking the other side. Reese was next asked to speak. With hindsight, he realised that he should have reserved his defence, as lawyers always recommend. At the time he admitted he might have held his cards in different ways at different times, and this could happen during the bidding of a single hand. He suggested instead that they check the match records. 'Go through the records,' he told them, 'and see if there is any indication of collusive play. I don't recall any clever psychic bids or brilliant leads. I know we made a lot of mistakes, particularly against Italy. Do you think we couldn't have done better in that match if we had had a cheating system?' This referred to the fact that they had lost heavily against Italy.

Alan Truscott was next to speak. He said he had examined the match records. He produced out of his pocket various bits of paper on which he had jotted down different hands, selecting from these eight hands where he felt their bidding or opening lead might have been influenced by knowledge of the heart distribution. His evidence concluded the proceedings for the first session. The committee said they would meet again later.

On leaving the committee room, Reese came across Schapiro in the sitting area of the hotel. 'What's all this bloody nonsense about?' Schapiro asked him. 'God knows,' Reese replied, and went on, 'I didn't know what to say, did you?' 'I just said it was balderdash,' Schapiro replied. Schapiro's interview had only lasted a few minutes. Then Swimer came up to them, telling them he didn't want them to play again until everything had been cleared up. Reese and Schapiro went to the dining room to look for the rest of the British team but none of them was there. They went to the bar instead and had a drink with Jeremy Flint. 'Boris was in a state of shock,' said Flint afterwards. 'He kept on repeating, "This is a nice state of affairs."'

The rest of the British team still didn't know what was going on. Reese came across them in the hotel lounge before the afternoon session, looking perplexed and worried. 'Nobody has told us what's happening,' said Konstam. 'All we know is that there has been some protest and that you and Boris are not playing.' As other people were standing near them, Reese didn't want to go into details. Swimer had met them and told them they would be playing in the same formations as that morning and afternoon, but wouldn't give any reason why, and then at one point said to the team, 'I don't want you to have anything to do with Reese and Schapiro.'

As Reese commented later, many people found it hard to understand why the rest of the team did not support them immediately and refuse to play on. Flint commented, 'I didn't realise it was so serious, or I would have insisted on a team meeting. As it was, I felt we were jockeyed out of any discussion and more or less steam-rollered into playing on.' But, as Flint's remarks show, it looked, at that stage, to be only a temporary storm. Their priority was their current match. 'Win that first, and argue later' seemed to be the prevailing policy.

Later that afternoon Reese and Schapiro were summoned to the second committee meeting, this time a meeting of the Executive Committee of the World Bridge Federation. Everyone who had been present in the morning meeting, except for von Zedtwitz, who had left on other business, was there, plus Dr Labougle of Argentina, Perroux, the Italian captain, Hammerich from Venezuela, and General A. Gruenther, Honorary President of the World Bridge Federation. Gruenther, an avid bridge player and previously referee at the Culbertson–Lenz match in the 1930s, had been Eisenhower's Chief of Staff and bridge partner during the Second World War. Gruenther opened the proceedings. 'I want you two gentlemen to feel that you have all the protection and advantages you would get under your own British system.' He asked for Swimer and Butler to submit their evidence in more detail. Swimer said he had watched the first ten hands of the evening session against Argentina and had taken notes of the number of fingers showing on the back of the cards of both players. Reese, in his later account, commented: 'A pantomime followed in which he read from his notes and Hammerich, holding the match records, turned over the pages and echoed the numbers called out by Swimer. ('Reese three fingers' – 'Reese three hearts', 'Schapiro two fingers' – 'Schapiro two hearts', and so on.)

Butler explained that he had watched the second half of the same session from a chair beside the table. He likewise read from his notes. Butler's record was necessarily incomplete. For instance, when the first hand was being played, he was climbing through the ropes and could not have observed the signals and at one point his view had been obstructed by a spectator. ('That's right,' Schapiro said afterwards of this unlikely happening. 'A spectator jumped onto the table and got in Butler's way. I remember it distinctly.')

Reese could see that, despite the gaps in the story, the evidence against them was mounting. 'What strikes me, as a layman,' commented General Gruenther at one point, 'is that you don't seem to make any violent rebuttal of these charges.' 'Well, you tell me, General,' Reese replied. 'How *does* one rebut this sort of accusation?' Reese's later comment was: 'Indeed, that was the difficulty. If somebody says you made certain movements and there was a pattern to it, what can you answer? You can deny it, but you cannot disprove it. To take a comparable situation, suppose that when you come in after a game of golf you learn that someone has reported to the club secretary that on three occasions you improved your lie in the rough. How can you defend yourself? However much you deny it, the moment is past and the damage is irreparably done.'

Many later commentators on the proceedings, notably in articles in American magazines, also wondered why Reese appeared to treat these accusations so coolly. His sang-froid was noticeable. In his defence Reese later said: 'I have too keen a sense of the ridiculous to perform the motions of conventional indignation.' And, referring to his partner, 'One might have expected Boris to be more demonstrative, but in moments of stress he relapses into paralysed silence.'

Discussing their match against Italy, Reese reminded the committee of their poor showing, an argument surely against the value of cheating. Turning to Perroux, Reese asked him if the Italians had had any suspicions at the time. His question was translated into French for him by the Argentine delegate. '*Absolument non*,' was Perroux's reply. Butler then allegedly made a remark, later widely quoted, but which he later denied making: 'You have an ingenious mind,' he is said to have told Reese. 'You invented the Little Major. Perhaps that was not as successful as you hoped, and so you invented the Little Heart.' Reese and Schapiro then left the committee room. A lengthy discussion ensued. General Gruenther said he had been greatly impressed by the checking of the heart suit from the notes produced by Swimer and Butler. Three or four examples could well have been coincidence, but when in nineteen successive hands the signals coincided, he said he felt convinced of the evidence.

By now the tournament was buzzing with rumours. The general public, who had arrived in large numbers for the final day, had no reason to suspect that anything was amiss. Many of them, carrying programmes or books, asked for Reese's autograph. 'May be more valuable than you think,' Reese reflected to himself as he signed for them.

Rumours of a pending announcement were circulating. Reese had some messages to write for his newspapers so he decided to go along to the press room. This had space for about four people to sit and type. The committee was in session next door. Whenever the typewriters were silent, conversations from the adjoining room could be heard clearly. Perhaps this, more than indiscretion on the part of committee members, accounted for the frequent leakages of information.

After a while the committee secretary came in, holding a sheet of paper on which the committee's statement was written. She hesitated when she saw Reese. Then she read out the statement: 'Certain irregularities having been reported. The Appeals Committee fully investigated the matter and later convened a meeting of the Executive Committee of the World Bridge Federation. The Captain of the British team was present. As a result of this meeting the Captain of the British squad decided to play only K. Konstam, M. Harrison-Gray, A. Rose and J. Flint in the remaining sessions and very sportingly conceded the matches against North America and Argentina. A report of the proceedings will be sent to the British Bridge League.' There was one abstention from the vote, Perroux, the captain of the Italian team.

Reese, having noted the contents, went on with the article he was typing. Dick Frey, editor of the *American Contract Bridge League Bulletin*, sitting next to him, telephoned his own account to a news agency, describing it in great detail. Reese was relieved that the committee had omitted both his and Schapiro's names. But the other journalists present moved quickly on to the story. 'Finger signals' were mentioned in news agency messages, and newspapers all over the world embroidered on the official statement. 'From that moment we were "dead",' Reese wrote. The other correspondents, who had been in the press room when the statement was read, soon melted away to transmit their own messages and, when Reese looked up after finishing his article for the *San Francisco Chronicle*, he found he was alone.

The committee's statement was read out on Bridgerama and the audience learned of it that way. Reese wrote: 'It required some nerve to stay around in the public rooms now. My friends thought it courageous, my enemies shameless.' Indeed, many did wonder about Reese's reaction and his apparent insouciance after the announcement was made – his continuing to write his newspaper articles and his aplomb in the face of these accusations. Such demeanour can be easily misread, but those who knew him felt it was typical of the man.

On the morning following the committee meeting and the announcement, Reese was still up in his room in bed. London was about five hours behind Buenos Aires, so the story had not broken there yet. Local newspapermen in Buenos Aires pressed Reese and Schapiro for interviews. Both, while denying the charges, refused to comment on the action of the British officials. Newspapermen asked Schapiro what plans he had for the future. He said it was a miserable tournament anyway and he never wanted to play championship bridge again. Reese said he had not made up his mind yet. The morning papers in London had already been printed, but the daytime papers had yet to come out. Reese got his first telephone call at about 8.30 a.m. local time from the foreign editor of the *Evening News*. Others soon joined in. By midday he had had enough and told the hotel telephone operator, 'No more calls.'

Dick Frey then appeared at his door with a proposition. Frey had his 'we're-all-professionals-in-this-together' air. He sat down and told Reese that the American magazine *Sports Illustrated* was doing a big coverage of the event and was prepared to commission an article from Reese giving his side of the story. The fee was temptingly high, so Reese agreed to do it and wrote out his piece for *Sports Illustrated* later that afternoon. Aware that American opinion might be against him, he let loose some of his grievances: 'I say nothing personal about the people involved in this case, but the world of tournament bridge is full of envious and evil-minded maggots that no self-respecting stone would shelter.'

Downstairs he met Schapiro and they went off for lunch at the golf club with members of the Italian team. The Italians were sympathetic and succeeded in raising Schapiro's spirits. The official banquet at the end of the tournament took place that evening but neither Reese nor Boris attended. Reese never liked such events anyhow. 'Always an exceedingly boring function which starts late and proceeds interminably.' They had dinner at their hotel instead and went for a long stroll afterwards. When they got back at eleven o'clock, dinner-jacketed stragglers from the cocktail party were still on their way to the banqueting room. 'You certainly cast a pall over the proceedings,' Jeremy Flint told them the next morning. 'Even under the stimulus of alcohol nobody had much to say.'

On their walk Reese and Schapiro discussed the incident in their usual abrasive way. 'It's your fault,' Schapiro told him. 'You annoy them all with your aloof manner. You don't make any effort to mix with the other teams.' 'I can't talk their blasted lingo like you,' Reese replied. 'Besides, I've got something better to do in the mornings than run round telling everyone how well I played the night before.' Schapiro, a gifted linguist, was well known for his sociability. Reese admitted he was not 'a naturally good mixer'.

The British team was set to leave Buenos Aires that day to fly to Rio de Janeiro to play two friendly matches against Brazilian teams en route to England. There was some talk of abandoning the fixture, but, as all the arrangements had been made and the present disputes had nothing to do with the Brazilians, the team went. Some felt this was unwise and thought that Butler and Swimer should have returned straight home to make their report. Reese and Schapiro returned to London the following day. The aeroplane journey in those days took about twenty hours, with four stops and two changes of crew. As they left Lisbon, a man in the seat behind them offered them an English newspaper with a full-page spread: 'Bridge Aces Say, "We are Not Cheats"'.

At Gatwick Airport they were met by a battery of thirty cameramen, and radio and television reporters. Friends from the bridge world came to greet them as well. Reese appeared on the BBC *Tonight* programme. The interviewer asked him if, leaving the present case aside, it was possible to cheat in tournament bridge. Reese, aware that there was a caption beneath his picture stating that he completely denied the allegations made at Buenos Aires, felt that there was no harm in responding. He said that it was actually very easy to cheat at bridge without being detected, giving as examples a simple gesture, a positioning of the hands or cards or head as means of conveying to one's partner whether one was weak, medium or strong in relation to the last bid made. A system of spacing between the cards held in the hand could convey any number of messages about strength or distribution. After writing down the contract at the end of the bidding, a player could leave his pencil at an angle that asked for a particular lead. Reese later commented, 'Apparently it was somewhat naive of me to illustrate these possibilities. I learned later that simple-minded members of the public had gathered the impression that I was demonstrating our own cunning devices.'

Back in England they received support from many quarters. They had a fond welcome at Stamford Bridge greyhound racing track from their old friends, the bookmakers. Newspapers for which Reese wrote articles backed him up. The committee of Crockford's card club, having already sent them a cable of support in Buenos Aires, pledged their support. However, Reese knew that, despite these encouraging signs, some players in Britain would be happy to see them brought down, not least professional rivals with an eye on their writing jobs.

The World Bridge Federation at their meeting in Buenos Aires had turned the matter over to the British Bridge League, which had to decide what to do next. Its Executive Council is composed of delegates from the English, Scottish, Welsh and Northern Ireland Bridge Unions. An emergency meeting of the Council was called for 30 May, the day after Butler and Swimer were due back from Rio. Butler took his accustomed place in the chair. He had his notes of the proceedings at Buenos Aires and was ready to give the meeting his version of what had occurred. However, Council members pointed out to Butler that his status was now that of a witness, and a new chairman was appointed for the meeting. As no official report from the World Bridge Federation had yet been received, the Council decided not to hear any unofficial account of those proceedings. So Butler gave an external account of the sequence of events, the meetings and the statement that had been issued.

The Council favoured the idea of an independent inquiry. At their second meeting, Louis Tarlo, a solicitor who had been captain of the British team at the European Championships at Baden-Baden in 1963, reported that Sir John Foster, QC, MP, had expressed willingness to act as chairman of such an inquiry. The League accepted this offer and the press was so informed. Reese and Schapiro appointed Eric Leigh Howard, a golfing friend of Reese and also a bridge expert, as their solicitor. Tim Holland, of Crockford's Club, agreed to support their defence 'in every way', a welcome relief to them. This enabled them to instruct Leonard Caplan, QC, as counsel. The solicitor for the British Bridge League was John Pugh, a friendly rival of Reese and Schapiro in the bridge world. He took Reese aside to say that he was open-minded about the case and had taken the job only because, if he did not, somebody else would. The BBL's counsel was Simon Goldblatt, a young advocate with some knowledge of bridge.

Sir John Foster was, in Reese's words, 'tall and shaggy, with a slight suggestion of a scholarly gipsy, resonant of voice, most courteous in manner'. He asked if he could be assisted by a colleague of the same status as himself and proposed General Lord Bourne. 'He is a man of the world with plenty of common sense. I sat with him on another case recently. I know his wife plays bridge.'

The inquiry began at the beginning of December 1965. Caplan's opening speech described the world of top-class international bridge. 'It is a world in which there are extremely strange passions and extremely strange antagonisms at work, a world in which there are few, it appears, if any, great players who are not subject to envy and malice by other players who have not reached their heights. It is a world where the weapons of that envy and of that malice have been found not infrequently to be the false trumped-up accusation of cheating.' He said it was a world in which Reese, by common consent regarded as 'perhaps the very best player in it', and Schapiro, 'who is hardly perhaps greatly inferior as a player', have been almost 'magically free from accusations of this kind, notwithstanding their pre-eminent position and notwithstanding the kind of jungle this world is'.

Caplan took the line that two such eminent players would hardly need to cheat or exchange only marginally important information about the heart suit in such a crude way, when so much more important information could be exchanged more simply. Equally, if they were cheating, they would surely have swept the board. Yet the results proved otherwise. Later Reese and Schapiro appeared as witnesses. Reese described the events of the two meetings, the committee's announcement, the way the story was circulated to the world's press. Then came the long task of dealing with the technical evidence, the thirty-five hands where it was alleged that their bidding or play had been, or might have been, influenced by knowledge of the heart suit. Photos from the play taken at the table were also shown.

The opposing counsel, Goldblatt, tried to insist that Reese was influenced by the relative failure of the Little Major, and that the alleged cheating code gave him 'a somewhat similar pleasure and advantage' to that enjoyed by the Little Major. Reese contested this. The Little Major was 'an exceedingly complicated intellectual affair', whereas there was nothing intellectual or interesting in exchanging knowledge about the heart suit. Reese could see no connection. Asked in what light he regarded cheating at bridge, Reese replied that most people wanted to do well at bridge in order to satisfy themselves that they were cleverer than the other person. 'If you take that pleasure away, such as it is, I personally cannot see any pleasure in winning at all.'

Other witnesses were called for both sides. The inquiry dragged on. Finally the day of judgement arrived. Reese, Schapiro and their solicitor assembled first at Crockford's Club and drove to the inquiry in Tim Holland's Rolls-Royce. The Council had been sitting for most of the afternoon. Reporters and cameramen milled around. Reese and Schapiro passed the time discussing bridge hands, the afternoon's racing, the possible outcome of the judgement, the significance of the delay. The London correspondent of the *New York Times* wrote, 'The sang-froid of great card players served them well. An outsider could not have guessed that this was possibly the most important moment of their lives.' Finally the result was announced and a statement read out for those assembled:

> The joint report by Sir John Foster and Lord Bourne into certain allegations of cheating at the World Championships in 1965 made against Messrs Reese and Schapiro was received by the Council today. After full discussion of the arguments and recommendations by Sir John Foster and Lord Bourne the finding in the report that Messrs Reese and Schapiro were not guilty of cheating was accepted. A copy of the report will be sent to the World Bridge Federation.

Reese and Schapiro were relieved and gratified. The second inquiry had cleared them of charges of cheating. They headed back for Crockford's Club for a celebration. Next day came news of the American reaction. Charles Solomon, President of the World Bridge Federation, doubted whether they would accept the decision. The repercussions of the verdict spread far and wide. Becker, Hayden and Truscott issued a joint statement which began: 'After lengthy consideration the British have seen fit to exonerate two of their representatives in World Championship play, despite the testimony of leading bridge personalities including the captain of their own team and the chairman of the British Bridge League.' Truscott, Hayden and Becker were to join forces later to publish their accounts of what happened in Alan Truscott's book *The Great Bridge Scandal*.

Truscott was in an invidious position as he had known Reese and Schapiro for nearly twenty years, having first met them in 1946 when, as a twenty-one-year-old and still wearing his naval officer's uniform, he had entered a bridge competition in Harrogate, Yorkshire, and encountered Reese and Schapiro in the final round. Truscott always remembered admiring Schapiro's courage in bluffing him on one hand by opening, vulnerable, with a psychic bid. On the train back to London they all shared a compartment and five years later became team-mates in the 1951 trials for the British team. Truscott had later contributed to the *British Bridge World* which Reese edited. In 1962 Truscott, having played for Great Britain in the New York World Championships, decided to stay on in America to edit the *Official Bridge Encyclopaedia* for the American Contract Bridge League. He soon became bridge correspondent of the *New York Times.* On the international bridge scene, his relationship with Reese and Schapiro remained on good terms, even though, as he acknowledged, he once or twice heard comments in the USA about their honesty. He dismissed these 'with considerable indignation' and thought no more about them. He was therefore both 'astonished and disturbed' when Becker and Mrs Hayden took him into their confidence in Buenos Aires.

Truscott was at Buenos Aires as a journalist for the *New York Times* and missed a scoop on the story as he had decided that it would be improper for him to cable his story to his paper while it was still under consideration by the official body. When he eventually got back to New York he was irritated to discover that the front page of the *New York Times* on Monday had carried the story of the cheating, not under his byline but using a wire-service story sent through by a local 'stringer' ahead of the official announcement. On his last day in Buenos Aires Truscott had an unexpected encounter with Reese. Reese was standing on his own in the hotel lobby and beckoned him over. Truscott had no idea what was coming. It turned out to be a civil offer to send him some hands from the forthcoming European Championship in Ostend which Reese was due to attend. Truscott accepted gracefully. Reese was being his usual enigmatic self, courteous and beguiling at the same time. Truscott's justification for publishing his own account, *The Great Bridge Scandal*, was, as he wrote in his preface, because: 'Reese has implied that I and other witnesses for the prosecution manufactured evidence against him. The facts show that if he is innocent he must be the victim of a gigantic international conspiracy. This book is my reply on behalf of the "conspirators".'

Rixi Markus was another outsider to enter the fray. At the time of the

Buenos Aires incident she was thousands of miles away in Venice on a working holiday to finish her book *Aces and Places*. Some time before she had become English agent for *The Bridge World*, the magazine founded by Culbertson in 1929. She had been a good friend of Culbertson, and was a friend too of its present editor, Sonny Moyse. Moyse had a standing commission with her to describe European reactions to any especially noteworthy incident in world bridge. When the scandal in Buenos Aires broke, he naturally asked for her views on the affair. Initially she felt she was not qualified to judge as she hadn't been there, but privately she felt the accusation had to be unfounded, as she could not imagine Reese and Schapiro cheating unless, as she put it, 'they had lost their minds'.

Moyse had already published in *The Bridge World* an article entitled 'The Case Against Reese and Schapiro', which showed eight hands from Buenos Aires and claimed that they proved the cheating allegations. In Rixi Markus's view they did nothing of the sort, and she sat down to write an article challenging it entitled 'The Case *For* Reese and Schapiro' which set out to demolish Moyse's piece. She sent it to Moyse for publication, enclosing with it a personal, hand-written letter in which she set out in unequivocal terms her assessment of the whole affair, including her opinion of the behaviour of the non-playing captain, Ralph Swimer. She sent both these documents to him from Venice and, having sent the article and letter off, thought no more about it.

On her return to London she was puzzled to hear rumours circulating that Ralph Swimer was going to sue her for libel. She then discovered that Moyse had published her private letter, intended for his eyes only, in *The Bridge World* instead of the article she had written and which she had planned for publication. She went to consult her lawyer who agreed that the published piece did contain one phrase which could be interpreted as libellous. The alleged defamatory words were: 'When Swimer was told by the (all-American) trio that Schapiro and Reese used signals, etc. he readily believed that was so, and when he went to watch them he saw what he was told to see . . . I like Ralph Swimer and consider him a decent and honourable man but he was an utter failure in his duties as a captain. How can I ever play for my country when my captain becomes a party to a conspiracy to convict me of a crime?' Mutual friends tried to settle the matter out of court, but she felt the conditions demanded by Ralph Swimer were more than she could put up with.

So the libel case went ahead. It came to the High Court in February

1969 and lasted for nearly two weeks. It received wide coverage in the national press, her picture appearing on the front page of *The Times*. Ralph Swimer claimed his reputation had been damaged by her words, particularly the use of the word 'conspiracy'. In evidence Rixi Markus compared his behaviour with that of the captain of a football team who accuses one of his own players of a foul. If he were in genuine doubt of the legality of his team member's play, he should have summoned the tournament director, not immediately sided with the opponents. Rixi Markus claimed that as a reporter she was entitled to express her opinion, that what she had said was what she believed, and that she had not meant it to be malicious.

The judge impressed on the jury that Rixi Markus was a world figure in bridge and so anything she said, or wrote, carried great weight and would therefore, if detrimental, be doubly damaging. Reese attended the court and wrote: 'Rixi was not the most responsive of witnesses. She was there to have her say, and she had it, despite the admonitions of her own counsel, the protests of the other side, and the instructions of the judge.' In his summing-up, the judge, so Rixi Markus felt, was not on her side, seeing her as 'a hard-bitten professional' and Swimer as 'a comparative innocent, an amateur doing his best in difficult conditions'. The judge also refused to allow testimony from Reese and Schapiro, or from her chosen expert witness, a French international tournament director, on the grounds that this was a libel action and was not concerned with whether the cheating accusations were true or false.

The jury deliberated for many hours, returning several times to request clarification from the judge on various points. The longer they deliberated, the more hopeful Markus became. Eventually the judge asked the jury if they thought they would ever be able to reach a decision, even if they had as much time as they wanted. For a moment there was complete silence in the courtroom, then from the second row of the jury came a woman's voice: 'It's no use, my Lord. We're never going to agree!' 'Be silent, madam,' said the judge sharply. 'Only the foreman is allowed to speak for you.' 'I'm afraid it's true,' said the foreman. And that was the end of it. It was a hung jury and the judge dismissed the case. From Rixi Markus's point of view, it was, 'if not a total victory, certainly a satisfactory result'. Swimer as plaintiff had to pay the costs of both parties. He could have renewed the action before another jury, but declined to do so.

The Foster Inquiry had put the World Bridge Federation on the spot with its 'not guilty' verdict. After learning of their finding late in 1966, the World Bridge Federation President Charles Solomon had stated at the time, 'It is doubtful that the World Bridge Federation can accept the decision of the London hearing . . .' and at their annual meeting in 1967 their Executive Committee reaffirmed its earlier guilty verdict. Effectively Reese and Schapiro were still banned from international competition and the following year, 1968, the British Bridge League, with the ban still in force, decided as a result not to play in the World Team Olympiad of that year which was taking place in Deauville, France.

Despite the absence of British teams there, many leading British bridge personalities attended. At a morning press cocktail party, a new, ingenious bridge instructional device was being shown to participants and journalists. Four of them were asked to try it out for a deal. Alan Truscott, who took part in the trial, takes up the story: 'To my surprise I found myself sitting opposite my old English partner, Tony Priday, for the first time in six years. There was a slight shock at the first trick when it appeared that there were two aces of diamonds, a mechanical error which was soon put right. There was a bigger shock at the fifth trick when I looked up from my cards to see that my partner's head, jacket and shirt were all extremely wet, and at the same moment he stood up and screamed, "Rixi," in a moist mixture of surprise and irritation. Mrs Markus had entered the room, seen him consorting with me – "the enemy" – and expressed her indignation by emptying a glass of water over his head.' The after-effects of Buenos Aires were clearly still around, but from the following year onwards Reese and Schapiro started playing international competition again.

Terence Reese and Boris Schapiro

♠♥♦
♣

Terence Reese was born in 1913 in a flat above the restaurant that dominated Epsom High Street. His mother's family owned a well-known chain of cafés and restaurants, with branches in several Surrey towns. She was a capable woman and Reese had fond memories of her. 'Without being priggish, she had the disposition of an angel; I don't believe it was possible for a selfish thought to find its way into her mind.'

With both parents working hard – his father had started off working in a bank but after marriage had moved into the family catering business – and a brother much older than himself, Reese developed a loneliness that was to be with him all his life. He was precocious as a youngster. At the age of six he used to travel on his own to his kindergarten at Sutton, four miles away, supposedly in the care of an older pupil on the train, but he avoided her. When his mother issued the standard warning about not talking to strange men, his father remarked that it was the strange men who should be warned against trying to talk to Reese.

His parents had originally met as 'First Gentleman' and 'First Lady' at a whist drive. Thus Reese was brought up in a card-playing household. His parents taught him auction bridge at the age of seven one summer on holiday at Lulworth Cove, in Dorset, but he had to dismount from his chair and retire behind a cushion to sort his cards out, thirteen at a time being too much of a handful. From then on they played *en famille*, his mother and himself, the keen ones, on one side against his father and brother who played 'with weary condescension', as Reese put it.

He was a useful games player at Bradfield College and got his colours for both cricket and football. From there he won the top classical scholarship to New College, Oxford. His mother had started to run a bridge club at her hotel, Merrow Grange, near Guildford, where he learnt contract bridge. She became a leading light of Surrey bridge and a popular tournament director. Reese later commemorated her with the Anne Reese Cup.

At Oxford University there was little organised bridge, so with another player in his college, Charles McLaren, he formed the University team. In his last year, 1935, he played a challenge match against Cambridge University led by Iain Macleod, the future politician. This was the first inter-varsity match and *Bridge Magazine* offered to sponsor it. It was played over 100 boards at the Albany Club in Savile Row. The match began in a tense atmosphere as there was a gallery of experts watching including A. E. Manning-Foster, editor of *Bridge Magazine*, and Colonel Walter Buller. Colonel Buller (as Reese later commented, 'no publicity agent could have invented a better name') was the proponent of 'British Bridge' and the best-known figure in the game in England at the time, writing trenchant, blustery articles in the *Star*, the London evening paper. The Oxford team won the match, having a stronger second pair than Cambridge who, as Reese put it, 'played with aristocratic languor but no great skill'. Both *Bridge Magazine* and *British Bridge World* carried reports of the contest, yet managed to muddle up the teams, and misspell the colleges.

Reese got a double first in classics and when he came down from Oxford he worked for ten months at Harrods as a 'university trainee', but cards increasingly lured him away from his traineeship and soon dominated his life. When the bridge writer and player Hubert Phillips asked him to write for *British Bridge World*, of which he was editor, Reese accepted. Before long he had sketched out the plan for his first book, *The Elements of Contract*, nominally in collaboration with Phillips. He wrote most of it during a fortnight at Lynmouth, in North Devon, where his father had now moved to run a restaurant and hotel business. His job with *British Bridge World* paid only two pounds a week, and to supplement his income he played bridge most evenings at Lederer's Club, in Upper Berkeley Street. This was followed by lengthy discussions with other players at the all-night Lyons Corner House at Marble Arch. Bridge hands were scribbled on paper napkins and fiercely discussed. Another diversion was greyhound racing and he would spend many evenings at White City. He had always been very keen on this sport. Even in Oxford days he used to slip away twice a week to the Reading track, sometimes sharing in a book by supplying capital to a bookmaker who had a pitch – profitable in summer, hard work in winter.

It was at this time that he came across S. J. Simon, the bridge player and author of *Why You Lose at Bridge.* Simon's attitude to money was even more cavalier. A late riser, he would descend from his flat off Baker Street in the early afternoon and take a taxi to the afternoon greyhound meeting at Stamford Bridge. There he would meet up with other bridge-playing aficionados such as Pedro Juan and Reese. When Simon's bets went down, as they usually did, he would grab hold of an acquaintance, hold out his grubby paw and say 'Give dollar'. With this he would hail another cab and return to his workplace at Lederer's Club, where his credit was still good. Lederer's Club had moved to new premises in the Bayswater Road and was re-named the Tyburn. 'They used to hang criminals on this site,' Reese once remarked after losing an eight-hundred-point penalty. 'Pity they ever stopped.'

Reese kept up his busy writing schedule with regular articles for *British Bridge World.* His articles on play were much appreciated and were advanced for their time. He also set competitions. Once, replying to a questionnaire, a reader described them as a lottery, while another, one Basset Scott, said that they 'helped those with brains to use them, and those without to realise the omission', a remark Reese treasured. The war came and Reese still managed to play bridge as he was employed for a time by his fellow bridge player, Pedro Juan, at a factory making black-out curtains. Once playing at Crockford's a loud bang was heard from the direction of Whitehall. A moment or two later, an officer rushed into the card room. 'My God! They've got the War Office!' 'Not intentionally!' drawled Reese as he dealt the next hand. After the war Reese became more widely known as an author, bridge player and broadcaster – his was the voice of bridge on the radio presenting *Bridge on the Air* on Radio 3, a programme which lasted for twelve years.

His best-known book, *Reese on Play*, was published in 1948 and did more than any other book to establish his reputation. It came about in a curious way. His older brother was then a master at Wellington and had written two history books for the educational publishers Edward Arnold, whose head was interested in bridge and invited Reese to submit an outline for a book. Reese sent him his chapter on squeeze play and *Reese on Play* was commissioned as a result. Seven years later

Reese suggested to the same firm that his *Observer* articles might be put into book form to be called *Observations on Bridge* but this was turned down. The editor said his public were expecting something new from him. *The Expert Game* was the result – with its fond dedication to his mother 'who taught me bridge – and many other things I learned less well'. In all he wrote, or collaborated in, eighty-three books and was the *Observer* bridge correspondent for over fifty years. As a reviewer he was known for his caustic wit and astringent comments. One review of a book entitled *Twelve Lessons on Bridge* ran to no more than: 'The author should hasten to take them.' His influence on modern thinking on bridge has been as important as anyone's.

The post-war years marked his most successful time as a player. He began his famous partnership with Boris Schapiro in 1944. They hit it off immediately. He found that playing with someone as intense as Schapiro was good for his game. Reese had a more intellectual, analytic cast of mind but their views on bidding were similar. At the card table, Reese was more like an academician, studious and diligent, reminding people of the classical scholar he had been. He was always strong on logical analysis. His single-minded concentration at the table was famous and all his energies were bent to the task in hand. There's a story that Schapiro and other players once put up the money to pay for a prostitute to sit naked opposite him at the bridge table in Schapiro's flat in Eaton Square while Reese was playing a hand. Reese didn't even notice. He was apt to chew his tie when confronted with a difficult hand and, at times, to slide down in his chair until he appeared to be reposing on the small of his back. Aside from chewing his tie, he had an insatiable passion for salt which he would cast over his food lavishly – he nearly always had boiled eggs for lunch. Drinking didn't agree with him and one glass of sherry would make him tipsy. Cricket and golf were other passions. When a test match was in progress, it would take a very important, or lucrative, card engagement to lure him away from his television. He played other games just as effectively: chess and poker, and in his later years backgammon, which almost replaced bridge for him as a pastime.

As an organiser of tournaments he was both efficient and sagacious, with an easy manner at the microphone, giving the impression that he was the supreme master of his medium, but he didn't suffer fools gladly. His speeches were always eagerly awaited but, when moved, his voice tended to soar suddenly into a sort of falsetto. Reese never took his achievements too seriously. There was an Olympian calm to him. Tall and slim, with a thin face dominated by a sharp-cut nose, his manner was marked by a superciliousness that could be humorous or mordant. Victor Mollo gives this vignette of him at the bridge table at the Eccentric Club. Having tabled his hand as dummy, 'He still looks pained, of course, and winces occasionally, but he spares me the scathing remarks which run through his mind. He simply won't understand that being, unlike himself, a poor card holder, I can't afford to bid as soundly as he does.' And Mollo ends, 'Terence admits that he is lazy. What would happen if he were not? It's an awesome thought.'

Bridge, for him, was a challenge that called for maximum powers of attention. The lonely boy had found his *métier* and he was sticking to it. Yet it was not all single-mindedness. He married happily later in life and was always a genial companion, as I can remember when I went to talk to him about Culbertson. He met his wife Alwyn, some thirty years younger than himself, at the *Guardian* Tournament at the Europa Hotel early in 1969. He discovered that she lived in Blackpool and that they had friends in common there. He mentioned he was coming up for the Open Golf at Lytham that July, and would be staying nearby with the Robinsons, well known in Lancashire bridge. She said she would call him at their home. She did, and later in the year moved down to London where they were married the following January. Reese takes up the story: 'At this time Alwyn was engaged in opening a new branch of her firm in Manchester. On the day before the impending nuptials the head of the firm, an admirer, spend hours trying to dissuade her from the venture. Finally she weakened and rang me at the Eccentric Club in London, where I was playing rubber bridge. Perhaps it was all a mistake, was I absolutely sure, etc. According to her story, I replied, "Not now, dearest, I am in the middle of a hand." Whereupon she replaced the receiver and said, "That settles it. I am going to marry that man."' It was a happy marriage, Reese's comment being: 'I have been lucky beyond all expectation or desert.'

Reese's Little Major system caused quite a controversy when it first appeared, as we have seen in the Buenos Aires incident. Here is his description of it: 'Towards the end of 1962, Boris and I played in the first of the popular Canary Island tournaments. In the aeroplane going over, the Little Major was born. It had seemed to me for some while that if one approached the whole subject of bidding without preconceptions there was no reason why, to indicate a spade suit, a player should bid one spade, or, to indicate a heart suit, one heart. It must, in general, save a round of bidding if you start with a lower call to indicate your real suit. In the Little Major an opening bid of one club signifies a heart suit, an opening one diamond either a spade suit or a strong no trump. Our first idea for one heart and one spade was to use these bids in a purely obstructive sense – on one, two or three cards in a limited hand. That is how the system gained its name. We soon found, however, that it was impossible to dispense with these bids in a constructive role. The system underwent many changes, but the general picture at the end of two years was as follows:

One club	In principle, a heart suit. To this, one diamond is a negative response but may also be the first move on a big hand. (This duality, by the way, can easily be attached to any of the modern one club systems.)
One diamond	Either a spade suit or a 16-19 no trump. One heart is a negative response but may also be the first move on a big hand.
One heart	Either a strong hand, usually 20 points upwards, or a controlled psychic on balanced hands in the 3 to 6 range.
One spade	Limited opening with length in both minors.
One no trump	Normal no trump type, 13 to 15 throughout.
Two clubs/two diamonds	Limited opening, 12 to 15 with a fair minor suit, no four-card major.
Two hearts/two spades	Fairly strong major-minor two-suiter.
Two no trumps	Equal to a weak three bid in a minor or a strong minor two-suiter.

Reese acknowledged that for slam bidding the Little Major was not so well equipped but it was very strong in the game and part-score area and 'created many problems for the opponents'. The Little Major licence was withdrawn after two years, on the grounds that not enough players were playing the system to justify its renewal. Reese abandoned it then.

Reese grew increasingly deaf in his later years and died, aged eighty-two, in 1996. With Schapiro he won in all four European championships and the 1955 World Pairs Championship, and in Britain seven Masters Pairs and the Gold Cup eight times. Schapiro remembers him for his extraordinary powers of analysis. 'He played from learning, study and method. He never made a mistake.'

Schapiro's own introduction to bridge was in the unlikely setting of the Doncaster Conservative Club while he was still an undergraduate studying engineering at Sheffield University. After the Russian Revolution he had come to Britain from his native Lithuania where he was born in 1909. His family supplied horses to draw carriages and omnibuses in many of the capitals of Europe. From early on in his bridge life Schapiro acquired the reputation of being 'irrepressible'. As Guy Ramsey wrote: 'The central core of his personality is aggressive self-confidence. The compact body is held with a certain arrogance of posture; the regular features are embellished with a small, almost foppish moustache; the short pipe round which his lips clamp so truculently alternates with a long cigarette-holder. The prominent eyes are balanced by a slightly undershot jaw which gives pugnacity to his whole expression.'

His mischievous side was often in evidence, as well as a liking to shock, all part of his ebullient, impulsive personality. He had a reputation as a *coureur de femmes* with a favourite catch-phrase: 'What about a spot of adultery?', mostly said in jest but likely to alarm an elderly lady who cut against him for the first time. A story in this connection tells of the time when Schapiro was a member of a team taken by Reese to Leicester to play an exhibition match in honour of Mollie Cole, a doyenne of Midland bridge. On the Sunday morning, Mrs Cole, who was also the wife of the Chief Constable of Leicester, threw a cocktail party for the Londoners to meet local notables. The visitors' book was produced, and the Londoners all wrote down their names, addresses, date and a comment. When it came to Schapiro's turn, he was, for once, at a loss. 'Too early to think. Give me something to say,' he demanded. But none of his team was feeling bright enough to think up anything for him. So Schapiro fell back on his familair catch-phrase, which he scrawled on the page. Ramsey describes the *dénouement*: 'The silence as it was glimpsed by the assembled Leicester big-wigs was like the icy breath of the Humboldt Current. It was Dimmie Fleming who saved the situation. As she wrote her own name in the space below, she put an arrow pointing to Boris's extravagance and subjoined: "But will he ever be adult?" ' Nevertheless Schapiro was always appreciated for his geniality and bonhomie, and forgiven quickly for his excesses. As a bridge player he has had a remarkable record, not just with Reese. He was always an instinctive player, able to do the right thing at the right time without needing to know why.

Skid Simon

—♠♥♦—
♣

One of the most entertaining characters on the bridge scene in the 1930s and 1940s was 'Skid' Simon. He also wrote one of the best books on bridge, *Why You Lose at Bridge*, published in 1945. He was born Simon Skidelsky in 1904 in Manchuria, but arrived in England with his parents after the Russian Revolution. In appearance he was short, unkempt, with saturnine features, pulpy flesh and a shock of black hair above a loose, sensual mouth. Yet women loved him. He lived in a flat in Baker Street in a state of unmistakable squalor. Empty food containers lay scattered around and porridge and claret were his staple diet. He was often unshaven, his hands stained with nicotine. He wore goggling glasses. He smoked seventy cigarettes a day, ash liberally sprinkled on his jacket. He had a potbelly. Yet his attraction to others was undeniable. After dinner in Crockford's Club he could be seen, a balloon glass of brandy in one hand and a cigar in the other. He would approach women and say, 'Give light, darling.' He never really lost his Russian accent. Nor a Slavic indolence – he would take a taxi from Piccadilly Circus tube to Crockford's, a mere quarter of a mile away, and all of it downhill. His thick, unmistakable Russian accent was characterised by the omission of the definite article, a habit retained from the Russian, and by the absence of pronouns. A typical sentence would run: 'Bid impeccable spade; butt-in, two H; partner, Free Cluck (three clubs). Pass. Self, what? Self, Free Die (three diamonds).' It needed some interpreting.

Yet he was indisputably a fine writer, one of the best on bridge, with a column in *Punch*, the *Observer* and the *Evening News*. He also had several humorous novels, often with a bridge theme, to his credit, many in collaboration with the ballet expert Caryl Brahms. The titles included *Bullet in the Ballet* and *No Bed for Bacon*. Unkind friends thought he took this novelist side of himself too seriously and would mock him by calling him 'The Famous Author'. Yet he had a brilliantly incisive and creative mind. For a hobby, he liked dog racing and would wear his 'lucky' red shirt over a bright blue one whenever he went to White City, regardless of the weather.

At the card table he was a stickler for ethics. Any underhand dealings, or sharp practice, would elicit a prompt rebuke. 'Can't do that, laddie.' If his partner delayed unduly while bidding, Skid would reprimand him, 'Expect me to bid after a trance like that?' and give him a swift brush-off, 'Palooka'. Worse still, if an opponent veered towards malpractice, Skid would let him know his feelings in no uncertain manner: 'Thank you very much, Mr So and So,' the 'Mr' being drawn out with deliberate slowness as in a gangster movie.

Guy Ramsey, a friend and fellow bridge player, remembers watching him lose his cool: teacup in hand, his recent cigarette hissing in the saucer, tea spilling on to the carpet, he stood in a petulant rage because the waiter had brought milk instead of lemon. At other times, during the play of hand, if a king was found to be on the wrong side of a finesse, Skid would blurt out: 'Someone's going to be murdered.' For many bystanders and players alike the threat seemed real.

He played regularly at the Acol Club, in Acol Road in Hampstead, and contributed to the formation of the system so named after the street and club. After a night's session there he would slowly walk around the nearby streets with his partner J. C. H. Marx, arguing and discussing the evening's play. He was a nightbird in any case, rarely going to bed until the small hours. The Acol system was indeed born out of these talks and late-night walks.

He was an international bridge player. He played for Great Britain in the 1939 European championships, his partner usually being Maurice Harrison-Gray, the pair resembling Don Quixote and Sancho Panza. He was imaginative and tactical as a player, his cunning often leading opponents astray. Iain Macleod, the politician and co-founder of the Acol system, termed his bidding 'feline'. He was like a cat, insidious but determined.

He married Carmel Withers, very English, tall, always carefully groomed in tweeds and pearls, and diffident in manner. She had a passion for solving crossword puzzles, and could solve them quicker than most, especially the difficult ones by Torquemada or Ximenes. They were a close couple and lived in Bickenhall Mansions off Baker Street. But many of his habits were incurable and he neglected his health, rising at lunchtime, and breakfasting either at 3 p.m. or 3 a.m.

He died in 1948, aged forty-four, and his wife died a year after him in 1949, never having fully recovered from her loss.

Terence Reese recalls his death :

> One evening about a year later I took part in a television programme on the European Championship. Skid, who was one of the participants, was much bothered by the studio lights, which generated an uncomfortable heat. The next morning I had a phone call from Gray's wife, Stella, with the very sad news that Skid had died during the night. Stella was speaking from Skid's flat in Bickenhall Mansions and his wife, Carmel, came to the phone. I asked if there was anything I could do to help on the professional side – for example, by ringing Skid's agent or letting them know at the *Observer*, where Skid had a column. The *Observer* asked me to write a piece about him for the following Sunday. In this I described the television date: 'He had a new tie for the occasion, buttercup yellow. "Thought was Technicolor," he said.' I commented on his distinctive style – the omission of the personal pronoun, the disregard for syntax – and ended: 'His humour always touched the human comedy, but never with malice. For example: At a pre-war congress a lady who held an ace and was on lead against seven no trumps neither doubled nor led the ace. The contract was made and the story of the double omission quickly went the rounds. It was Skid who pointed out that she must be acquitted on at least one count. If she was not going to lead the ace, he said, she was quite right not to double.'

Skid Simon's book *Why You Lose at Bridge*, published by Nicholson and Watson in 1945, begins with a Portrait and an Introduction.

PORTRAIT

You are the ordinary club player.

You have a fair amount of playing ability, which you imagine is greater than it is. A smattering of all the more popular systems. And a pet system of your own (probably a variation of the 'Two Club') which you play whenever you manage to cut one of your favourite partners.

Your bidding is adequate and your defence quite shocking.

You have no ambition to become a master player, but you like winning.

You do not keep accounts and tell everybody that you think you are about all square on the year.

You lie – and you know it.

INTRODUCTION

Why You Lose at Bridge

There are two primary reasons:

(a) Lack of technical skill.
(b) Losing tactics.

It is not the object of this book to do much about the first. It is probably too late to do much about it anyway. You've been playing bridge far too long now to start learning how to play your dummies better. You've been making the same mistakes quite happily for years and you've every intention of going on making them. You don't want to know how to make a contract on a 'double squeeze, dummy reversal, throw-in'. You don't believe there is such an animal.

And quite right, too. I sympathise. Bridge is a game and you play it for pleasure.

You can well afford to leave such highly technical plays to the expert, the would-be aspirant to the first post-war Bridge Championship. Let him enjoy himself with them, together with his despairing psychics, his ever-weakening three bids, and all the advanced arguments for interminable refinements in carefully complicated systems that made competitive bridge such a nightmare before the war, and caused Master Players to lie awake nights regretting that they had not played the seven of spades and won the match instead of the five and lost it.

I know. I've done it.

Simon's conclusion to *Why You Lose at Bridge* was: 'Try and play your own type of game better, that is all. If a "one Club" system suits you – stick to it. It will still be a filthy system, but if you like it, you will get your best results with it. For it is better to play a bad system well than a good system badly.'

Simon was a co-founder of the Acol System in pre-war days. Here in 1938 he describes its essence :

ATTITUDE OF MIND BY S J SIMON

The Acol System has often been described as an attitude of mind. It is never easy to explain an attitude, but I feel that I must have a stab at explaining this one.

The Acol attitude comes half-way between two schools of thought. The first and most popular school, whom I call the scientists, believe that bidding is essentially a duet between partners, an exact science subject to immutable laws, and that the more one learns of those laws the more accurate will bidding become. The second school believes in no conventions and common sense, the more you have got the more you bid, and, when hard-pressed in argument, that all these feature showing conventions are nothing but cheating anyway and, in the words of Mr James Agate, there is no difference between them and looking at your wrist watch to tell partner you hold all four aces. What Mr Agate of course ignores is that bidding, say, a conventional Four No-Trumps uses up a tempo, while looking at your wrist watch does not.

The Acol attitude has realised that bidding is not an exact science but a scientific estimation of mathematical probabilities. It has also realised that the probabilities to be estimated include the probable actions of opponents, who regrettably happen to be present, and that the entire language for estimating is limited to 35 bids (One Club to Seven No-Trumps), and that that is not nearly enough to paint a complete picture of the hand most of the time or even part of the time. It has therefore realised that there is a limit to the accuracy any system can reach and that no system can hope to be completely accurate all the time.

Accordingly it has thrown that particular ambition into the gutter, where the scientists can scramble for it and set itself out to evolve a loose flexible style of bidding which, though not as accurate as some systems on certain types of hands, will in the long run achieve better results over all types of hands both by the aid of its own bidding machinery and opponents' mistakes.

OPPONENTS' MISTAKES!

These words form an essential element of the Acol attitude.

As I have so often pointed out and will no doubt be pointing out again, there are two objectives in bridge. The first is to make the best of your cards, the second to prevent the enemy making the best of theirs. The first is clearly the more important, that is why a certain amount of scientifically planned bidding machinery is necessary to a system. But to ignore the second entirely, as the scientists do, is to ignore the major element of bridge. The competitive element.

The Acol attitude believes that this theory of probabilities should be borne in mind throughout the whole gamut of bidding, and that even at low levels there are situations where it will pay on balance to withhold information from partner and risk missing the best contract, rather than tell partner something which may be of no value to him and risk opponents profiting from it.

This has nothing to do with system or system bids. It is entirely an attitude of mind which believes that in the long run a perpetual bit of extra puzzle to the enemy is more profitable than a bulk of mainly useless information to partner.

You will find the system has been built to fit the attitude. A system with a few set pivotal bids, a minimum of forced responses, and the maximum of room for manoeuvring as the logic of the situation dictates. A system concentrated on the bidding of everyday hands in a manner to combine a sufficient accuracy with the best chance of harassing opponents. A system rich in light opening bids and even richer in sign offs, always ready to start one jump ahead of opponents, and equipped with masses of brakes for back pedalling if the jump gets too dangerous. A system resigned to occasional bad results, because it is aiming at the best results on balance and will not squander any of its machinery on the occasional big hands when it can more profitably be applied to the bidding of the much more frequent every day hands.

In short a system for bridge players and not for parrots.

Skid Simon's last bridge book was *Design for Bidding* in 1949. His inimitable style was still to the fore in the Introduction:

There is a distinct tendency in modern bidding to treat opponents as an afterthought.

Except for such established gambits as pre-emptive bids and third hand psychics, the entire attention is focused on the passing of accurate information to partner. Rigid bidding routines with every response bristling with inferences are being built up to present partner with a perfect picture of the hand.

About the only admission that opponents still exist and may be ill-mannered enough to interfere with the presentation lies in a contingent variation of the responses.

Give a partner a perfect picture of the hand. That is the main object. Anything else comes a bad second.

Bidding is not an exact science. It is an estimation of probabilities. There are not two players but four. They are not a quartette working harmoniously together to achieve a double dummy result but two opposing pairs concentrating on getting the best of each other. To attempt to reduce this contest to a portrait of twenty-six cards may be a fascinating exercise but it is not an advance in the art of bidding.

It is merely bad bridge.

Here is a summary of the Acol System by another of its co-founders, Iain Macleod, from his book *Bridge is an Easy Game* (1952).

SUMMARY OF THE ACOL SYSTEM

GENERAL

The Acol System has two main objectives:

1. To make bidding easy for your partner.
2. To make bidding difficult for your opponent.

It is based on Approach Forcing, but with several system bids peculiar to itself. It believes in light opening bids, light informatory doubles and in natural bidding whenever possible. It treats all big hands as separate problems and – if necessary – improvises a bidding sequence to interpret them. The Milton

Work count (ace = 4, king = 3, queen = 2, jack = 1) is used. In no trumps a ten may be counted as ½ point.

OPENING BIDS OF ONE OF A SUIT

If there is a probable game even if partner cannot reply to a bid of one, then you must open with a stronger bid. The lower limit, except for freak holdings, is covered by these general requirements.

1. Always bid with fourteen points.
2. Always bid with thirteen points unless your shape is 4-3-3-3 and you are vulnerable. A pass here is optional.
3. Always bid on twelve points with a fair five-card suit.
4. Always bid on eleven, and usually on ten, if you have one six-card or two five-card suits.

Below ten points only freak holdings qualify. *When in doubt – bid.*

NO TRUMP BIDDING

Open:	1NT Non-vulnerable 13-15
	1NT vulnerable 16-18
	2NT at all scores 20-22
	3NT at all scores ? (7-8 playing tricks).
	4NT at all scores ? (Conventional demand for Aces).
Raise:	1NT Non-vulnerable to 2NT 10½
	1NT Non-vulnerable to 3NT 12
	1NT Vulnerable to 2NT 7½
	1NT Vulnerable to 3NT 9
	2NT to 3 NT 4-5.
Rebid:	Opener rebids non-vulnerable 2NT to 3NT on 14.
	Opener rebid vulnerable 2NT to 3NT on 17.
Slam Zone:	The small Slam zone is around 34. Grand Slam 38.

RESPONDING TO A BID OF ONE OF A SUIT

Range for a one no trump response is 5½-9½. If one opening bid was one club the response shows 8-9½. One-over-one response normally not more than 16 and may be as low as 5 or less. Two no trump response 11-12½, and three no trump 13-15.

NO-TRUMP REBIDS

Rebid to two no trumps after one-over-one suit response or response of one no trump shows 17-18½.

Rebid to three no trumps after one-over-one suit response of one no trump shows 19.

If the response to your opening bid is at the two level these point counts can be shaded by about 1½ points.

TRIAL BIDS

Once the suit is agreed all other suit bids are forcing for one round.

TWO CLUB OPENING

Game forcing except for the sequence: 2♣ – 2♦ – 2NT which shows 22½-24. Partner raises on three points.

Two Club shows five high-card tricks. Negative response is Two Diamonds unless partner holds:

An ace and a king, or
king-queen and two kings, or
Two king-queens, or
Four kings, or
One king-queen and one king if either heads a six or a strong five-card suit.

With no biddable suit, but one of these holdings, respond two no trumps.

JUMP REBID

A jump rebid whenever a forcing situation exists shows a solid suit.

ACOL TWO BID

The bid of two of a suit (except clubs) is forcing for one round. The negative response is two no trumps. The opening bid shows eight playing tricks and the responses are at partner's discretion. As a rule you should make the same response at the appropriate level that you would have made to a bid of one (i.e. if you would have bid one spade over one heart, then bid two spades over two hearts). The response of three no trumps is a slam try, and the double raise shows a good hand, but without first round controls.

FOUR/FIVE NO TRUMP CONVENTION

Acol uses this convention in preference to Blackwood. It is *not*, however, used automatically on every slam hand, many of which are bid by direct methods or by cue-bidding.

Conventional bid of four no trumps shows: three aces or two aces and the king of a bid suit.

Conventional bid of five no trumps (preceded by four no trumps, shows: four aces between two hands.)

Conventional bid of five no trumps (not preceded by four no trumps shows: three aces and the king of a bid suit.)

RESPONSES TO CONVENTIONAL FOUR NO TRUMPS

Five no trump response shows: two aces or one ace and *all* the kings of suits bid.

If not holding one of these requirements, responder may either:

(a) Sign off in lowest suit bid, or
(b) Cue bid an ace or a void, or
(c) Encourage by bidding suit (not the sign off suit) at the five level, or
(d) Bid a direct slam.

Superstitions at the Card Table

—— ♠♥♦ ——
♣

Superstitions are very much part of card playing. In ancient days, it was considered unlucky to meet a woman on the way to a card game in case she was potentially a witch. Playing with a cross-eyed man was best avoided in case he had the evil eye. Cutting the cards crosswise was considered unlucky as this might 'cut the luck'. The origin of the word 'hunch' dates from olden times when a hunchback was viewed as lucky, a superstition going back to the grotesque dwarf god Bes of Ancient Egypt, whose amulet is still worn in the Mediterranean as protection against the evil eye. In Monte Carlo, a hunchback used to stand outside the casino and would sell the privilege of touching his hump to incoming gamblers.

Cards got their reputation as the 'devil's picture books' from their connection with fortune-telling and divination – not good for normal ecclesiastical business. Fishing-boat captains will often not allow cards on board and, if anything goes wrong, they are immediately thrown overboard. Miners consider them unlucky in the pit and will take care to remove any pack from their pockets before going down. Thieves will never steal cards for fear of incurring misfortune or detection.

To drop a card during the game can signify inviting a fall in one's fortunes. If bad luck persists, many players ask for a change of seats or call for a new pack, believing these changes will bring a change of luck. Others attempt to defeat bad luck by standing up and circling their chairs from left to right, this being the way of the sun, thereby attracting the sun's blessing upon the enterprise as per the ancient rite – it's also aimed to isolate the bad luck by encircling it. Others will simply twist their chair while not moving from it. Sometimes a sufferer from bad luck will place a handkerchief upon his seat and then sit upon it, thus providing himself with a new basis of operations, and therefore a fresh start.

Superstitious players have been known to place a badger's foot in their right-hand jacket pocket. Some have tried to cancel their opponents' luck by surreptitiously placing a used matchstick in the ashtray and then equally unobtrusively placing another crosswise upon it, thus crossing out their luck. People have been known not to want to play against the grain of a wooden table, and some believe that a black ace falling to the floor during a game is a sign to stop playing. As regards choice of seats, some players refuse to play with their backs against the wall, or near a mirror. Having cut the highest card for seats, most players stay where they are. If the cut card was an ace, this becomes more of an imperative because of the saying: 'You must never insult an ace.' Having lost a rubber, many prefer to change seats. Others are obsessed by the run of the table or the rub of the green as it's called. Again, after the cut, most players stick with the cards they have cut with. Some prefer to 'consult the oracle' by drawing one more card from the deck. If it's a red card, they choose red, or black, if black. Similarly with seats: after a winning rubber, most winning pairs prefer to keep the same seats and same cards. After a losing rubber, they'll try to change both. Some cards are considered unlucky – the ace of spades, the queen of spades (the death card), the jack of diamonds, the ten of clubs, and nine of diamonds (see below). A misdeal is often counted unlucky. On the score pad some players won't put their names on the top of the ledger for fear of 'jinxing' themselves. Many variations exist as to where winning totals are written in on the score pad. Some players are very particular about shuffling the cards in a certain way, or positioning the pack before and after the cut, or using a certain pencil for scoring and for no other purpose. Rixi Markus and Giorgio Belladonna both believed their pens had magical qualities and would keep moving them in synchronisation with the ebb and flow of their fortunes. But this moves us into idiosyncratic territory, particularly in the choice of garments worn, for which there are any number of superstitions.

Beginner's luck is recognised by all. It is an ancient superstition based upon our primeval ancestor's superstitious awe of the magic properties of new things, in this case the new player.

LEGEND OF NINE OF DIAMONDS

The nine of diamonds has always been known as the 'Curse of Scotland'. Various theories for the use of this term have been put forward. One was that 'Butcher' Cumberland wrote the orders for the bloody Battle of Culloden in 1746, in which the Highland chieftains were defeated, on the back of a nine of diamonds card. Another is that the order for the Massacre of Glencoe in 1692, when the Campbells slaughtered the Macdonalds, was signed on the back of this card, and a third is that it derived from the nine lozenges that formed the arms of the Earl of Stair, who was especially loathed by the Scots for his connection with the Massacre of Glencoe. None of these explanations, however, is authoritative.

History of Cards

I am sorry I have not learned to play at cards. It is very useful in life: it generates kindness and consolidates society.

Dr Johnson, *Tour to the Hebrides* (11 Nov. 1773)

The history of playing cards is also shrouded in mystery and folklore. One legend has it that they were invented by terminally bored queens and concubines of the imperial Chinese harem of early medieval times. It is believed that the inventive ladies fashioned their pastime from some fertility rite, calculated to call down fruitful blessings on the royal couch or to foretell the outcome of the night watch. Indian myth tells that playing cards were invented by an equally bored and irritable wife of an Indian maharajah, whose endless days of idleness were made more unpalatable by her husband's habit of pulling at his beard. It is claimed she hit upon the idea of playing cards, something that would both alleviate her boredom and keep the maharajah's hands occupied.

According to a Chinese encyclopaedia of 1678, playing cards were invented in China in the reign of Emperor S'eun-Ho, around AD 1120. They probably had four suits – coins, strings of coins, myriad strings of coins and flowers. The game was called 'Chinese money'.

Some writers say playing cards were invented at an earlier date. Professor T. F. Carter discovered in 1925 a reference to an augury being drawn from cards in AD 969–979, also in China, with the pack divided into four suits, fourteen cards in each, which was used for paper money as well as for games, and also, it is believed, for divination. The existence of tarot cards bears testament to the degree with which cards and divination, and indeed diabolic influence, were intertwined in times gone by.

Long before bridge was heard of, playing cards were used in many forms of gambling and in fortune-telling, acquiring an unsavoury reputation of being associated with all sorts of vices, worldly or otherwise. In 1432 St Bernardo of Siena preached the first sermon against them, attributing their invention to the Devil, an attitude later taken up by the English Puritans. The Devil's Picture Book and other names indicate the horror with which they were regarded by the virtuous and religious.

'There is a legend telling how the sailors with Columbus,' writes Catherine Perry Hargrave in her book *A History of Playing Cards*, 'who were inveterate gamblers, threw their cards overboard in superstitious terror upon encountering storms in these vast and mysterious seas. Later, on dry land they regretted their rashness and, in the new country, made other cards out of the leaves of the copys tree, which greatly interested the Indians.' This seems to be more than a legend, for Garcilaso de la Vega (*Historia de la Florida*, Madrid, 1723) tells that the soldiers of Spain played with leather cards in the 1534 expedition. Cards were known to the early Mexicans as *amapatolli*, from *amatl* meaning paper and *patolli* meaning game.

Those who claim cards came to Europe from China believe it was due to the Venetian trader Niccolo Polo, or even his famous son, Marco. Marco Polo returned to Venice from the court of Kublai Khan in 1295 and, according to some accounts, brought with him playing cards from the East. Other writers say that cards were brought by gypsies from India returning to Europe with Alexander the Great via Persia and Arabia into Egypt (hence their name), or by the Saracen invaders of Sicily or the Moors who lived for centuries in Spain. Early European cards used to bear symbols of a wand, a cup, a sword, and a ring (symbolising money), similar to those of a Hindu goddess.

The gypsy link ties in with another theory of the origins of European cards – that they came from Egypt, or the Mameluke empire to be precise. The Mameluke suits were goblets, gold coins, swords and polo sticks, suit-marks believed to be ancestors of those eventually adopted in the European suits. Polo being then unknown in Europe, these were transformed into batons or staves, which together with swords, cups and coins, are still the traditional suit-marks of Italian and Spanish cards. The four suits of the cards represented the cornerstones of medieval society, the knights (swords), the churchmen (cups), the citizens (coins) and the countrymen (batons).

Cards began to be manufactured in Europe in the fourteenth century, notably in Nuremberg, Augsburg, and Ulm in Germany. Italian tarot cards may have predated the German cards as they are mentioned in an

Italian manuscript dated 1299. One theory has it that the present emblems of the four suits (clubs, diamonds, hearts and spades) arrived via tarot itself, which had rods (wands), shekles (or pentacles), cups and swords respectively. Johanna, Duchess of Brabant, mentions cards in the Netherlands in 1379, and cards were known in Spain at least as early as 1371. The Moors or Saracens may have brought cards to Spain and Italy, but the attempt to show a resemblance between the Spanish word for cards (*naipes*) and the Arabic word for a prophet (*nab*) is not well founded.

Fifteenth-century German card makers experimented with suits based vaguely on Italian ones, also representative of the four tiers of medieval society. They eventually settled for acorns, leaves, hearts and bells (hawk-bells), which remain in use today.

The French card manufacturers had different ideas which are more familiar to modern bridge players. Around 1480 the French started producing playing cards by means of stencils, and simplified the German shapes into four: *piques* which were the tips of the knights' lances (they looked like spades to the soldiers who brought them from France to England); *coeurs* which alluded to the church; *carreaux* were arrowheads of bowmen; and *tréfles* were the trefoils or clover of agriculture. Spades may reflect the earlier use of Spanish suit-marks, from the Spanish word *espada* meaning sword, and clubs are what the Spanish suit of staves actually look like. Diamond is not only the shape of the arrowhead, but may perpetuate connotations of wealth from the older suit of coins. Eventually these shapes were adopted by English card makers, though some of the concepts altered, as did the names as translated into the Anglo-Saxon tongue.

During the fifteenth century, cards seem to have caught the imagination of the ruling and rising classes of Europe – perhaps as a new kind of war game in which women could do battle on equal terms with their menfolk. Prints have survived of more than one duke playing cards with his duchess and there is other evidence. New technology met the new demand, and large numbers of packs were manufactured in many European cities by the new process of wood engraving and coloured stencils. Cards thus became cheaper and plentiful.

Cards probably reached England later than the other European countries. Chaucer, who died in 1400, never mentions cards, although he enumerates the amusements of the day: 'They dance and they play at chess and tables.' The earliest clear-cut reference to playing cards in

England dates from 1463 when manufacturers of playing cards petitioned Edward IV for protection against foreign imports, and were favoured by an appropriate edict. Kings Henry VII and Henry VIII played cards, and the costumes on today's English and American court cards are those of this period. Henry VIII, with his curling moustache and divided beard, is reputed to be the model for the four kings in the pack. In 1495 Henry VII issued an edict forbidding his servants and apprentices from playing cards except during the Christmas holidays – among his private expenses at the time are several entries for loss of cards. During Elizabeth I's reign a tax was levied on the making of playing cards. She granted a monopoly in card making to Ralph Bowles and then, in return for royal protection from imported cards, promptly demanded a 'recompense' of three shillings per gross, or a farthing a pack. This generated a healthy income for the Crown.

In the reign of Queen Anne card playing seems to have attained the full tide of its popularity in every part of civilised Europe. In England it had become both fashionable and popular. The game of ombre was favoured by ladies, while the gentlemen preferred piquet. Clergymen and country squires played whist, and the labouring classes played all fours, cribbage, etc. Tax on cards went up to three pence a pack during Anne's reign to finance a potential war against Spain. It was doubled to sixpence in 1711, continuing upwards to three shillings a pack in 1801.

The ace of spades in the pack was officially stamped to indicate that the tax had been paid. In 1765 the ace became the obligatory 'duty card' when a new method was introduced. The Stamp Office would keep a stock of pre-stamped aces of spades, and card-makers were instructed to print their decks short of that one crucial card. When the tax for the packs was paid, the Office issued the ace of spades to complete the pack, and the deck could then be sold. The tax was abolished in 1960, when duty was back down to three pence per pack. Yet today, most packs still display the ornate ace of spades of the manufacturer's design.

The present pack of fifty-two cards, arranged in two black and two red suits, probably derived from the early Italian tarot packs, in which there were four suits with ten sport cards and four court cards – king, queen, cavalier and knave. The knave has been variously represented by a valet, and still carries this name, although modern usage changes it to the jack. The joker, a character also found in tarot, was introduced into the deck of regular playing cards from America, which was used for the game of euchre there. Originally, the joker was just a blank extra card in a pack, but later it was seen as an opportunity for a little humorous expression.

Another commentator has written of the packs of fifty-two cards that, 'The twelve honours of the pack are emblematic of the twelve signs of the zodiac, also the twelve months of the solar year, and each of these is divided into thirty degrees, as the honour cards are equivalent to ten in value, and if we multiply thirty by twelve we get 360, the number of days in the ancient Egyptian year, and equal to the number of degrees into which the equator is still divided. The colours red and black answer to the great division of the year into two equal parts, from solstice to solstice and equinox to equinox. The four suits indicate the four seasons. The whole number of cards in the pack is fifty-two, equal to the number of weeks in the year, and the number of cards in each suit is thirteen, the same number as the weeks in each quarter of the year.'

Kem Cards

♠♥♦
♣

Cards were originally pasteboards, made out of two thin sheets of paper pasted together with a black paste. Two sheets had to be used since a single sheet of heavier paper would become transparent if the player had a lamp behind him. The black paste helped to make the cards opaque. In the late 1870s, double-headed cards were first introduced, that is, cards which could be read from either end and with indices at both corners making it possible to recognise the card without needing to see its entire face. Until then a player had had to hold the card the right way up and would usually only know what the card was by looking at the full face of it.

With the spread of contract bridge in the early 1930s, greater numbers of playing cards were needed. Traditional pasteboards quickly got dirty and their edges became frayed and had to be trimmed down. They seldom lasted long enough and soon had to be thrown away. Manufacturers didn't mind this as it meant more business. A major change came about with the introduction of plastic cards later in the 1930s, and this unexpected development also enabled Culbertson to make more money out of this than from his books.

The story starts one morning late in 1933 when Culbertson was in his apartment at the Sherry-Netherland Hotel, New York. Two foreign-looking gentlemen, both strangers to him, were let in by the maid. The first to introduce himself was Siegfried Klausner who was brandishing a pack of playing cards in his hands. With him was his assistant Robert Caro.

'At last, Herr Culbertson, we manage to talk to you. We've been trying to see you for two months.'

'Why didn't you go and see my merchandising man?'

'We've seen him already.'

'Did he turn you down?'

'Yes. Only you, Mr Culbertson, have the imagination for this.'

Such an opening gambit was bound to appeal to Culbertson and he listened to Klausner's story intently. Klausner was a Viennese who, a few years before, had invented a new process for manufacturing playing cards out of plastic acetate. The pack he was carrying in his hand was an example of this. Normally, acetate cellulose is transparent but Klausner had devised a means of making it opaque, which was essential for playing cards, and being plastic gave them better durability. Klausner, himself a chemist and keen bridge player, had limited resources. After patenting his invention in Austria and selling shares in it to various individuals and companies, Piatnik, the Austrian firm of card manufacturers, deliberately bought him out so as to kill off the product. Luckily, or shrewdly, he had retained the American rights, which was why he was in New York.

Hearing this, Culbertson first thought he might do a deal along similar lines with the US Playing-Card Company with whom he had good contacts. They held a ninety per cent monopoly of the manufacture of playing cards in the USA, and might well have been prepared to put forward a sizeable sum to buy out this new invention and kill it stone dead, as Piatnik had done in Austria. But as Klausner went on talking something else stirred in Culbertson's mind. He sympathised with him as a European struggling to make his way in America, remembering his own early years and efforts to get established. Culbertson could foresee distinct commercial possibilities. He studied the samples Klausner showed him. The printing on them was coarse and the backs looked ordinary and poorly designed, but when he picked them up and shuffled them he noted their fine snap and the smoothly textured sheen on the face-side. They promised to be long-lasting and good to use. Not only did they need no trimming but they could be washed as well, making them virtually germ-proof, unlike their paper counterparts. Of course, they would be more expensive than existing cards. But Culbertson's view was that, in America, you could sell anything for any price so long as it was good. Sold for three dollars, as opposed to twenty cents for a paper deck, they would need to last twenty times longer. Klausner assured him they would.

The more Culbertson looked at them, the more he could visualise the cards in a streamlined version to suit the American market. Despite the early hour and the unwelcome intrusion, he told Klausner he would do business with him. Their initial agreement was for Klausner and Caro to have a seventy-five per cent holding and Culbertson twenty-five per cent. That afternoon Ely got in touch with a personal friend of his, Jack Dreyfus, President of the Celanese Corporation, to ask him to supply them with acetate cellulose. He explained how Klausner had been to see him, but Dreyfus warned him that it might be difficult to arrange, as his firm had a cartel agreement with a German firm linked to Piatnik. Culbertson kept at him over the next few days and eventually got Dreyfus to agree.

Now that he was taking charge, Culbertson wanted the deal recast. He suggested a corporation be set up with his having the seventy-five per cent holding and Klausner twenty-five per cent. Klausner was in no position to argue and had to agree. Next, Culbertson undertook to locate a printer, not an easy task as printing on opaque cellulose was in those days an undeveloped technique. Eventually he found the Western Playing-Card Company, who agreed to take on the contract.

He never had any doubts about merchandising. He already had his established chain of distribution and outlets via his bridge organisation and bridge teachers in department stores throughout the USA. Culbertson also brought to the enterprise his own unique method of financing. Rather than go through the tiresome business of regular accounts and balance-sheets, he hoped to finance the whole operation out of his personal income. In business matters, Culbertson was an unashamed optimist. Economic forecasting was based on the unshake-able principle that everything would come right in the end. Fortunately his income stood up to it initially. Albert Morehead, his right-hand man, later calculated that for the year 1933 to 1934, the joint income of Ely and Josephine amounted to over $300,000 per annum, made up of (the figures are approximate) $140,000 from royalties on his books (mainly the best-selling Culbertson *Summary*), $85,000 for his movie shorts, $40,000 in other royalties, $22,000 for newspaper and magazine articles, $10,000 for lectures and $10,000 for miscellaneous endorsements.

Richard Frey became Sales Manager for Kem cards in 1935 with a one per cent share in the company (Albert Morehead was already on ten per cent of all the Culbertson enterprises). But hard as they tried to promote Kem cards, the expected breakthrough never came. The American public resisted the idea of paying that much for a single pack of cards. Culbertson was worried as he had staked heavily in Kem cards. Then, like a *deus ex machina*, Theodore W. Herbst suddenly appeared. Herbst was a German by birth who had lived in the USA for some years and in 1931 married Cynthia Kuser, the daughter of a prominent and wealthy senator from New Jersey. They lived in

Barnardsville, New Jersey, and mixed with a rich and affluent social set. It was this as much as any strong business sense that was a direct cause of Herbst's interest in Kem cards. Herbst did not have a job so that when, as often happened, they were invited on friends' yachts and to country-houses, and businessmen there began to discuss their latest acquisitions and dealings, Herbst felt very left out. He resolved to find himself a business. Through Robert Caro whom he knew personally, he heard that Kem cards were going through a difficult stage and sought out an introduction to Culbertson.

Culbertson initially remained cool and impassive. He enquired about Herbst's background and his reasons for wanting to buy Kem cards. Then he decided on a campaign of subtle psychological warfare, a campaign of nerves directed against Herbst and his advisers. For the best part of 1935 there were manoeuvres and counter-manoeuvres, approaches made, a tentative price suggested and then the matter was dropped for weeks, even months. Culbertson based all this on his view that the longer he waited and delayed, the more Herbst would want to buy the company. When, eventually, in January 1936 an offer of $300,000 was made, Culbertson unhesitatingly turned it down. Jo and his business associates were surprised and dismayed. To them it seemed a fair price. Kem cards might eventually be worth more but his present financial state was in such a parlous condition – he had a floating debt of $200,000 – that a sale for $300,000 seemed like a godsend. But Culbertson would not hear of it. He wanted more, much more. Moreover, he sensed that the other side had heard of his financial difficulties and were trying to buy him out cheap – nothing was more likely to offend his pride.

The atmosphere changed from parlour bridge to a game of bar-room poker. If he lost, Culbertson would be several hundred thousand dollars worse off, but if he won, he would make a fortune. He decided to up the ante and told Herbst that the company was worth at least one million dollars, take it or leave it. Weeks and many anxious hours passed in the Culbertson camp before he got a reply. Their best offer, they stated, was $400,000. Culbertson reckoned this was a tactical mistake on their part. The sudden jump of $100,000 revealed their unmistakable intention to buy. Jo, however, by now was getting desperate. She berated him for putting their and the children's welfare at risk. As she saw it, this sum would not only pay their debts but leave them $200,000 in addition. But Culbertson turned a deaf ear to her entreaties.

Two months elapsed and even he became nervy. His creditors were pressing. Then came a final offer of $500,000, cash, for all the rights. 'Gentlemen,' Culbertson told Herbst and his associates, 'you're getting warmer, but you're not hot enough.' The other side were furious. As they rose to go, one of them said, 'Well, Mr Culbertson, I guess that ends the matter,' and threw the proposed agreement on the floor. Culbertson took this as a good sign. 'Did you see the way they threw that agreement on the floor and not at me? It shows they're still interested,' he commented.

Another three months passed. By now it was January 1937. All around him feared the opportunity had been lost for good. But Culbertson still held on. His intuition told him they were still interested. His view all along had been that Herbst was emotionally committed to buying Kem for reasons of social prestige, and would not want to back down now. Money, so far as Herbst was concerned, was not the main issue. In the meantime, Culbertson upped the stakes by putting in a couple of home-made 'forcing bids'. First he let it be known that another company, a phantom buyer, was interested in Kem. Then he made sure the newspapers announced that he and Josephine were due to leave for Europe in the spring of 1937 to play in the World Championships in Budapest.

His strategy had the desired effect. Ten days later an offer of $600,000 came through – again in cash. 'Gentlemen,' he told them, 'you're getting hot, but not hot enough.' Finally, in frustration, they asked him to name his price – something he had been careful to avoid doing all these months. 'My price is $600,000 cash, and . . . ' They waited.

'. . . you'll want to use my name and experience, won't you?'

'Of course. But we won't pay a cent more.'

'That's up to you. But I wouldn't be doing justice to my name and business sense if I took less than five per cent gross on all the money received by you.'

'For one year?'

'No,' Culbertson said blandly. 'For fifteen years.'

They snorted, muttered 'ridiculous' and walked out. This time Culbertson's nerves really were on edge. Jo pleaded ceaselessly, and even Al Morehead was frantic. Culbertson waited tensely at home. The next evening they returned and said they would do business. In the end, the price was lowered by ten per cent in return for the fifteen-year personal royalty on Kem cards. Lawyers on both sides were closeted for twenty-four hours before the final contract was drawn up. Culbertson was taking no chances on a last-minute change of mind. The revenue from Kem cards was to become his main source of income up to the time of his death, and the basis for his personal fortune.

Murder at the Bridge Table

♠♥♦
♣

Marital strife at the bridge table reminds us of the precariousness of human relationships. The starkest case came with the Bennetts in 1929. John and Myrtle Bennett were living in a fashionable Park Manor apartment in Kansas City. They were a well-off couple who had been married for eleven years. John Bennett was thirty-six years old, a highly paid perfume salesman with the Hudnut company, with a yearly salary and commissions earning him more than $35,000 a year – a more than comfortable income in those days. On Sunday morning, 29 September 1929, Bennett went out to play eighteen holes of golf at the exclusive Indian Hills Country Club with his friend and neighbour, Charles Hoffman, who lived in the same apartment building. Afterwards, their appetites whetted, they went back to the Bennetts' apartment for an ice-box lunch. An afternoon bridge foursome was proposed, since they were regular bridge partners. 'As the game went on,' Mrs Hoffman later recalled, 'the Bennetts' criticisms of each other grew more and more caustic.' Then the famous spade hand was dealt. The cards were as follows:

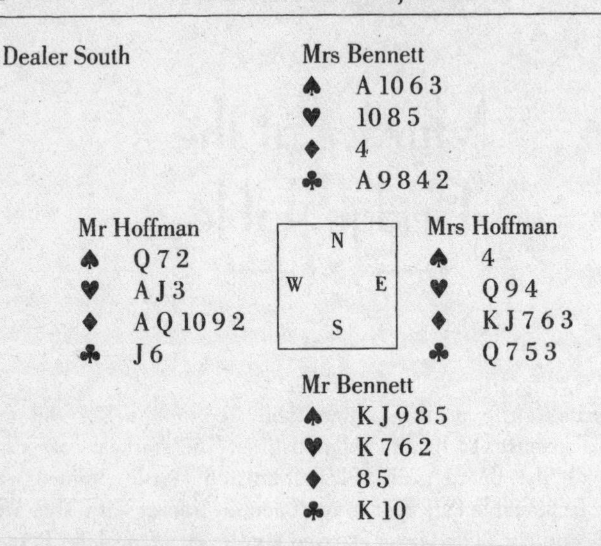

Bennett as dealer opened and bid, rather ambitiously, a spade. Hoffman on his left overcalled with two diamonds. Myrtle Bennett as North, with her good spades and two aces and a singleton, promptly raised to four spades. Mrs Hoffman passed, as did Bennett and Mr Hoffman. Hoffman on lead played his diamond ace, then switched to the jack of clubs once he saw the shortage of diamonds in dummy. Bennett as South won with his king of clubs and set about clearing trumps. He led the jack of spades but when Hoffman on his left failed to cover with his queen, declined to finesse and put up dummy's ace. He then played a second round of spades leading the ten from dummy and when Mrs Hoffman showed out, went up with his king. He then ruffed his losing diamond in dummy and then led the ace of clubs followed by the nine. Mrs Hoffman played the queen over the nine, Bennett ruffed with the five of spades and was overruffed by Hoffman's queen. Hoffman next played the ace of hearts and then led a low heart. Bennett won with his king but found he had cut himself off from dummy's good clubs. He had a further heart to lose and ended up one down.

Mrs Hoffman takes up the story. 'This seemed to infuriate Myrtle Bennett and she began goading her husband with remarks about "bum bridge players". He came right back at her. I don't remember the exact words. This kept up for several minutes. We tried to stop the argument by demanding cards, but by this time the row had become so pronounced that Bennett, reaching across the table, grabbed Myrtle's arm and slapped her several times. We tried to intervene, but it was futile.'

Mrs Hoffman said Mrs Bennett kept up her refrain, repeating over and over again, in a strained sing-song voice, 'Nobody but a bum would hit a woman.' Then her husband suddenly had enough, and jumped up, shouting, 'I'm going to spend the night at a hotel. And tomorrow I'm leaving town.' Mrs Bennett then turned to the Hoffmans and said, 'I think you folks had better go.' The Hoffmans started to leave. As they were putting on their coats in the hall, they saw Mrs Bennett dash into the bedroom where her mother, Mrs Alice Adkins, was resting, and pull the family automatic from a drawer. Her explanation to her mother was that, 'John's going to St Joseph and he wants to be armed.' Meanwhile Bennett had gone to his 'den', near the bathroom, to pack for his intended trip.

Mr Hoffman was still adjusting his muffler in the hall when he saw Bennett alone for a moment. He advanced towards him, hoping to say a word or two to calm things down. The two men were in conversation when Mrs Bennett appeared, automatic in hand. Bennett saw her and immediately ran to the bathroom. He slammed the door hard behind him but two bullets pierced the wooden panelling. Hoffman, rigid with astonishment, stayed where he was in Bennett's den. Mrs Hoffman, hearing the shots and standing by the hallway, ran out of the apartment, and began pounding on the door of the next apartment. Now Bennett left the bathroom and was trying to head for the entrance door himself when he was hit by a further two bullets. He staggered to a chair moaning, 'She's got me.' Then he slumped unconscious to the floor. Mrs Bennett was by now standing on the other side of the living room, the gun dangling loose from her fingers. As Bennett fell, she ran towards him. By the time the police arrived, they found her still there, bent over her husband's body, sobbing uncontrollably.

Mrs Bennett was held on a charge of first-degree murder. She came to trial later on in February 1931. The case attracted widespread publicity. She had contrived to acquire the services of a distinguished and powerful local attorney as her lawyer, whose display of forensic skill, combined with the jury's lack of knowledge of the intricacies of contract bridge, brought about her acquittal. She claimed in court that the pistol had gone off accidentally when she stumbled against a chair. The jury were out for eight hours – some of that time, it was alleged, being taught the rudiments of bridge by jurors who knew the game. After her acquittal, Mrs Bennett even managed to get $30,000 life insurance money for her husband.

But from then on Mrs Bennett had difficulty finding bridge partners. Alexander Woollcott, also from Kansas City, recounted in his book *While Rome Burns* that when she did eventually find one, her new partner, unaware of her past history, made an intemperate bid and as he put down his hand, began to say to her, 'You're probably going to shoot me for this, but . . .' By the time he looked up, she had already fainted.

Ely Culbertson, keen as ever to assert his authority as bridge expert, gave his view on the murder case. In *The Bridge World* he wrote: 'We have heard of lives depending on the play of a card and in this case it was literally true. Mr Bennett had overbid his hand, but so kind were the gods of distribution that he might have saved his life had he played his cards a little better.'

Culbertson explained his view in more detail and proposed a better line of play. After Hoffman's diamond ace, and the shift to the club suit, Bennett should have taken stock when he started to draw trumps. 'Here again he flirted with death, as people so frequently do when they fail to have a plan either in the game of bridge or the game of life,' wrote Culbertson. 'He still could make his contract and save his life. The proper play before drawing the trumps would have been to establish the club suit, after ruffing the last diamond in the closed hand, upon which to discard losers in his own hand. Suppose Mr Bennett, when he took the club trick with his king, had led his last diamond and trumped it with one of dummy's small trumps. He could then lead a trump and go up with the king . . . Now he would lead the club ten, and, when East followed suit, his troubles would be over. He would play the ace of clubs and lead the nine or eight. If West put up the queen, Mr Bennett should trump and let East overtrump if he pleased. If East, after winning this trick, led a heart, the contract and a life would be saved. If he led a diamond the same would be true. A lead of the trump might still have permitted the fatal denouement but at least Mr Bennett would have had the satisfaction of knowing that he had played the cards dealt him by fate to the very best of his ability.'

For all his technical concern, Culbertson, the master of publicity, was really out to promote the soundness of his Culbertson System, above all the need for two and a half honour, or quick, tricks to make an opening bid. This Bennett had failed to do, and, in Culbertson's eyes, he had sealed his own fate. Culbertson concluded: 'Scientific tests and the concrete experience of millions of bridge players have proved that a hand must contain two and a half honor tricks for a sound opening bid. The hand Mr Bennett dealt himself had barely two honor tricks, and, while it is infrequent that the penalty for unsound bidding is as severe as this, all bridge players have learned by sad experience that behind this rule there is both logic and safety.'

Culbertson elsewhere had written once that he was 'all for bridge fights between married couples. It's a fine way to blow off steam and get rid of the millions of little differences and big differences which dam up in both parties and are the real reason for bridge fights.' Maybe he really felt this, or was he once again protecting his system and ensuring that bridge could apply to any situation? An article that appeared in *Harper's Magazine* at the same time took a different line: 'As for domestic discord, bridge never broke up a home that was not ripe for disruption anyway. If your wife is a very much better player than you, or a very much worse player, you had better not play with her.'

Jo Culbertson, always a foil to her husband, argued the question of marital discord with the cartoonist H. T. Webster in an article that appeared in *The Bridge World* in 1930. She saw bridge more as a marital solace. Webster, sometimes tongue in cheek, begged to differ. Webster commenced their discussion by commenting: 'I can't say that the bridge murder cases surprise me, or fill me with regret. After the scenes that I have witnessed between ordinary gentlemen and their wives, over the great American table sport, murder often seems an anti-climax!' Jo then acknowledged that bridge quarrels did crop up, but felt that bridge was an excellent thing for couples. Through bridge, they can learn a fine self-control. 'Perhaps, like Mr Culbertson and myself, they have made a rule never to discuss bidding or plays while the game is on. In other cases, I feel that bridge performs an even more valuable function. It is a lightning rod, a safety valve that releases pressure. It simply brings out the ill feeling that has gathered in the irritations of family life. But it does so in the impersonal atmosphere of a mental game, instead of in the awful emotional privacy of family rooms. It is a real crime reducer and divorce suppressor. Many a quarrel that would have left a disfiguring scar is dispersed by bridge into an impersonal argument and easily forgotten. Why forget the melodramas of family life in general, and exaggerate them so illogically if they happen at the bridge table?'

Webster took the opposite view: 'The result is so disproportionate to the cause. Bridge does not seem to me to release pressure, but to increase antagonism, to increase competitiveness, of which there is always enough in modern marriages. But for this reason bridge is one of the true American comedies. Married people exhibit tantrums at bridge that could never occur at a family dinner table. They are charmingly comic, but these exhibitions, with the neighbors looking on like that and all prepared to gossip later, make it harder and harder for these people to adjust their matrimonial problems. You can get over almost anything that happens when you are all alone. But when all a family's friends have seen them fight, their social and their inner life become more and more involved. And, lady, what makes you think that bridge quarrels are more impersonal than other quarrels? The arguments that are initiated at the bridge table continue far into the night.'

Jo disputed this: 'No sensible person ever takes bridge quarrels seriously. The bridge table is the only place I know where the sexes are absolutely equalized. Nothing counts here but skill. I really think that bridge has done more for feminism than the women's party or all the suffrage movements. It has taught men and women the practical experience of thinking and playing on equal terms, and they like it.'

Webster admitted that as a cartoonist he would see things differently: 'You must excuse me if I think in pictures rather than in generalities. When I think about bridge equality I think about poor old Henpeck, being sat upon twice as hard by his wife. If she is a worse player, she makes him suffer. If she is a better player, she flays him alive. And where is the dominant male more successfully dominant than at a bridge table? Overbidding egotists show their self-esteem twice as much as usual. I really think that as many people play because of the pleasure they get out of a decidedly unhealthful exhibitionism in the matter of family quarrelling as because of any liking for the game.'

Jo wasn't to be outdone: 'If they didn't do it there they'd do it somewhere else. You get a married couple across the bridge table, and you have one set of frayed inferiority complexes competing with another set. But the beautiful part of bridge is that, unlike life, the villain usually gets shown up at once. Your overbidding egotist usually loses, a fine object lesson. The wife who is more intelligent than her man, but at a loss in daily existence because she is not a good fighter, has a chance to get her compensation, to show her excellent mind.'

Webster queried this: 'One would actually think from your conversation that people learn lessons and get better. Does the egotist stop overbidding? The blustering fool bluster less? And what about the women who drop half their allowance at bridge, or the men who lose more than they can afford – and Baby gets no new summer rompers?'

'Bridge is the light wine and beer of gambling,' said Josephine. 'Dice lie idle in the cigar stores and poker chips get dusty since bridge became so popular. Women and men who used to play the races and the stock market now get rid of the gambling urge at bridge. And because, as I have said before, it is a game of skill, it is less vicious than other gambling. And why always think of the morbid cases when so many people play in a self-contained happy way and have a grand time at the game with no bad results?'

♤♡◇
♧

Murder of a different kind but still with a bridge connection took place in 1920 with Joseph Elwell. Joseph Bowne Elwell (1873–1920) was, in his day, the principal American authority on the original game of bridge (bridge-whist) and on the early form of auction bridge. However, he is remembered chiefly as the victim of one of the most celebrated murders of the century.

On the evening of 10 June 1920, Elwell had a quiet dinner with some friends at the Ritz Hotel. The party – Mr and Mrs Walter Lewisohn and Miss Viola Kraus along with Elwell – were celebrating, with appropriately muted enthusiasm, the decree of divorce granted that day to Miss Kraus from one Victor von Schlegell. Mr von Schlegell, as it happened, was also celebrating (by an odd coincidence, at the very next table) in the company of his new fiancée. After dinner both the Elwell group and, by another coincidence, von Schlegell and his lady friend, went to the roof of the New Amsterdam night club to see the *Midnight Frolics*, and again nothing occurred to disturb the festivity of the occasion. At about two in the morning Elwell, having bidden his friends goodnight, took a taxi to his home at 244 West 70th Street. Despite persistent rumours of adventures en route, all the cab driver could remember was that his passenger requested him to stop at a newstand so that he could buy a *Morning Telegraph* – perhaps to see if the Republican Convention in Chicago had settled on a presidential nominee. Elwell arrived home about 2.45 a.m.

Shortly after 8 a.m. on 11 June 1920, Elwell's housekeeper arrived at the house he occupied alone on West 70th Street. She found him barefoot and clad in pyjamas, slouched open-mouthed in a chair, fatally shot. The postman had come at about 7.30 a.m. and an opened letter had fallen from the dying man's hand on to the floor beside him. He had thus received the bullet wound in his forehead apparently not more than an hour earlier. The motive was not robbery because none of the considerable amount of money and jewellery in the house was touched. Several women had keys to the house, as he was separated from his wife. The case received wide publicity, 'Who killed Joseph Elwell?' continued to be asked in the popular press off and on for months, and has since been the subject of several books and countless more articles. Officially the murder was never solved, though it is generally believed that the police knew the murderer but had insufficient evidence. Several novelists used the setting of the case for mystery novels in which they supplied their own solutions. The spurned mistress and cuckolded husband or lover remained favoured candidates, but it was inevitable that someone would suggest, whimsically, that rival bridge writers ought to be investigated. More soberly, it was later conjectured that Elwell had been heavily involved in bootlegging and perhaps failed to pay for several thousand cases of whisky he had purchased from tight-lipped gentlemen in black suits.

The case bore a superficial resemblance to that of the violent death of another legendary gambler, Arnold Rothstein, some time later. But in Elwell's case there was such an embarrassingly rich superfluity of suspects and clues that the police were lost in a wilderness from which they never emerged.

Elwell began his career around the turn of the century as one of the first teachers of bridge, and quickly became a favourite of high society in New York City and Newport, Rhode Island. He was a regular high-stake player at the Whist Club of New York and other clubs, and he and his regular partner, Harold S. Vanderbilt, were considered the strongest American pair from about 1910 to 1920. He was part of a select circle of whist players in America who became leading theoreticians of the auction period. He amassed a considerable fortune, chiefly through speculation in Wall Street, and at the time of his death owned more than twenty race horses. He wrote many books that went through many editions, such as *Elwell on Bridge* (1902), *Advanced Bridge* (1904), *Practical Bridge* (1906), *Bridge Axioms and Laws* (1907), *Auction Bridge* (1910), *Elwell's New Auction Bridge* (1920).

For his astonishing rise to prosperity, he chiefly relied on his skill and luck at other games, most notably baccarat, and the stock market. Despite his fame as a high-flying playboy in later life, his earlier books are among the best of their time and his interest in bridge continued unabated into the period of auction.

Elwell was playing in Mexico when a spectator (they didn't use the word 'kibitzer' in those days) interjected a remark: 'Mr Elwell, you did something just then that's absolutely forbidden in your own book.' 'My book,' said Elwell, 'was written for beginners. I am an expert.'

He was handsome and charming. A chauffeur recounted later that Elwell, riding on the back seat of his car, was able to pick up on the streets of New York virtually any girl he wished merely by opening the door and saying, with extreme conviction, 'Why, I haven't seen you since Palm Beach!'

♤♡♢
♧

Bridge playing incites powerful emotions. In the four cases that follow, the violence happened away from the bridge table itself but each protagonist was a prominent bridge personality.

The first occurred around midnight on Thursday, 19 July 1984, at the Sheraton Washington Hotel, site of the ACBL Summer North American Championships. Interest in bridge quickly disappeared when the word spread like wildfire that bridge player Edith Rosenkranz had just been kidnapped from an underground parking garage when saying goodbye to a young woman friend. The incident left thousands of bridge players at the tournament in dismay, and soon provoked nationwide interest and sympathy.

Edith spent about forty-three hours in captivity, mostly in the van used for the abduction. The Washington police and the FBI searched everywhere for her. Meanwhile, her husband, Dr George Rosenkranz, negotiated with the kidnappers for her return, and paid a ransom reported to be one million dollars.

Edith was finally released unharmed. After the ransom was picked up, the kidnappers drove her into Washington and let her out at the corner of 15th and Constitution. 'When they let me out,' Edith said, 'they told me not to look back. They told me to just wait there for about five minutes and my husband would be along to pick me up.' The kidnappers were apprehended immediately afterwards by FBI agents and Washington police, who had secretly kept the designated drop area under surveillance. The ransom money was recovered.

Edith and her husband George made a tour of the playing rooms on Sunday evening to express their thanks to all the players for their assistance and co-operation during their ordeal. Edith was her usual self, quiet and soft-spoken, and apparently in good health and good spirits. George made a moving speech in each room, and wherever they went the two were greeted with a standing ovation.

Earlier on Sunday, Edith and George were the subjects of a major press interview in the main ballroom of the hotel. They had to face some two dozen television cameras, scores of microphones and innumerable reporters and cameramen. They were escorted to the main table by a posse of police and FBI, and then the questions began. Edith was asked if the kidnappers ever said what would happen to her if they did not get the ransom money. 'They said they'd kill me, or bring me back. One of them said he was going to make sure they brought me back,' she said. George talked with a great deal of emotion when asked how he managed during the ordeal. 'I had faith in God, faith in my wife and absolute faith in the people who were working on the case. I prayed. I prayed for guidance. I convinced myself that there was no sense in losing control. Control in such a situation is the most important thing. I looked at it as just one more crisis in my life.' 'I have no feeling of fear now,' Edith said. 'I have feelings of relief and confidence.' She was asked if the ordeal would change her way of life. 'I hope not,' she replied in a subdued voice.

After a two-week trial that included three days of dramatic testimony by Edith Rosenkranz, the jury deliberated for three hours before finding Glenn Wright, forty-two, and Dennis Moss, twenty-six, both of Houston, guilty on thirteen counts, including kidnapping and conspiracy to kidnap. The jury did not accept the defence arguments that Wright was insane at the time of the abduction. They also rejected Moss's contention that he was coerced into taking part in the kidnapping – Wright, Moss claimed, had threatened to kill him.

Both Wright and Moss took the stand during the trial. Each portrayed the other as deeply involved in the kidnapping and eager for the ransom. Wright gave his testimony despite being told by his attorneys and Judge Gasch that he was not obliged to do so. Under oath, Wright said that he felt he had to kidnap Mrs Rosenkranz because his only other option was suicide. But during cross-examination, he was asked, 'If in July you'd won a million-dollar lottery, you wouldn't have kidnapped Mrs Rosenkranz, would you?' 'Probably not,' Wright replied.

Dr Rosenkranz, the founder of the Syntex Corporation, a pharmaceutical firm, was one of American bridge's most successful players and the author of several bridge books. In what the *ACBL Bulletin* described as a kind of poetic justice, his team still managed to overcome the heightened tension caused by the kidnapping to capture the prestigious Spingold Knockout Teams title in Washington at the same time. George and his regular partner Eddie Wold took no part in the play after Thursday night, but were granted special dispensation and received full credit for the team's victory.

♤♡◇
♧

Florence Osborn, writer, columnist and bridge editor of the *New York Herald Tribune* from 1936 until the newspaper was discontinued in 1966, and of the *New York American*, died of stab wounds in a domestic tragedy in Mount Carmel, Connecticut, on 20 April 1985. Her husband Harold, sixty-nine, was charged with homicide after being released from the intensive care unit of Yale–New Haven Hospital where he was treated for apparently self-inflicted wounds. Later reports said he was transferred to the psychiatric unit of a veteran's hospital where he was being held under guard on a $250,000 bond.

Florence's maiden name was Fitch, and her first husband, Lewis Osborn of New York, was a bridge teacher and writer, author of two books on *How to Play Duplicate* and *Expert Bidding* published in 1932 and 1934. He was tournament director of the Algonquin Club in New York, scene of the famous Round Table where Dorothy Parker and other wits such as George Kaufman gathered. He had also donated the Lewis Osborn Trophy for the Southern New England Pairs Championships and was a contributor to *The Bridge World* magazine.

Lewis Osborn died, and when Florence married Harold Schwartz, a

Second World War veteran, she retained the name of her first husband and Schwartz changed his surname to Osborn. A former *New Haven Register* copy-editor, he was also a professor of mathematics at Quinnipiac College. Mrs Osborn was a lecturer in the humanities and taught liberal arts subjects at New Haven College.

Besides her bridge column and her work as bridge editor for the New York newspapers, she was the author of many magazine articles, published a book and was a contributing editor to the *Official Encyclopedia of Bridge*. She also conducted a bridge interview programme and made many television appearances.

♤♡◇
♧

Kathie Wei and Judi Radin had been a world-class bridge partnership for seventeen years beginning in 1975. Among their achievements was winning the 1978 World Women's Pairs Championship. Having lived together as a couple for some time in an elegant Manhattan apartment, in February 1992 they had an explosive and violent lovers' tiff. Police arrived to find sixty-two-year-old Kathie Wei nursing her wounds and applying first aid to herself in one room and thirty-nine-year-old Judi Radin staunching the flow of blood from a wound in her head with a towel in another. Radin had just hit her partner with a silver Chinese exercise ball.

Judi Radin had always been the stronger player in the partnership. She had been a top-class bridge player ever since her days at Columbia University, New York. Her bridge prowess brought her to the attention of Charles Wei, a wealthy Chinese-born shipping and transportation magnate, with a strong interest in bridge. He was based in New York and had met his future wife Kathie while she was working as a nurse in a New York hospital where he was having treatment. They soon discovered a shared interest in bridge, and Wei, more of a theorist at bridge than a player, was keen to promote his system and needed expert players to do so. Kathie was going to be the first and Judy Radin was brought in as both her coach and partner. The plan was for the three of them to launch themselves on the international game.

Kathie was born in Peking, China, in 1930 but fled the country in 1949 following the Maoist revolution and went to the USA. Her father had spent time in the USA as a young man attending the University of Michigan where he got a doctorate in sociology and agriculture. He went back to China and lectured in sociology at Yenching, one of China's major universities. The university had been founded by an American, was supported by American contributors, and was mostly staffed by American-born faculty members. So Kathie was brought up in an English-speaking home and an American-influenced environment.

Kathie had three sisters. Each of them had both a Chinese name – Hsiao-hue, Hsiao-ven, Hsiao-ving and Hsiao-ching – and a Western name as well – Alice, Katherine, Victoria and Joan. Her mother was a strong, ambitious and capable woman. She was the daughter of a Shanghai merchant and had joined the ranks of the first emancipated women in China in the 1920s. Kathie said of her, 'I have never known a person of stronger will and have never met anyone more skilled at controlling the people around her.'

Kathie married while still in China and had three children by her first husband. After she left China she didn't return to the country until 1981 when she visited her father and mother in Hankow where they were living. She had not seen them for more than thirty years.

Charles Wei was born in Shanghai in 1914. He too had left China after the revolution and had gone to Formosa (Taiwan) where he learnt bridge and developed his Precision Club System. He was the non-playing captain of the Taiwan team in the World Olympiad in 1964. He then moved to New York from where he built up his shipping empire.

A professional agreement was drawn up between the three of them. Radin was promised one-third of all subsequent profits. Wei planned to use his wife's glamour and good looks as part of his campaign to establish her as a bridge personality. But there was a secondary motive as well. Besides promoting his 'Precision' bidding method, he wanted to further his business interests. The trio travelled the world and in 1978 Radin and Kathie won the World Pairs Championships. They also won the North American Pairs Championships. In the world of bridge, they were soon famous and became household names.

Radin was the anchor of the partnership and was considered one of the best woman players of all time. Kathie Wei expanded her interests in bridge to include promoting bridge links with China, the country of her birth. She was also one of the main influences in starting the China Bridge Association, and in founding China's bridge links with the West.

Here again Wei's secondary motive came into play. The China operation was not simply one of bridge promotion, but part of his plan to expand his shipping empire. When Kathie played against Deng Xiao

Ping, the supreme leader, and other members of the upper echelons of government in the People's Great Hall in Beijing, Wei used these bridge occasions to develop his business contacts.

Deng had acquired his passion for bridge as a young man. In 1920 when he was sixteen he was a hard-working student at one of the best secondary schools in the city of Chongqing. The reward was an opportunity to work and study in France. He worked for a time at a Renault factory and at a rubber-footware plant in Montargis, south of Paris. It was during this time that he acquired a lifelong fondness for both croissants and bridge.

Bridge became legal in China in 1979 after a thirty-year ban. The game is now widely played at every level. Xiao Ping was honoured as the *Bridge Personality of the Year* during the World Championships at Port Chester, New York, in October 1981. The IBPA chose Deng because he has 'set an example to the Chinese people who are quickly finding out that bridge playing can lead to international friendship through membership in the World Bridge Federation'. With the support of Xiao Ping, the People's Republic of China became a member of the World Bridge Federation and the Far East Bridge Federation. During Deng's leadership in the 1980s, bridge playing in China went from almost nothing to being the nation with the greatest number of bridge players in the world. China was to host the world championships in 1995.

Elsewhere in the world, the same arrangement was made. The trio went to Israel, and once again Radin, was promised the same profit from the shipping business. It was an unwritten deal and few in international bridge knew of this dual role of one of the world's top women's partnership.

The more they played bridge together, the closer the two women became. They moved from being partners to close friends and then lovers. Their affair started. Judy Radin had been married to Mike Radin, also a bridge player. Charles Wei died, Radin divorced her husband and then moved into Kathie Wei's elegant apartment on East 64th Street in Manhattan. Their bridge success and the relationship continued. At tournaments they always shared the same hotel room. For Radin, the relationship had become official. Both women had gone to lawyers and signed 'a living contract'. Radin received specific fees and bonuses for the bridge relationship. She was also promised a quarter of Kathie's multi-million-dollar estate in her will.

Then in 1990 the personal relationship began to sour. Radin claimed that Wei was jealous. 'Anybody I was friendly with or went out with, she believed I was sleeping with. She was obsessed with jealousy and was afraid of losing me. I was not allowed to bring any friends into the house. One of my friends called the apartment "The Forbidden City".'

Yet their business partnership still prospered, that is until the events of 20 February 1992. Radin's lawyer Helwell described what happened. 'Wei basically "cold cocked" Radin on the morning of 20 February with one of those silver balls. Radin simply defended herself.' In the court documents, Kathie claimed she was walking out of the bathroom when Radin began haranguing her about money. 'Radin brutally battered and beat me with the silver balls, which are used to increase hand strength. I was pounded to the floor and left bruised and bleeding.' Kathie said she eventually staggered to her room and fell unconscious.

Curiously, after their fracas Radin tried to play down her relationship with Kathie. She said, in a dismissive way, 'It was a casual thing, a joke. She initiated sex to control me, to keep me as a bridge partner.' Wei, in her court documents, also tried to play it down and claimed she couldn't remember having sex with Radin. Radin contested this, 'You don't have a long-time love affair with someone with amnesia.' She added, 'Mrs Wei is not a very sexual person. The attraction and turn-on wasn't sex, it was bridge. There was sex, but nothing serious.'

The court documents also included 'Exhibit 1' – a Valentine Day card with a photograph of a woman with short-cropped black hair reclining nude on a bed. Wei had submitted this, alleging that Radin 'supplied herself with a home guest of dubious character'.

In the end, the court judgement upheld the contract and Judi was awarded a substantial financial settlement. There is still a great deal of animosity between them – they don't speak to each other (they hiss) and Radin is aggressively derisory whenever Wei is within hearing distance.

Barry Crane

♠♥♦
♣

Barry Crane, the man widely considered to be the greatest matchpoint player of all time, was found dead by his housekeeper on the afternoon of Friday, 5 July 1985, in the underground garage of his home at Studio City, California. He had been bludgeoned to death. His naked body was found wrapped in a sheet. Bloodstains showed that the body had been dragged from his third-floor bedroom down to the garage. In the bedroom, signs of a struggle were evident and an *objet d'art* stained with blood lay on the floor. This could have been the murder weapon. Crane's wallet was missing, but the house otherwise had not been ransacked, nor were there signs of forcible entry.

On the day he was murdered, Crane had played in the Bridge Week Regional Tournament held in Pasadena. After the game, he dropped some of his fellow players off at a restaurant and went on alone. He was driving a rented car as he had lent his own car, a Cadillac, to a friend. After that, no information about his whereabouts ever came to light. Searching for a motive or a lead, the police went to the tournament the next day, impounded all the entries and questioned numerous players and officials, but nothing emerged.

Crane was by far the most prolific winner the game has yet produced. Flying to tournaments all over the country, sleeping on planes, playing with many different partners, he picked up points at almost every tournament he attended, and amassed the staggering overall total of 35,084 American Contract Bridge League master points, fully 11,000 points ahead of second place. He overtook Oswald Jacoby as the all-time leader in October 1968 and improved his position every year. He was prolific, almost promiscuous, in his search for bridge points and achievements. It is this promiscuity which may have underlain his eventual undoing.

Born Barry Cohen, on 11 November 1927, he came from a well-off Detroit family. His father, a staunch Republican, owned a theatre building which showed early silent movies. His was also a card-playing family. Crane went to the University of Michigan and he married young – to please his father, so it was said. But this marriage, and a second later one, ended in divorce, with a daughter and a son from them. Crane changed his name from Cohen in the early 1950s once he had moved to Hollywood. He trained at the Pasadena Playhouse as a tyro director. One evening, playing bridge with a film producer, Frank King, they were about to play a slam contract doubled, when the club's lights went out. As the club steward made repairs, the players engaged in small talk. 'How would you like to go to Spain?' King asked him. 'Make this contract,' King then said, 'and then come to my office in the morning.' The next day, Barry appeared at the producer's office and soon found himself on location in Madrid, his film career on its way.

In time he became a very successful television producer and director. His credits include *Hawaii Five-O*, *The Six Million Dollar Man*, *The Bionic Woman*, *Police Story*, *Mannix*, *Born Free*, *Harry O*, *Hung Fu*, *Dallas*, *The Incredible Hulk*, *Mission Impossible*, *The Magician*, *Trapper John MD*, *The Streets of San Francisco*, *Jessie*, *Wonder Woman* and *Joe Forrester*. He would play bridge on the film set with actors and producers in the intervals between takes. As a director he was known for his boldness, his organisational skills, his memory, his speed and efficiency, and his practical approach to problems. It was the same story at the bridge table too. At the bridge table he had certain mannerisms. He always opened his cigarette packs from the bottom and kept his scorecard and score slips in an especially neat and tidy way. There was always a half cup of coffee in his hand. His dress sense was flamboyant and he could usually be seen with a scarf round his neck and his half glasses tipped on the end of his nose. He had a distinctive way of pronouncing 'No Bid'.

But Crane also was a mystery, and secretive. He was one of the least visible of the top players and was practically unknown to the general bridge-playing public outside the tournament world. Though he mellowed in later years, he could be impatient, vitriolic even with any who showed signs of struggling with the subtleties of the system he preferred to play. His regular partner was Kerri Shuman. She once said that playing with him was like being on a merry-go-round. 'Like a high. But I know how to handle him when he gets mad. I realised that it was temporary and I just tell him off sometimes. "Oh now, Barry, stop being like that."'

Crane wasn't sociable. He declined to mingle with the crowd.

Whereas most players would go out after a session to a restaurant and eat together, Barry would be as likely to take himself off to a movie or go to his hotel room to read a best-selling novel. Conscious of his weight, he was choosy about what he ate. He was known as a loner, which may explain the unknown identity of his eventual assailant. Crane was not always liked. In the highly competitive world of tournament bridge, Crane was certainly envied for his success, and many disliked, or misread, what they saw as his aloof, insensitive and supercilious manner. They resented his achievements. Some disliked the ruthlessness of his play, which they viewed as designed to kill off weaker players. Moreover, he was an amateur among pros, and wealthy enough from his TV shows to pay his own way, another source of grievance. Some of the enmity was realistic. Crane's competitive drive put people's backs up. There were reported incidents of gamesmanship and other self-serving tactics during the 1984 Top 500 race, and Crane himself once spoke of himself thus: 'I can be malicious, petty and vindictive – but I'm a good friend.' Not for nothing was he known in the bridge world as 'The Whiz'.

Charles MacCracken, a former tournament director, remembers encountering Crane and his partner of the day, with Barry in the middle of a stern lecture about one of the few hands that had proved costly that day. The last thing he heard was, 'We could have had 900 today if you'd only . . .' On another occasion, Barry was holding forth with considerable animation about his partner's errors during the session, 'If you and I are going to play bridge, we are going to play my way, because when we play my way we win.'

Partners' reactions to playing with Crane were always interesting. Mike Passell said, 'I play with Barry once a year just to remind myself of how much I hate playing with him.' Jeff Meckstroth went one better. After playing with Crane in a two-session regional event just because he thought he should play at least once with 'Mr McKinney', Meckstroth tore their convention card into ribbons and threw the pieces at Crane, making it very clear that he would never play with him again. Crane's partnership rules were expressed in such quips as: 'No safety plays', 'Only Jesus saves', 'Never play me for the perfect hand', 'The queen lies over the jack in the minors, under the jack in the majors'. If his partner broke a rule and was right, Crane would say nothing, but if his partner broke a rule and was wrong, he would scream 'like a wounded eagle', as one of Crane's partners put it. 'Barry loved to scream. I think that was partly a personality malfunction, and partly because Barry loved to show he was the boss.'

In the year Crane died, 1985, he stayed completely out of sight for the first couple of months. Nobody knew where he was or what he was doing. Finally he started to play. He was in good form, winning constantly, even though he was not playing with his best partners. Apparently, he had taken time off to be alone and regroup. Crane's team had reached the final stage of the tournament on the day he disappeared. Kerri Shuman, his long-time partner, then played as his substitute, and his team went on to capture the event. When news of his team's victory was announced to the tournament on Saturday, the room, which had sunk into a listless silence on the Friday night, burst into applause. To this day, the murder has not been solved, although the view is taken more and more that it was a gay killing.

Train Bridge

—♠♥♦—
♣

Bridge has always been played on trains. In the early 1930s when contract first came in, Culbertson saw it as a useful launching pad for his System. Four passengers sitting down to play bridge would ask each other 'Do you play Culbertson?' and the game would be on. Since then commuter bridge has been popular everywhere, especially in the USA and especially on the Eastern seaboard. A crisis occurs when a rubber is still in progress and the station has been reached. The New York–New Haven–Hartford Railroad was a case in point. In 1930s hearings before the Connecticut Public Utilities Commission, Roscoe T. Noyes of the New Haven Railroad company testified that train No. 367 New York–Old Greenwich was often late because train bridge players refused to get off promptly on the homeward trip. The Commissioner H. B. Strong told Noyes, 'If you would continue once and leave them on, that would do it.' Noyes, a wiser man, answered loud and clear, in a voice ringing with shock: 'I don't think we could do that, Mr Strong.'

The Boston and Maine Railroad once went so far as to run a special train from Boston to Montreal and back, entirely for the playing of train bridge, an occurrence which prompted H. I. Phillips to draw up his own train schedule in the *New York Sun*:

a. Stops to take on kibitzers.
ss. Will not run on Washington's, Lincoln's or Lenz's birthday.
b. Extra fare train. Carries supply of good fourths at bridge.
c. Has buffet, oversized ashtrays and ample supply of pencils.
d. Engineer of this train makes good fourth, and becomes available after passing through tunnel.
e. Stops at Merriwell Junction to empty ashtrays, throw out dead cigars and drop passengers who have trumped partners' aces.
zz. Will not run on Aug 10, Sidney 7th, Ely 11th or Oswald 25th.

The New Jersey Central in former days fixed up special cars for bridge. The cars had built-in bridge tables, air-conditioning and a freezer for beer, cokes and other refreshments. Originally books of contract bridge were supplied, but they were found to be inapplicable to the game, and were soon discarded.

The Blackwood Convention

—♠♥♦—
♣

Easley Blackwood was so fearful of his name becoming known for his invention of his Blackwood Convention that he asked for the name of Ernest Wormwood to be used instead. The reason for this was that he was in insurance and held a senior post as the manager of the Metropolitan Life Insurance office in Indianapolis. He felt that if his bosses knew that he was seriously involved in a risky game such as bridge, his career might be in jeopardy. When he devised his system in 1933 he had to keep quiet about it.

Blackwood had thought up the basics of his convention while playing in an Indiana bridge tournament in 1933. There was a muddled hand when both he and his partner each thought the other had the ace of spades. They had eventually bid up to seven spades, gone down and lost the tournament. It was a turning point for Blackwood. His system – probably the most used convention in bridge – was born out of that occasion. Yet when he first attempted to test the system shortly afterwards in a tournament in 1933, he and his partner were barred from play.

Easley Blackwood was born in Birmingham, Alabama, in 1903. Blackwood's interest in bridge began at the age of eleven when he played auction with members of his family. His interest increased with the birth of contract, but his activities in the business world – he had joined the Metropolitan Life Insurance Company soon after school – limited his attendance at regional bridge tournaments.

Once known about, his system caught on by word of mouth. Blackwood felt he ought to 'patent' it. He sent a letter early in 1935 describing it to *The Bridge World*. His letter stated, 'Should you see fit to accept the enclosed manuscript, please use the *nom de plume* of Ernest Wormwood and do not reveal the name of the writer.' He went on, 'Since I first suggested this bidding, it has been adopted by a number of Indianapolis players – Rollie Buck, Larry Welch, Joe Cain, Edson Wood and others. At the recent tournament in Cincinnati they were using this bid and explaining it to their opponents. Mr Buck informed me that Johnny Rau of New York asked for a detailed explanation of the convention and became extremely enthusiastic about it, going so far as to state, "This convention will sweep the country within six months." . . . Possibly an article in the *The Bridge World* crediting this convention to Ernest Wormwood would forestall the use of this convention in the book of some other writer . . . Please consider this letter of a confidential nature and do not reveal to anyone either the contents of this letter or its author.' He included the outlines of the convention as we now know it.

The Bridge World replied as follows.

THE BRIDGE WORLD
Incorporated

Mr E. R. Blackwood May 24, 1935
Room 1411
11 South Meridian Street
Indianapolis, Ind.

Dear Mr Blackwood:

We read your article with interest and enjoyment, but we fear we cannot use it in *The Bridge World*.

While the suggestion is a good one, the four-no-trump bid will remain informative rather than an interrogative bid, and our subscribers are too prone to accept anything printed in *The Bridge World* as a recommended change in the Culbertson system, unless it is specifically part of another known system.

We hope that you will at some time submit another manuscript to us, for judging by the merit of this one, we are sure that we can make use of it.

Yours sincerely,
THE BRIDGE WORLD
[signed]
Albert H Morehead,
Editor

For the next three years Culbertson rejected the Blackwood Slam Convention, nor was it written up elsewhere in books or magazines on bridge. But gradually, by word of mouth again, players across the nation started using Blackwood. A short paragraph by George Beynon in an article on 'Bush League Bridge' in *The Bridge World* in August 1938 stated: 'In rubber bridge, Indiana plays "wide open" with an abandon that is a joy to watch. But it tightens up in duplicate. The Hoosier state is the home of Blackwood, author of the Blackwood Convention for the showing of aces after a four no trump asking bid, and kings after a five no trump bid by either partner. The convention enjoys considerable popularity – except [sic] in Indiana – proving that a prophet is not without honor save in his own country.'

In the 1938 printing of *The Gold Book*, Culbertson admitted the Blackwood Convention had 'a number of sturdy adherents', and then in September 1938, *The Bridge World* published a fuller account of it. When Culbertson visited Indianapolis in 1939 he presented Easley Blackwood with a copy of his recent autobiography and inscribed it, 'To my friend, Easley Blackwood whom I'm trying hard to digest in my system, Ely Culbertson.' He told Blackwood at that time that he had made some $100,000 out of his book on the Culbertson Four/Five No Trump Convention. Blackwood's system never directly brought him in any money, though obviously he came to include it in the books he later wrote, such as *Blackwood on Bridge*. In 1949 Culbertson gave up and said that when a pair announced it was playing the Culbertson System, it should be assumed that the Blackwood Convention was being played. By 1950 most books on bidding had a section on the Blackwood Convention, and recommended its use.

As Blackwood said in his book *Bridge Humanics: How to Play People as Well as the Cards* (1949), the story of his slam convention was essentially the story of the politician who was overwhelmingly elected to a public office despite the bitter and violent opposition of all 'experts' of press, radio and the political parties. 'Everybody was against me,' he said, 'but the people.' Richard Frey, his contemporary, wrote: 'Of course, there is no such thing as patenting a bid and collecting a royalty on it, but if Blackwood had a nickel for every time his bid was properly used he'd be a rich man indeed; if he had a nickel for every time it was misused, he'd be a multi-millionaire . . .'

Politics

♠♥♦
♣

Culbertson was fascinated by the link between cards and politics. He wrote: 'I have always been fascinated by the bizarre world of cards. It was a world of pure power politics where rewards and punishments were meted out immediately. A deck of cards was built like the purest of hierarchies with every card master to those below and a lackey to those above it. And there were "masses" – long suits – which always asserted themselves in the end, triumphing over the kings and aces. In bridge every play was in itself a problem of force and timing.' (*Total Peace*, 1943)

In fact, his first introduction to cards came through politics when he was a young man, a student in Russia. Like many middle-class youths he had joined in revolutionary politics and had been involved in the first Russian revolution. He was caught by the police and imprisoned in 1907, along with other, older extremists. His imprisonment was a dramatic moment: 'Four men are seated around a makeshift card table. They are playing vint, a Russian card game derived from whist. One of them, the dealer, is to be executed next morning. Each player concentrates with rapt attention – not because of the high stakes but out of a sense of dedication to the task in hand.' Culbertson was then a mere sixteen, awaiting a possible death sentence for revolutionary activities.

As he listened to his fellow prisoners discussing the future of Russia, not with any sense of recrimination about their own misfortune but trying to plan ahead in a relentless spirit of enquiry, he was strangely elated, dimly aware that he was witnessing something vitally important to him, the first coming together of the powerful combination of cards and politics that was to shape much of his life. Dawn approached and the game was still in progress. The thud of hobnailed boots was heard in the corridor and their cell door was thrown open by one of the guards and a name called out. The oldest of the group, Ureniev, aged forty, got up to leave and as he reached the door, beckoned to Ely and said, 'Goodbye, Illiusha. There is no sense in these revolutions. Concentrate on vint.'

Culbertson made his name and fortune out of bridge and then changed tack in the second half of his life and returned to his first love, politics. At first people were reluctant to take his political views seriously – they had grown used to him as the flamboyant showman of bridge. He felt his own qualifications were impeccable. As he put it, he had studied at six great universities, attended the little red school house of three forlorn revolutions, had read deep and widely in philosophy, history and economics, and also stood in bread lines, picked fruit, planted corn, panhandled, and gambled scientifically for a living. For him the connection between bridge and politics, each regulated by 'force and timing', was manifest.

By the late 1930s, he had developed his own peace plan – an international umbrella organisation, the World Federation, as he called it, its powers restricted to one aim: to prohibit and prevent war. To this end each nation would be required to give up its 'sovereign' right of waging war and would be guaranteed to be defended against aggression. The world would be broken up into eleven Regional Federations, decided on a geo-political basis. A World Peace Force would keep the peace according to a Quota Force Principle, each Regional Federation supplying a proportional National Contingent.

Culbertson's plan had undeniable merits. It did attempt to tackle, on a worldwide scale, the issue of the preservation of peace. Its emphasis on active shared responsibility between all participating nations was an attempt to avoid the kind of creeping nationalistic aggression that, Culbertson argued, was to lead to the outbreak of the Second World War. Its emphasis on Regional Federations – the idea had come to him from the Swiss model – seemed its strongest point. The faults of his plan were typical of the man. It tended to be rigid and autocratic, structured so that if you tampered with the parts, the whole would cease to function.

To get his scheme off the ground he looked around for associates. The one he came closest to inveigling on his side was Bertrand Russell, who, early in 1940, had been offered the post of Professor of Philosophy at the College of the City of New York, but his appointment had been quickly blocked by Mayor La Guardia and the local Catholic hierarchy who viewed Russell as an atheist and unfit to teach the citizens of New York. The Jesuit weekly *America* referred to him as a 'desiccated, divorced and decadent advocate of sexual promiscuity'. A lawsuit was brought by a Brooklyn taxpayer, Mrs Jean Kay, calling Russell's appointment a 'Chair of Indecency'. This was where Culbertson came in. He sent Russell a letter offering to pay his salary himself. It was the beginning of a long friendship. Russell describes their first meeting in his autobiography:

> I found Culbertson in a flat in New York overflowing with secretaries and clacking typewriters. He worked all day and half the night and was obviously endangering his health by overwork. For visitors he provided exquisite food and drink, but he himself could not touch alcohol and his diet was Spartan. He had a divorced wife who lived in the flat immediately above his, and popped in and out of his flat in the friendliest manner. He regarded bridge solely as a means of procuring money to be spent on the crusade. He is one of that very small company of men who, having decided in youth to make a fortune and then do good work, not only succeed in making the fortune, but when they have made it still retain the public spirit of their youth. Such men are as admirable as they are rare.

Russell and Culbertson had certain traits in common. Both had a dogmatic side and stuck to their ideas irrespective of public opinion. Both were womanisers. But Culbertson exhibited for Russell something that he too must have shared – the child in the man. 'It is the child in Culbertson which has caused me to feel for him a warm affection,' Russell later wrote in 1950. 'The survival of the child in the adult is one of the characteristics of really remarkable men, and is perhaps the chief cause of the affectionate devotion they inspire. Something of the child exists in every man who has strong impersonal passions which dominate his life, for such passions outweigh the instinct of self-preservation, and lead to heroic actions from which a sensible adult would shrink.' In the same article, Russell described Culbertson as 'the most remarkable, or at any rate the most psychologically interesting, man it has been my good fortune to know'.

Russell's mention of the child in Culbertson and the strong impersonal passions which dominated his life give us a clue to his bridge playing. There is the strong play element in bridge as in many games: the childlike rapture of being presented with goodies, the fresh deal of cards with its eternally renewed promise of bounty (aces, kings and queens), the burgeoning relationship with partner cultivated as some sort of mother substitute who will supply necessary needs. Then there is the ruthless side, a strong component of any child's existence, the child who is determined to get what he wants, the child who pushes all opposition out of the way, who bids and makes his game ruthlessly excluding all others. Bridge permits this single-mindedness, this out-manoeuvring of opposition, of opponents or siblings. The laws of the game, with their restraint and elegance, keep this savagery on track.

Culbertson kept up his political interests through the post-war years and right up to his death in 1955. As we shall see, the link between bridge and politics has always been strong.

Hilaire Belloc's lines echo this:

> The accursed power which stands on Privilege
> (And goes with Women, and Champagne, and Bridge)
> Broke – and Democracy resumed her reign;
> (Which goes with Bridge, and Women and Champagne)

The Tory politician Iain Macleod was a passionate bridge player of international standard and played a crucial role in bridge history by helping to formulate the Acol System in 1939. Iain Macleod learnt to play bridge at the age of nine in the early 1920s. He came from a card-playing Scottish family. His father Dr Macleod introduced contract bridge at home soon after it arrived in England and was something of a gambler himself, a poker player and breeder of horses. Macleod went to school at Fettes, just outside Edinburgh. There Macleod was at his happiest indulging in pastimes that engaged his quick wits and good memory. He organised a bridge 'school' in his study, even taking some of the time allocated for his prep to play the game and then quickly completing his school work in half the remaining time. Macleod invariably showed a profit, having relieved fellow members of his house of any loose change that remained from their weekly shilling allowance. After Fettes he went on to Cambridge University.

At Cambridge, Macleod used his phenomenal memory, always the hallmark of a good card player, to study racing form. Newmarket was nearby. In later life Macleod kept up this passion for racing and, while editing the *Spectator* in the mid-1960s, would always insert tips for the Derby in his editorial, and go regularly to Sandown on Saturday afternoons. Racing in its way connected him with politics. Both dealt with possibilities and probabilities, the art of the possible, as Balfour called politics. Odds featured in Macleod's everyday conversation, as if he was always assessing the chances of a political option, or of a play at cards.

Bridge played a major role in Macleod's university life at Cambridge; indeed, it dominated his life throughout the 1930s. The first inter-varsity match against Oxford was his brainchild. In his final year, he was playing cards one evening with a second-year student at Magdalene, Colin Harding, and when they finished Macleod stayed on and, as they chatted, suggested challenging Oxford at bridge. Macleod nominated himself as captain and Harding as honorary secretary. Harding wrote to *Isis*, the Oxford magazine, issuing the challenge. Macleod made sure it had maximum publicity. 'A contract bridge league has been formed in Cambridge,' *The Times* announced in its bridge column on 17 November 1934, 'with a view to promoting duplicate matches. The first Oxford and Cambridge bridge match has been arranged and will take place in London next month . . . Cambridge men who are interested should communicate with Mr Ian [sic] Macleod, Caius College, Cambridge.' The match was finally held three months later in February 1935 at the Albany Club, Savile Row, in London's West End. Macleod captained the Cambridge team while Oxford was captained by Charles Maclaren (later Lord Aberconway) and included Terence Reese. Michael Noble, who, like Macleod, was to become a Tory cabinet minister, played for Oxford. Oxford won by 3,800 points.

Macleod's bridge playing meant, for him, having a good time. When Cambridge arranged a match with Leicester, Macleod arrived in Harding's room to go to the match. Harding was mixing cocktails but had to leave momentarily to answer a telephone call. During his absence Macleod consumed most of the 'White Lady' cocktail Harding had been preparing in his shaker. By the time Harding returned, Macleod was out for the count. When the other team members appeared, Harding suggested that they should leave him behind, at which point Macleod rallied and declared, 'Macleod drunk is better than anybody else sober.' At the lunch that followed, Macleod was so drunk that he had trouble finding his mouth with his fork. Having finally made their way to Leicester, the Cambridge team discovered that their opposing captain was a vicar. Harding hurriedly ordered plenty of black coffee, but to little avail. When Macleod finally met his opposite number, he tried to light a cigarette but fumbled with his box of matches and finally spilled its contents all over the floor.

Bridge nevertheless got Macleod his first job after Cambridge. While at Cambridge his team had played a match against the English Bridge Union, and one of their team was Bernard Westall, chairman of De La Rue, the City printing firm that manufactured both playing cards and bank notes. Macleod's talent at bridge and his geniality impressed Westall who offered him a post with his company after leaving university. Macleod, still without a future career in mind and fearing a poor degree, accepted immediately. In fact, he only got a lower second, much to his father's chagrin. His father had worked his way up in the world from a poor background, and had acquired his medical standing through his own efforts. Having spent money providing the best education he could afford for his son Iain, he was not pleased.

Macleod joined De La Rue in the summer of 1935 but soon had a double life. By day, he worked for De la Rue in Bunhill Row, and at night headed for the excitement of London's night life, principally to the bridge tables at Crockford's in Mayfair or at Lederer's Club in Bayswater. Getting to work on time at eight in the morning soon became a struggle. When he did put in an early appearance, he was often in no fit state to work and spent much of the day trying to catch up on sleep. By evening he had usually perked up and would sometimes ask his work colleagues to join him on his night out. By their standards, he was doing well. He was already making more money from cards at night than they were paid for a day's work. He once told a colleague, without boasting, that the previous night he had won £100 at cards, this at a time when the average male annual earnings were around £200 per year, and Macleod's wages at De La Rue were a mere £3 a week. As with most card players, losing runs inevitably came along and he would be reduced to asking his father to help him out. Whenever the morning post brought a begging letter from him, Harry Thurlow, Dr Macleod's long-serving factotum, used to warn Iain's brothers to keep well out of their father's way.

Macleod was popular at De La Rue, generous to a fault, handing out free cigarettes and buying drinks for drivers when he went out on deliveries with them. His appalling timekeeping, however, meant his job was constantly at risk. But when a massive order for bank notes from China came in, Macleod relished the challenge. Although it interfered with his bridge weekend, he threw himself into the task, working overtime through the night to have the shipment ready for Southampton on the Monday morning. Eventually, though, his habits and nocturnal life got the better of him and he was fired by Westall. Then he became a bridge devotee. He first attempted to pacify his disappointed father by offering to read for the Bar. It was a promise not kept. Too much else was on offer. The bright lights of the West End beckoned and, as a twenty-two-year-old, he wasn't going to resist them.

By now he had come across some of the leading bridge players of his generation, Maurice Harrison-Gray, Jack Marx and S. J. Simon. At the bridge club in Acol Road, Hampstead, he spent long hours with them devising a new system of bidding, based loosely on Culbertson, but which also incorporated several new features. Much of it was concocted late at night and jotted down on anything to hand, from cigarette packets to tablecloths. They soon named their system Acol after the road of its birth. Along with Terence Reese, who had been on the opposing side in the first Oxbridge varsity match, Macleod was regarded as one of the most promising players around. The year after leaving Cambridge he played internationally for England, not Scotland, in the four-nation home countries Camrose Cup. At the bridge table he was seen as a forceful, but not reckless, player, logical and considered in his play.

Macleod soon got a job working during the afternoons and evenings as a host at Crockford's, then located in Hertford Street, Mayfair, in their 'ten shillings room' – ten shillings a hundred was the highest stake allowed in the club. One of his tasks was to keep an eye on those coming in, which meant keeping a weather eye out for professional card sharps. He had to oversee the tables and, if members needed a fourth for bridge, he would be asked to join them. He was young, attractive and popular, and members were soon keen for him to do so. He had tidied up his appearance since coming to work for Crockford's. Although paid little, his food and drink were free and he could make money on the side playing as a partner. After Crockford's closed, he would go off to play poker, usually for high stakes. One night a friend, Michael Fraser, watched him lose steadily, and left, unable to watch any more. As he left, he saw Macleod sitting there, hunched, in-drawn and apparently emotionless. Six hours later he met him again in the street, triumphant now, having won back his losses and more.

With money to burn, he quickly spent it. A night's card playing at Crockford's might be followed by the midnight cabaret at the Café de Paris, and then on to one of the West End's less savoury drinking clubs around Shepherd Market. This hedonistic stage ended with the declaration of war on Sunday, 3 September 1939. The next day, Macleod, Harding and their friend Tommy Gay, went to a deserted Crockford's. For all they knew, this might be the last time they would play cards together and they therefore played a high game for imaginary stakes. At the end of the evening Macleod had 'won' £50,000, Harding £10,000 and Gay had 'lost' £60,000. Not serious money and Gay never had to pay up, but it was a symbolic ending to a particular phase of his life.

Eight days later, Macleod enlisted as a private soldier in the Royal Fusiliers at a recruiting office at Acton, West London, and kept the taxi waiting while he did so. He gave the taxi driver his King's florin, a two-shilling piece given to all those who enlisted, to keep as a tip. Time elapsed before his posting and he enrolled as an ambulance driver since bombing raids were expected nightly over London. He was interviewed by Eve Mason, an attractive woman of twenty-four, whom he later married. But this was during the 'phoney war', so he had little to do and spent his time at ambulance headquarters working out bridge hands. One day, a mysterious message, apparently in code, was found on a slip of paper on the floor and prompted a full-scale alert and spy scare. Nerves were jittery at the time anyhow. An intelligence officer was sent to investigate. He questioned Macleod and showed him the 'message'. It read 'Ax, Kxxx, Qxxx, KQx'. Macleod immediately recognised it as a bridge hand he had scribbled down and thrown away – not as a plot to overthrow the monarchy.

He went with the British Expeditionary Force to France and was wounded in the leg in the fighting before Dunkirk, which gave him a slight limp for the rest of his life. His subsequent war-time service included becoming Staff Captain at Dover, a posting to the Staff College, in 1943, and being part of the Planning Staff for the invasion of France on D-Day, where he actually landed on D-Day itself.

After the war he went into politics, an ambition since University days. He contested the Western Isles seat as a Tory in the 1945 election. Despite the romance of its name, he came bottom of the poll – 'with the greatest ease', as he put it. Politics took more and more of his attention. In 1948 he was made a member of the Conservative Secretariat, a sort of Shadow Cabinet, specialising in questions of national health. This ran alongside his bridge interests. In the 1950 election he was returned as Tory member for Enfield. He kept up his bridge as an MP and still made money out of it while a backbencher, despite the demands of frequent late nights and the need to remain within reach of the Commons Division Bell. His opponents in St James's clubs generally had more money than sense and Macleod would usually win. Bill Deedes, another member of the same intake, used to rib Macleod when he appeared in the Commons smoking room in the evening, 'Have you been robbing them again?'

In 1951, Macleod led, as non-playing captain, the British bridge team to the Venice European Championships. He was due to take part in further trials when he was created Minister of Health, the post for which he had trained for so long. He was the youngest Minister of Health ever to hold office. This meant, of course, that he had to give up serious bridge and also had to resign from his *Sunday Times* bridge column which he wrote as 'Yarborough' and for which he was paid £500 per annum, although it usually took him no more than half an hour to write each weekend. His book *Bridge is an Easy Game*, however, came out in 1952, and is rated among the best bridge textbooks ever written. The title, which implies that bridge is an easy game provided people don't complicate it, epitomises Macleod's own approach: challenging, keen on paradox, yet accurate and to the point. There's a copy in the library at Number 10 Downing Street which bears Macleod's inscription on the fly leaf: 'This is the only book in this place that is certain to profit its reader.'

Macleod built a strong reputation as a debater in Parliament, even when confronting his formidable predecessor at the Health Ministry, Aneurin Bevan. He continued to play bridge in London clubs, notably at White's in St James's Street, before his workload as Minister of Health became too much. Indeed, he caused something of a scandal when staying up all night playing bridge. Members were shocked at the Minister of Health, of all people, behaving in this way. Nevertheless his winnings from bridge usually helped to subsidise his family holidays.

As a bridge player Macleod played with courage, flair and imagination, sometimes to the point of recklessness, but it was a recklessness firmly based on technical knowledge and self-confidence. He would bid his cards high – always avoiding the use of the plural ('two heart', 'four no trump') – and often stopped abruptly when he judged that he had pushed his opponents too far to make their contract. He could size up a hand and calculate the odds very quickly and was always prepared to gamble, and perhaps go down if he thought the risk was justified. One evening he was playing in an important match at

Crockford's and he asked his wife Eve to come and watch the game. At great inconvenience she arranged to do so and sat patiently, though uncomprehendingly as she was not a bridge player, by the table for two or three hours. No one paid the least attention to her and eventually, tired and discouraged, she took the last bus and underground back to Enfield. Some hours later Iain arrived home by taxi and greeted her rather petulantly: 'I asked you to come and watch me play and I was very disappointed when you didn't.' His concentration had been so intense that he was quite unaware that she had been sitting a few feet away from him for most of the evening.

At the bridge table, on the other hand, he could at times become almost lethargic, taking up a semi-recumbent attitude like his contemporary, Terence Reese, apt to sprawl, sitting on the small of his back. He often chewed a pencil as opposed to Reese's preference for a tie. Reese wrote of him: 'Macleod's outstanding characteristic, at the table or away from it, is a dynamic aggression. He is always on the attack. Of all the players I have ever known, he most exactly mirrors his character in his bridge – in both there is a pugnacity that seems reckless but which is, in fact, founded upon profound knowledge – sometimes self-knowledge – and justified self-confidence.'

Macleod died in 1970 at the age of fifty-seven when many considered him a future prime minister.

Here are some extracts from his book *Bridge is an Easy Game* to give a flavour of his distinctive writing style:

THE OPENING SUIT BID OF ONE

This is the foundation of bridge. Very rarely is it possible later to retrieve the consequences of a thoroughly bad opening bid. Partner is always entitled to assume when you open with one of a suit:

(a) That your hand is not good enough for a bid of two.
(b) That it is too good to pass.
(c) That the suit you name will normally be your best suit.
(d) That your hand is not one that should be opened with a pre-emptive (or shut out) bid.

If your bid ignores any one of these criteria it may prove

disastrous. The first thing to decide is the upper and lower limits of the bid: where the decision to open with a bid of one shades into the decision on one hand to bid two, on the other to pass. These limits cannot be precisely defined, and the deciding factor must always be one of personal judgment. A dozen influences may sway you: the state of the rubber or the match: the calibre of your partner and opponents: who is to play the hand.

COMPETITIVE BIDDING

There can be no competitive bidding unless you bid. So get into the bidding. Get in as quickly as you can and as safely as you can, but get in. Nearly always it's poor play to 'trap' by passing on a big hand. Nearly always it's silly play to hold back from the bidding until the opponents' bidding peters out. It may or may not do so, and even if it does the level is sure to be higher. So you should intervene readily and, if the balance of cards is against you, push the bidding as high as you dare as quickly as you can; you must steal bidding space from you opponents. We must – it's a favourite saying of Harrison Gray's – 'contest those part-scores'. We must worry our opponents and give them neither space nor peace. There must, of course, be some sort of safety level always in mind and Culbertson's 'Rule of Two and Three', as he calls it, is the surest guide. A player should expect then for a defensive bid to get within three tricks of his contract non-vulnerable and two tricks vulnerable. He should assume reasonable breaks, but also that his partner's hand will be near worthless to him.

PLANNING THE PLAY

Unless a contract is laid down there is usually an appreciable pause after dummy has exposed his cards. The declarer plans the play of the hand, and the defenders calculate cheerfully or gloomily at their prospects. Don't be in a hurry to play to the first trick. I'm no advocate of slow play and I believe that excessive analysis at bridge usually muddles the analyst. There is a great advantage in the smooth speed of such players as Kenneth Konstam and Leslie Dodds. But that is after the plan is made. For the moment we are studying dummy and making an appreciation of the relative values of the different lines of approach to a doubtful contract. You should do as much of your thinking as possible at this stage so that later you can play as confidently and easily and naturally as possible. Unexpected distributions or an unorthodox defence may, of course, make you switch your plans later. At least you should have a plan to switch. There is no surer mark of the bad – of the losing – player, than a hasty play from dummy at the first trick. Chew for a few moments over the opponent's bidding remembering, of course, that there is often as much to be learnt from a pass as from a bid, study the inferences you can draw from the opening lead, and then sum up your chances. Bridge hands defy exact classification if only because the combinations are too numerous. Experts play a hand as declarer more by drawing on the well of their experiences, than by book lore. Yet there is much about the approach to play that can be taught. In particular, there are two principles that should always guide you as declarer:

1. Play always so that any decision you have to take is taken as late as possible in the hand, and any decision the defenders have to take is presented to them at the earliest moment.
2. Always scheme and play to give the defenders as many chances of guessing wrong as you can contrive.

DEFENSIVE PLAY

There is a bigger gap between the expert and the good player in this field of Bridge than in any other. I doubt if there are half a dozen defensive players of the highest class in the country. An expert needs knowledge and flair and toughness and above anything else, endless practice.

DEFENCE IN THE END GAME

The key to successful defence is anticipation. It is fairly easy to see what end game the declarer is striving for. When you know that he plans to throw you in try and keep a safe exit card, and remember to unblock suit combinations so that your partner can if need be hold the trick. When he plans a trump reduction you can often defeat him simply by refusing to lead the suit that he wants to ruff, or by forcing him to use entries before he is ready. When, in either a genuine or a pseudo squeeze, declarer starts to reel off his trumps or an established suit, tell your partner at once, by your discards, which suits you can protect.

All this is negative defence, and as you will rarely be in the lead most defence in the end game is negative. Positive defence should take the form of an assault on declarer's entries and menace cards.

Lord Lever, a regular participant at the House of Lords versus House of Commons matches, is quoted as saying: 'Chess is challenging, but bridge is the stuff of life.' The Chinese President Deng Xiao Ping was an exceptionally keen bridge player, and played to a very high standard, always willing to intersperse high diplomacy with a game of bridge. Indeed, it was through his passion for the game, learnt when he was sent as a promising young Chinese student to Paris in the 1920s to work in a Renault factory, that China now has more players of the game per capita than any other nation in the world. Curiously, the Japanese were always thought to find bridge difficult – too much loss of face, too much reliance on apparent duplicity, both of which go against their culture.

Presidents and world leaders have been keen bridge players. Churchill was one and Dwight D. Eisenhower another, both in the White House and elsewhere. Warren Harding, his predecessor, was also absorbed by the game, in auction bridge days. In June 1923 Harding took an Alaska vacation. The corruption scandals that would brand his administration as the worst in US history were about to break, and he felt the tension. His Secretary of Commerce, Herbert Hoover, accompanied him and later wrote, 'As soon as we were aboard ship, he insisted on playing bridge, beginning every day immediately after breakfast and continuing except for mealtimes often until midnight. There were only four other bridge players in the party, so we soon set up shifts so that one of us at a time had some relief. For some reason, I developed a distaste for bridge on this journey and never played it again.'

Dwight Eisenhower first became interested in bridge when he was still a captain in the US Army in the early 1930s. As Supreme Allied

Commander in Europe during the Second World War, he played regularly. A key moment was November 1942 when the invasion of North Africa was about to take place. France had fallen and the Allies were planning to start the war on a different front. Some eight hundred Allied ships lay off the North African coast about to invade but were held up by incessant fog. Eisenhower was on board waiting with his senior officers feeling increasingly impatient and restless. 'Let's have a game of bridge,' Eisenhower suggested. They played – Generals Gruenther and Mark Clark and Commander Harry Butcher, Eisenhower's Naval Aide. The game continued for some hours until the fog lifted and the invasion could start.

During the war, Eisenhower seized what chances he had to play bridge, usually assembling the best players available among his staff officers to have a game. It was a favourite form of relaxation, but it was something more as well. As a general he was constantly having to make tough decisions. Bridge presented its own tough decisions but an error at bridge wasn't going to cost thousands of lives as it might on the battlefield. Bridge also played its part at the invasion of Normandy and the D-Day landings. Again, he used it as a pre-battle relaxation. After the war, still in Europe as NATO commander, he played again with General Mark Clark, now American Commander of Occupied Austria, and Gruenther, now his Chief of Staff, in a mountain resort in the Alps where they had been summoned for a tactical meeting. When they arrived, the first thing Eisenhower said was, 'Let's play some bridge.' It was his means of bonding them before their strategic meeting.

Once elected President of the United States in 1953, Eisenhower held a regular Saturday game of bridge at the White House, with Gruenther again as his usual partner. Gruenther was long considered the best bridge player in the United States Army. Years later Gruenther called Eisenhower one morning at seven to tell him to read the *New York Times* bridge column that morning because it included one of the hands Eisenhower had played. Eisenhower replied, 'I've already read it.'

The Saturday game at the White House usually began at 5 p.m. in the solarium with an interruption for a snack or sandwich at about 8 p.m., and then went on until 10 or 10.30 p.m. Oswald Jacoby was a regular player whenever he was in Washington, and, when asked how good Eisenhower's bridge was, deemed him 'superior – capable of holding his own in the best club games below the most expert'. Jacoby went on, 'I know a lot of persons who play good bridge. They have learned how the game should be played. But their play is wooden. The

President obviously plays intelligent bridge. He thinks about what he does and what he does is done with good reason. He's the nicest person at the bridge table that I've ever played with. He doesn't get excited about winning or losing but he plays hard. He plays better bridge than golf; he tries to break ninety at golf; at bridge you would say he does break eighty.' Golf was Eisenhower's other passion and there was a nice story that during his presidency his security guards soon realised that the safest place for them to stand while he was driving off the tee was in the middle of the fairway.

Eisenhower took his bridge seriously. He was a studious player always trying to do the right thing, and favoured a straightforward approach, with a simple bidding system. He liked to bid and play fast and decisively. He never tried to hog the bidding or play, as others in commanding positions have done. After his retirement from the Presidency in 1961, he continued playing at his houses at Gettysburg, Pennsylvania, and Palm Springs, California, up to his death in 1969.

♤♡♢
♧

Churchill played bridge in his younger days when auction was still dominant. Violet Bonham Carter recalled that he 'played a romantic game untrammelled by conventions, codes or rules. To cut with Winston was to both of his private secretaries a severe ordeal . . . Winston declared, doubled and redoubled with wild recklessness.' Early in 1941, Churchill was in Admiralty House when he was visited by Lord Beaverbrook and Lord Birkenhead. Two other MPs were already there and, as they waited for news, they decided to play bridge. A dispatch box was brought in which contained the news that Germany had declared war on Russia. Churchill got up immediately and went off to mobilise the British fleet. Lord Beaverbrook then took over his partly played hand, but Churchill did not come back that day.

Oswald Jacoby was in the middle of a bridge tournament in Richmond, Virginia, when the news of Pearl Harbor came through. He got up immediately, left the tournament and joined up, his extra-sharp bridge mind providing invaluable assistance at deciphering enemy codes when he worked for the Office of Strategic Studies.

♤♡♢
♧

Mention was made earlier of the inter-parliamentary matches in Britain. The first House of Lords versus House of Commons match was held in 1974 in the Chelsea Tower Hotel in Sloane Street. Rixi Markus was the moving spirit behind it, mainly through her close friendship with Harold Lever, MP for Manchester, later to become Lord Lever. Card playing within the Houses of Parliament up to that time had not been allowed, presumably for fear of its diversionary effect, though chess had been permitted. Yet historically many members of the Houses of Parliament were keen card players and gamblers – Charles James Fox would be a notorious example. Members of Parliament had instead gone to play elsewhere, mostly at clubs in St James's Street such as White's and Brooks's. The Palace of Westminster remained forbidden territory. Rixi Markus got together with a bridge-playing friend of hers, the MP Sally Oppenheim, and discussed the idea of an inter-parliamentary bridge match. Sir Timothy Kitson was captain of the Commons team, though he soon relinquished that role in favour of Sir Peter Emery. Lord Glenkinglas captained the House of Lords team, though when his health began to deteriorate not long afterwards, the Duke of Atholl took over. On Atholl's death the captaincy passed to Lord Gisborough.

The first inter-parliamentary match proved a very popular occasion, with the press turning out in force, and the BBC televising the proceedings. The match was won by the Lords. Thereafter it became an annual event, held until 1986 at the Inn on the Park, and subsequently at Le Meridien Hotel, Piccadilly, and the Portland Club. The House of Commons team usually won, thanks largely to Harold Lever, their most gifted player. In later years the Lords pulled ahead, mainly due to Harold Lever's ascension to the House of Lords. After the 1998 match the score was 13–11 in favour of the upper house.

Challenges from parliamentary teams abroad were soon received, the first coming from France. On this occasion the British team included the Duke of Atholl, the Marquess of Dufferin and Ava and Lord Smith, a surgeon who once removed thirty-four gallstones from the English bridge international Maurice Harrison-Gray with the statement, 'Enough for a small slam in no trumps'. The Commons were represented by Timothy Kitson, Anthony Berry (who was tragically killed in the Brighton bomb in 1985) and Kenneth Baker. Yet, as often with politicians, the problem arose of making sure everyone was in the same place on the same day for the necessary length of time. Just before the first French match, scheduled to be played at the Hotel

Normandy in Deauville, the French government resigned and the National Assembly was dispersed. Not enough proper French deputies remained to play. However, they had assembled a team whose members' political connections were less evident than their prowess at bridge. One man had even played for the French national team, and his link with politics was very tenuous. They were too strong for the British, who were mostly rubber bridge players, a game requiring different tactics.

Further invitations followed. The British team won against the Dutch in Amsterdam, and repeated their success in a return match in London. Rixi Markus was very much the organising spirit behind these occasions. She became like one of the team, 'and a very congenial team it was', as she once said. Further invitations came from Sweden, the United States, Morocco and elsewhere. In Dubai in 1982, they were flown first-class, all paid for by their hosts, and treated royally. In 1984 came an invitation from Washington to play against the US Congress. Rixi Markus assembled her best possible team: the Duke of Atholl, the Earl of Birkenhead, Lord Grimthorpe, Sally Oppenheim, Tony Berry, the Marquess of Dufferin and Ava and John Marek, their only Labour member and one of their best players who, unfortunately, managed to arrived at the airport without his passport. An extra player, Albert Dormer, stepped into the breach. He was really a well-known bridge expert with no parliamentary connections, but no one seemed to object to such flexibility. The US Congress team also included a few 'ringers' – a judge and at least one man who was not at the time in Congress, though he formerly had been. The festivities pleased the Americans. The Duke of Atholl, the British captain, had brought his own piper wearing the Atholl tartan to pipe them in to the opening reception. Confusion reigned among the Americans as to how to address members of the British aristocracy. One lady curtsied to the Earl of Birkenhead, asking politely, 'How do I address you, sir?' 'Call me Robin,' came back the reply.

The British team won the match comfortably and after their defeat the Americans wanted revenge. The return engagement was played in November 1985 in London. The Mayor of Westminster arranged the opening ceremony and, determined not to be outdone, had the band of the Coldstream Guards on hand, plus an Atholl piper. American Express sponsored the match and donated a silver cup from Garrards the royal jewellers, which, when the British side won, stood for six months in the House of Commons and six months in the House of Lords.

The story of parliamentary bridge reached a triumphant conclusion on 11 May 1987. Bridge was officially declared a proper recreational pastime for Members of Parliament. Members could now play in the room previously reserved only for chess, and Rixi Markus's long campaign, with the help of others, to make bridge a 'parliamentary' game had been successfully concluded. The first rubber ever to be played legally on those historic premises was played by Sir Peter Emery, John Marek, Cranley Onslow and Tim Sainsbury that very same day.

♤♡◇
♧

On the international scene, world bridge is now regulated by the World Bridge Federation which was set up in August 1958 at the European Championships in Oslo, Norway. There representatives of the American Contract Bridge League, the European Bridge League and the Australian Bridge League came together to inaugurate the federation. Baron Robert de Nexon of Paris, a French international bridge player, was named first President. Alvin Landy of the American Contract Bridge League was Secretary-Treasurer and Charles Solomon and Charles Goren were on the Organising Committee. General Alfred M. Gruenther, at the time President of the American Red Cross, agreed to serve as the Honorary President.

The first project of the World Bridge Federation was to be an Olympic Teams Championship to be played every four years at the time of the Olympic Games proper, and in the same city if possible. Thus the initial 'Olympic' was planned for Rome in April 1960. It was, in fact, played in Turin from 27 April to 4 May 1960 and was known as the first World Bridge Olympiad. This has continued to be played every four years. The inventor of contract bridge, Harold S. Vanderbilt, generously donated a trophy and also provided for individual replicas to be made for future winners.

The World Bridge Federation's primary aim, however, has been to provide a central organisation to bind together the National Contract Bridge Organisations (NCBOs) throughout the world. More specifically, its original objects can be summarised as:

1. To promote, foster, and control the game of contract bridge.
2. To apply the International Laws of contract bridge.
3. To promote and conduct quadrennial World Championship team

tournaments on the basis of one team only for each country (the Olympiad).
4. To conduct the Bermuda Bowl contest, in every year in which there is no Team Olympiad.
5. To promote and conduct quadrennial World Championship pair tournaments.
6. To conduct World Championship par contest.
7. To conduct such other contests as from time to time are agreed upon.

Other objectives in subsequent announcements have included:

- To oppose any religious, racial or political considerations which may from time to time threaten the well-being of our game.
- To update the bridge laws regularly, taking full account of views received from each NCBO. The Laws Commission will study all suggested changes, and a special committee will consider the possibility of modifying the scoring system.
- To reinforce ethical standards . . . 'The WBF is pledged firmly to do its utmost to see that its competitions are played according to the strictest rules of morality and sportsmanship . . . WBF can never accept lax standards. Our intellectual game maintains its value only when played with complete honesty.'
- To build a sound financial base.

To belong to the World Bridge Federation, member countries must have a minimum of 250 individual members, and belong to a zonal organisation. At present there are seven zonal organisations, each administering its own geographical area, and co-ordinating the National Federations of its member countries.

Zone 1 European Bridge League with 40 countries as members and 373,025 individual members.
Zone 2 ACBL North America with 4 countries and 167,413 individual members.
Zone 3 South American Bridge Federation with 8 countries and 5,859 individual members.
Zone 4 Africa, Asia and the Middle East with 21 countries and 17,703 members.

Zone 5 Central American and Caribbean Bridge Federation with 22 countries and 2,131 individual members.
Zone 6 Pacific Asia Bridge Federation with 10 countries and 69,323 individual members.
Zone 7 South Pacific Bridge Federation with 4 countries and 45,451 individual members.

This gives (1997 figures) a total of 109 countries and 681,018 members.

The World Bridge Federation is administered by an Executive Council consisting of delegates from the seven geographical Zones, plus the President. There are five delegates from the European Bridge League (Zone 1), five from the American Contract Bridge League (Zone 2) and one from each of the other five geographical Zones. Thus the Council has sixteen members, including the President.

The World Bridge Federation is present at the major international championships, such as the World Championships, which are held every two years between the best teams from the seven Zones above. The number of teams from each Zone is determined by the number of members of official bridge organisations within each Zone. On that basis Europe is allowed four teams, North America three teams, and the other Zones one or two each. The host country enters automatically, making sixteen teams in all.

Famous Hands

DUKE OF CUMBERLAND HAND

The most famous, and certainly the most notorious, hand in whist and bridge history has been the Duke of Cumberland hand. The Duke of Cumberland responsible has always been thought to be the second son of George the Third, William Augustus (1721–1765), who had a reputation as an inveterate gambler for high stakes. This hand is said to have been dealt to him at the very popular gaming rooms in Bath. The Duke's opponents goaded him into betting on the outcome, claiming that he would not win a single trick. The Duke, having seen his hand, went ahead and did so. It was said to have cost him twenty thousand pounds. This is the story, at any rate, related by Professor Richard A. Proctor in *How to Play Whist* (1885).

The Duke of Cumberland hand appears again in Ian Fleming's James Bond novel *Moonraker* (1955) where Fleming describes a bridge game at Blades Club in London. There Bond and Sir Hugo Drax, the villain of the piece, are to have their first encounter. Bond, with M., his superior and mentor as his partner, is matched against Drax and his henchman, Meyer, in a bridge game. Fleming so constructs his story that bridge leads to Drax's undoing. Fleming was always adept at this kind of scene-setting and his description of the occupants of Blades Club is no exception. A typical club player is General Bealey who 'doesn't know the reds from the blacks. Nearly always a few hundred down at the end of the week. Doesn't seem to care. Bad heart. No dependants. Stacks of money from jute.' Or the scruffy-looking Duff Sutherland, 'an absolute killer. Makes a regular ten thousand a year out of the club. Nice chap. Wonderful card manners. Used to play chess for England.'

Sir Hugo Drax is introduced, his hairy red face 'shining with cheerful anticipation' as he waits in the card room. Drax's aggressive side is soon in evidence and, as Bond comes up, he greets him by drawing a finger across his throat 'in wolfish pantomime'. Bond is determined to be his match and immediately challenges him to play for the highest stakes, five and five, namely £50 a hundred and £500 on the rubber. Bond wants to teach Drax a lesson that he will remember for the rest of his life.

The bridge game starts. The first rubber goes to Bond and M., who are £900 ahead. Drax and Meyer win the second rubber, cancelling the winnings of the first rubber and winning a bit more besides. Drax, his confidence returning, suggests raising the stakes to a hundred a hand. Bond agrees. Drax wins both that and the rubber. 'God is with the big battalions,' Drax tells him. Bond now feigns the effects of champagne and suggests raising the stakes to double that amount. As Drax watches Bond struggle to light his cigarette, he readily agrees. Bond then makes a small slam in hearts, and with M. winning the next hand with three no trumps they take the rubber. Bond grins at the sweating face of Drax, picking angrily at his nails. 'Big battalions,' he says, rubbing it in.

Bond now says this will have to be his last rubber as he has to get up early in the morning. Drax, still noticing the signs of intoxication in Bond, suggests trebling the stakes to fifteen and fifteen. Bond pauses before answering, making sure Drax will remember this moment before saying 'You're on.' M. cuts the cards and the game begins. Earlier Bond had warned M. to watch out for the time when he, Bond, would take out a white handkerchief from his coat pocket. This would be a signal for M. that he was about to be dealt a Yarborough, and was to leave all bidding on that hand to Bond. Drax cuts the blue cards to Bond, and M. sees Bond put the two halves together and place the pack near the edge of the table. M. then sees a white handkerchief appear in Bond's right hand, which he seems to wipe his face with. Bond glances sharply at Drax and Meyer, then the handkerchief is back in his pocket. Bond starts to deal.

The deal completed, Bond picks up his cards. He has five clubs to the ace, queen and ten, and eight small diamonds to the queen. Not much to look at. But it is the Duke of Cumberland hand which Bond has pre-arranged in the Secretary's room before dinner. The hand is as follows:

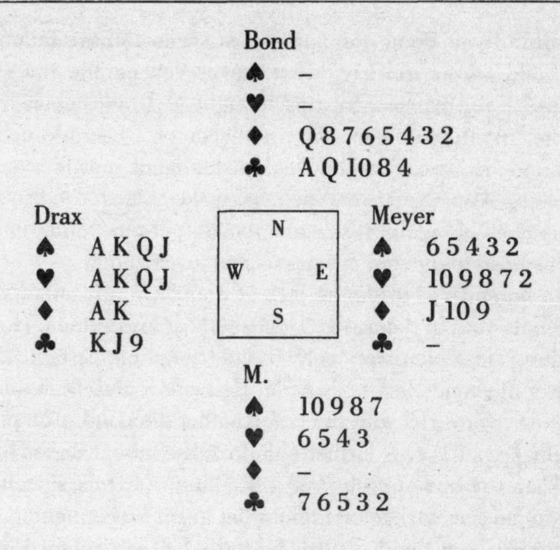

The trap is set for Drax. Bond watches as Drax thumbs through his cards, and then, in a state of disbelief, thumbs through them again. Bond knew what he had, a seemingly unbeatable hand – ten apparent top tricks with the ace, king of diamonds, the four top honours in spades, the four top honours in hearts, and three other strong cards, the king, jack and nine of clubs. Bond still waits before bidding, taking an almost sadistic pleasure in watching how Drax reacts to his huge hand. Drax lives up to his expectations. He watches him put his hand down on the table and take out a cigarette from the carton in his pocket without a care in the world. As he lights it, he looks slyly at Bond. 'I've got some good tickets here. I'll admit it. But then you may have too, for all I know. Care to have something extra just on this hand?' Bond scrutinises his cards, still sticking to his semi-intoxicated act. In a slurred voice he agrees. Drax offers to increase the stakes to a hundred a trick on the side. Bond, keeping up his befuddled pretence, takes another careful look at his hand, checking the cards one by one, and then agrees.

Bond was the dealer so it was his turn to bid first. 'Seven clubs.' Drax reacts as if hit by a bullet and hastily runs through his cards for reassurance. 'Did you say grand slam in clubs?' he asks. 'Well, it's your funeral.' Meyer, still nervous, passes, as does M., seemingly unperturbed. Drax doubles, spitting the word out of his mouth. He looks scornfully at Bond who now at last seems to have fallen into his hands. Bond moves quickly, 'That means you double the side bets, too?' 'Yes.' Bond pauses, looking straight at Drax, not at his cards. 'Redouble.' At that moment the first seeds of a horrible doubt enter Drax's mind. He takes another look at his hand, but is reassured by what he sees. At the very worst he must make at least two tricks. Meyer passes as does M. again, less convincingly perhaps. Drax impatiently shakes his head to indicate his pass, keen to get going.

Meyer, perspiring, leads the jack of diamonds. M. puts his dummy down with its void in diamonds. Drax snarls at his partner. 'Haven't you got anything else, you damn fool?' Bond trumps on the table and drops the king of diamonds in Drax's hand. He leads a club from dummy and Drax's nine is covered with the ten. Another diamond, trumped on the table, fells Drax's ace. A further club from the table catches his jack of clubs. Then the ace of clubs takes his king. As Drax surrenders this last trump, he sees for the first time what might be happening. His eyes squint anxiously at Bond, waiting fearfully for his next card. Has Bond got more diamonds? Surely Meyer must have them guarded as he led them? Drax waits, his cards now slippery with sweat. At this point in his story Fleming recalls how Morphy, the great chess player, used to never raise his eyes from the board until he knew his opponent could not escape defeat.

Now, like Morphy, Bond lifts his head and looks straight into Drax's eyes. Then he slowly draws out the queen of diamonds and places it on the table. Without waiting for Meyer to follow, he puts down the eight, seven, six, five, four of the suit and his two winning clubs. Drax's immediate reaction is to lurch forward and tear Meyer's cards out of his hand and throw them face up on the table, scrabbling furiously to find a winner. Defeated, he flings them down on the baize, his face now an ashen white, his eyes blazing with fury. He raises his clenched fist and crashes it down on the table among the pile of impotent aces and kings, then slowly rises to his feet, pushes back his chair and, glancing down at each player in turn, bids them each goodnight, his voice full of contempt, a gesture Bond finds oddly disturbing. 'I owe about £15,000. I will accept Meyer's addition.' With that he leans forward and whispers in Bond's ear, 'I should spend the money quickly, Commander Bond,' before turning away to leave the room hurriedly.

It's a first-rate piece of narrative, among Fleming's best, conveying the high drama of a tense rubber bridge game in a London club. The style is taut, with the right amount of detail and suspense. Kingsley Amis in the *Dictionary of National Biography* 1961–70 wrote: 'One cannot forget *Moonraker* for the vivid, rounded depiction of its villain, Hugo Drax, and what is probably the most gripping game of cards in the whole of literature.'

Fleming himself was a keen bridge player and played regularly in London at the Portland Club or at White's. In fact the model for Blades Club in this story is probably an amalgam of those two clubs, and with a dash of Boodle's thrown in. Fleming was very much a man's man, happiest in the world of clubs, whether playing cards in London or golf at Royal St George's, Sandwich, near where he lived after his marriage to Ann Rothermere in 1952. In fact, it was only this getting married at the age of forty-three that pushed him into becoming a writer. He, a bachelor all his life, felt he needed something to counterbalance the foreseeable demands of marriage. 'I was about to get married – a prospect which filled me with terror and mental fidgets. To give my idle hands something to do and as an antibody to my qualms after forty-three years as a bachelor, I decided one day to damned well sit down and write a book.' He did most of his writing at his house on the north shore of Jamaica, Goldeneye, which he had bought in 1946, and where he always managed to spend two months each winter. He would write in the morning and go swimming in the reef off his house in the afternoon. He would aim to write two thousand words a day and finish a book within six weeks. 'I never correct anything and I never look back at what I have written, except to the foot of the last page to see where I have got to. If you once look back, you are lost.'

A neighbour in Jamaica was Noël Coward, who had always been one of his heroes along with Beaverbrook and Somerset Maugham, another bridge player. Fleming admired these three for qualities they had which he lacked himself. As a writer he admired Maugham particularly, and used to go and stay with him at the Villa Mauresque in the south of France. His wife Ann was a close friend of Maugham as well and they often stayed there together. In a note she later wrote she describes one of these visits in 1954: 'Ian joined me at the Villa Mauresque, and was delighted by Willie's [Maugham's] company and well-planned day. There was a strange resemblance between them, the luxurious symmetry, the perfect martini served in a sunny garden, a high standard of cooking, a variety of menu, a choice of wonderful smells in the bathroom, soap, essences and shaving lotions. A curious feeling that they both regarded 'women' with mistrust. They both had a basic sadness and a desperation about life.'

Fleming died in 1964 still in his mid-fifties, his health declining through the excesses of his Bond-like existence. Bond was his *alter ego*, his answer to the never redeemed inferiority complex he felt towards his brother Peter, the travel writer, who had been *Victor Ludorum* at Eton and whom he always tried to emulate. Fleming redressed the balance by creating this idealised version of himself with Bond, of whom he wrote: 'Whenever he had a job of work to do, he would take infinite pains beforehand and leave as little as possible to chance.'

MISSISSIPPI HEART HAND

The second most famous trick hand dating from the days of whist was the Mississippi Heart hand. Variations of it used to appear in different editions of Hoyle's books from 1746 on, and the full deal was published in Thomas Mathews' *Advice to the Young Whist Player* in 1803.

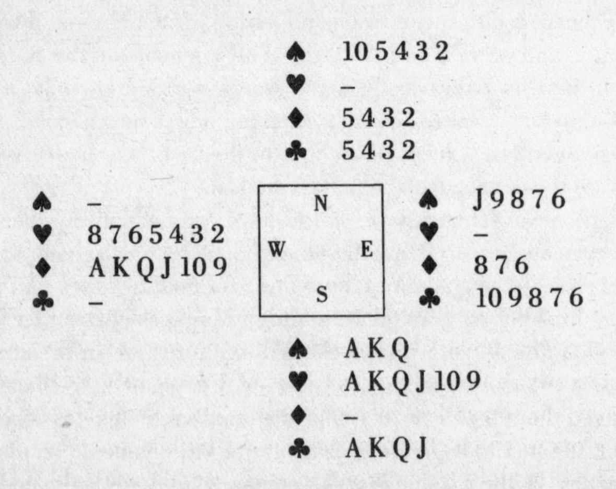

A diamond lead by West holds South to six tricks in a heart contract, and a game cannot be made in any denomination. South can make nine tricks in a spade contract or ten tricks in a club contract. This hand got its name from being used by card sharps on Mississippi River steamboats in the nineteenth century, who hoped to persuade South to make a heavy bet when hearts were trumps. The contract bridge player Charles M. Schwab, who donated an international bridge trophy in the 1930s, is reported to have once been taken to the cleaners over this hand and lost over ten thousand dollars.

Unusual hands have always intrigued bridge players. The chances of getting all thirteen of a suit are 6,250,000,000 to 1. Newspapers occasionally report this happening. This hand was dealt in Culbertson's first 'World Bridge Olympic' in 1932.

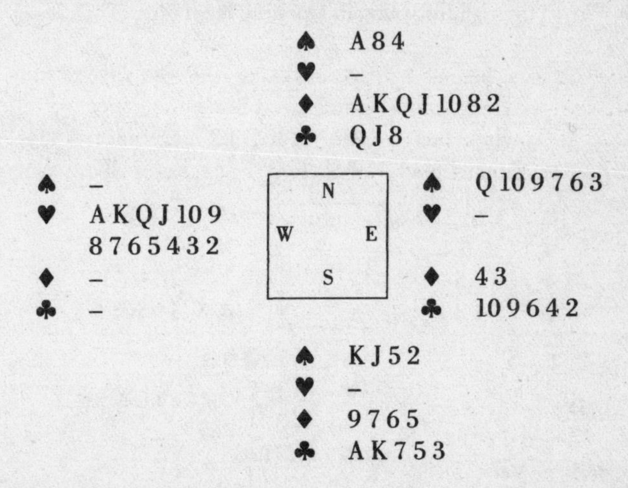

South opened the bidding with one club and the committee in charge of the event decided that West should not receive credit for having bid his hand correctly if he now bids seven hearts. Any other bid on his hand gave him par, regardless of the result, but a bid of seven hearts, pointing the way to a no-trump grand slam by his opponents, was out. The results achieved by various players were remarkable. In some instances South played the hand in seven no trumps and was, of course, defeated thirteen tricks, the West player facetiously leading the two of hearts.

At another table North played the hand at six hearts doubled and redoubled, his partner failing to decode his redouble as an SOS redouble. At still another table East rescued his partner from seven hearts doubled with a bid of seven spades. Elsewhere the bidding went: one club, two hearts, followed by three passes. Another West achieved a remarkable result by bidding two diamonds over South's opening bid of one club. This bid was followed by three passes in turn and, of course, North and South won all thirteen tricks.

Trick hands can appear in many forms. In this hand, North and South ended up in, and made, a slam contract in clubs holding only four trumps. Play it through for yourself. Opening lead: jack of spades.

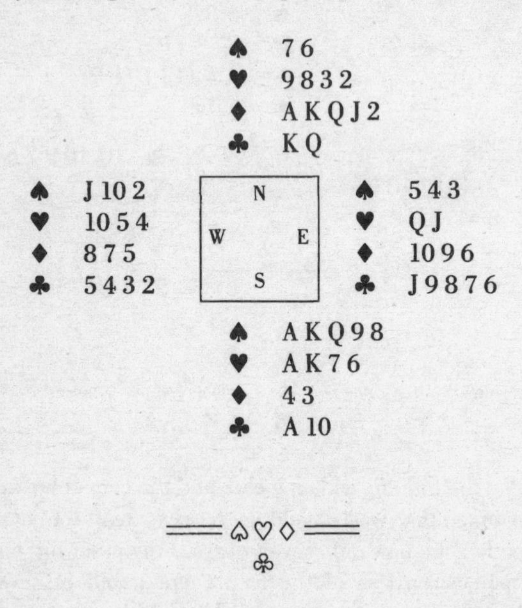

Here are six consecutive bids in the same suit in the same deal, and all of them logical.

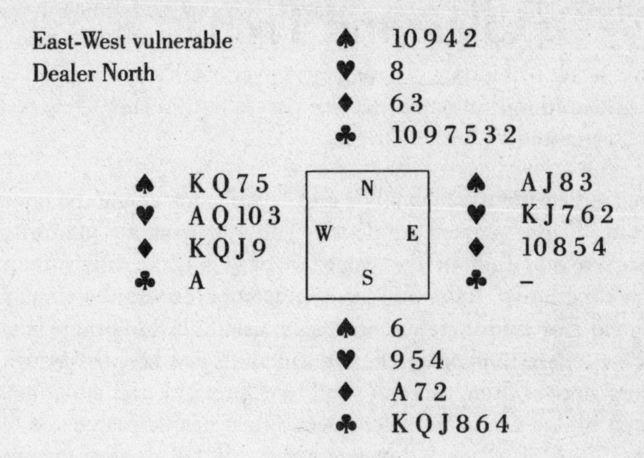

The bidding:

South	*West*	*North*	*East*
–	–	Pass	Pass
1♣	2♣(1)	3♣(2)	4♣(3)
5♣(4)	6♣(5)	Pass	6♥
Pass	Pass	Pass	

(1) West's overcall in the same suit as an opponent shows a powerful hand with club control.
(2) North's bid is made on distributional values and suggests a later sacrifice.
(3) East's club is a cue-bid, seeking further information.
(4) South is happy to sacrifice in five clubs.
(5) West's six club bid asks partner to choose the suit for slam.

The contract is cold.

Adler and Freud

—♠♥♦—
♣

Alfred Adler, the psychoanalyst and Freud's contemporary, once wrote: 'Bridge players are usually suffering from an inferiority complex and find in the game an easy way to satisfy their striving for superiority.' Adler was the originator of the term 'inferiority complex' and saw human relationships in power terms. Bridge was relevant as it offered opportunities for triumph (note how the bridge word 'trump' derives from 'triumph') and for supremacy over superiors. Adler found bridge useful in this respect. 'Most people play cards to waste time. Time, if a man is not courageous, is his greatest enemy. Bridge is a great invention. A little of it is relaxation, but a lot becomes a mental habit, an attempt to satisfy a striving for superiority. It offers an opportunity to conquer others.'

Not everyone agreed with Adler and Ely Culbertson, predictably enough, was quick to challenge him: 'The argument is, like his books, a half truth. Meaningless generalities which are so characteristic of any premature science like Dr Adler's psychology cannot offer intelligent people, such as the race of all bridge players, one-tenth of the mutual exhilaration that is found in precise and logical conditions which underlie any bid or play of the hand . . . A well-built slam bid or a squeeze play contains the same spark of superior intelligence and is stamped with the same subtle and profound inferences as the creation of a Gothic cathedral with its soaring towers, a well-written sonnet or a Burroughs bookkeeping machine.' Culbertson's soaring prose was designed to defend his corner but his exaggerated rebuttal misses some of Adler's essential idea. Adler's point that the struggle in bridge is about winning, about feeling on top, feeling superior, is worth noting. The appeal of bridge is that it can allow people to feel a sudden moment of glory, a fifteen minutes of fame. A winner basks in this reflected glory. Yet the structure of the game, with its inherent restraint, gives this momentary elation both dignity and justification.

As Adler pointed out, the urge to conquer asserts itself at the bridge table in its own unique way. Who hasn't enjoyed banging down an ace to win a trick and triumph over a helpless opponent? Who hasn't secretly gloated at the prospect of holding up that same ace, or a winning court card, before launching a *coup de grâce*? And who hasn't enjoyed castigating his partner with all justification for errors made? There is release in this, a momentary euphoria, as well as the establishment of superiority. Adler was right there.

Language too brings this out. Bridge is full of loaded phrases. 'We left them for dead', 'When he tried that finesse, I cut him up in little pieces', and 'I knew I had him, and I twisted him bit by bit'. The idea of the squeeze is excruciating in itself, the word itself conjuring up all sorts of tortured significance. Culbertson often taunted his opponents with his sharp, acidic tongue. 'I play men, not cards' was his motto. Hal Sims used to assert his superiority by threatening to climb over the table to get at an opponent. Since he was huge, the threat seemed real. Even Goren, normally a model of restraint and gentlemanly conduct, struggled at times to keep his simmering hostility under control.

Much of the appeal of bridge is that players can enter this other world to escape from reality. In the 1930s doctors began prescribing bridge as a palliative. Dr Harold Hays wrote in *The Bridge World*, 'From the doctor's point of view, contract bridge is the greatest outlet for excess nervous energy that one has at hand. There are thousands of people who are "bottled up", who are full of nervous explosive material which is in constant turmoil. Many such individuals get rid of this energy by contract bridge.'

One of Sigmund Freud's most famous patients, Ida Bauer, or 'Dora', became later in life one of Vienna's most eminent bridge teachers.

Dora came from a problematic family. Her mother was described as 'cold and withdrawn', her father as 'self-made' and 'hard-driving'. Her parents became estranged and she nursed her ailing father until she was twelve or thirteen, becoming unusually close to him. Dora was on very bad terms with her mother who displayed hysterical symptoms and suffered from 'housewife's psychosis'. This meant she was obsessed with cleaning and would refuse her family access to certain areas of the house. Because of his unhappy marriage, her father looked elsewhere for affection, falling in love with Mrs K., the wife of a family friend. Mr K. meanwhile made inappropriate sexual advances to Dora. Both her father's affair and these sexual advances were denied within the family. When Dora, aged fifteen, confided her distress about Mr K. to her father, he refused to believe her. The affair between her father and Mrs K. had become obvious to Dora when she was aged thirteen. The Ks and the Bauers had always been close, but her father's affair threw Mrs K. and Dora into even closer proximity and they spent many hours together. The adolescent girl clearly had a crush on Mrs K. who also suffered from ill health, in this case nervous disorders.

Earlier on, when she had stopped nursing her father, Dora started suffering from migraines, loss of voice and a chronic cough. Her affection for her father disappeared and her relationship with her mother deteriorated even further. She withdrew, felt tired and unable to concentrate. She ate badly and lost interest in her looks. She felt suicidal. After an argument with her father she became delirious, had convulsions, lost consciousness and could remember nothing of what happened. Finally in October 1900 Dora's father took her, then aged eighteen, to consult Sigmund Freud. Dora became one of Freud's principal cases, even though she stayed with him for only eleven weeks before she left him abruptly, perturbed by his seemingly intrusive and aloof style.

Freud felt her predicament was a classical oedipal one. Since Freud said nothing about Dora's mother's lack of warmth or maternal nurturing, and did not appreciate Dora's involvement with Mrs K., Dora felt hurt and misunderstood by Freud. Freud told Dora that her symptomatic cough expressed her unconscious fantasy that Mrs K. was gratifying her father sexually through fellatio. His interpretations centred on his belief that Dora loved Mr K. deeply, and unconsciously wished to have sex with him.

Dora recognised some of her repressed emotions concerning her father and Mr K. and in practice gained some temporary relief from her debilitating symptoms. After she left Freud, she soon got married, aged twenty-one, and had a son, who later in life became a famous conductor. Yet marriage and motherhood seemed to offer her little fulfilment. She became, like her mother, unhappily married, had a husband who was unfaithful, and also became obsessive about cleaning.

It was in her later years that she took up bridge. This followed on from the game becoming fashionable in Vienna in the 1930s. Soon playing and teaching contract bridge became the centre of Dora's life. She would teach other middle-class women, usually going out to teach them in their living rooms. Her partner in this intellectually absorbing and challenging occupation was none other than Frau Zellenka, the woman Freud had dubbed Mrs K.

It is as if, across the years, the two women had finally dispensed with their superfluous men as partners in favour of a new partnership game of complex skills and rituals. They had substituted bridge as a game whose essence is the mutual understanding of open, yet coded, communications. Dora, adept from her early years at keeping a secret, knew how to conduct herself in these new arrangements.

Freud might well have been impressed by Dora's fidelity to her friend Frau Zellenka. It certainly would have reinforced in him his belated conviction that Dora's secret love for her had been the deepest current in her emotional life. He might also have viewed Dora's choice of occupation as a bridge teacher as an example of that rarest of all psychological skills, successful sublimation.

Partnership and Psychology

♠♥♦
♣

The perfect partner, according to a cynic's definition, is he who stands by you through all the troubles you wouldn't have got into without him. Partnership misunderstandings occur mostly in the bidding. Is a particular bid discouraging or encouraging, forcing for one round or to game, or a sign-off? Artificial bids and conventions cause further confusion – for instance, what are the responses to a pre-emptive three bid or a cue-bid. Is a double for penalties or for take-out? Even a pass can cause complications nowadays as it might be a forcing pass. Partnerships do best to evolve their own guidelines, or rules, to get round these difficulties. Such a rule could be: 'Never make an ambiguous bid when an unambiguous one will do.' And, 'If an ambiguous bid happens, always go for the weaker interpretation – non-forcing as opposed to forcing, natural as opposed to conventional, take-out rather than penalty double.'

The essence of partnership psychology is to keep partner happy. Goren and Sobel knew this, as did Culbertson and Jo Culbertson. No amount of technical expertise can compensate for this. A player who berates his partner at every turn will diminish the partnership. Someone who encourages will have the opposite effect. Partnership is after all a shared experience.

Partnership harmony can lead to telepathic understanding. People often wonder whether husbands and wives have an advantage in this way. They might when things are going well, but often extraneous factors bring out resentments and old grudges that have been stored away, and partnership understanding can rapidly deteriorate. The Culbertson partnership was a case in point. When their marriage was crumbling in the late 1930s they still played together, but marital strife soon found its way on to the table. In the 1937 Budapest World Championships, for instance, a missed cue-bid by Jo virtually lost them the title.

Rixi Markus took this view of partnership: 'I have learned by bitter experience that unless you treat your partner as you would a good friend you will not achieve good results. It does not matter how little or how much he knows about the game: it is up to you to make him feel safe and confident in order to get his best game from him. Allow him to take part in the bidding and play, and do not treat him with disdain or indifference even if he is far below your own standard.' Zia Mahmood has this to say: 'Rather than worry about individual bidding system preferences, I preferred to know the individual characteristics of my partner. Was he cautious or aggressive? Was he a good declarer or defender? Modern or old-fashioned? Just knowing these things would be a huge advantage.'

Partnership, from a psychological angle, can be seen as a form of communication. A bidder gives out a piece of information, the responder reads the sub-text, not sure quite what it means, but stays with it and gradually works it out, reading all the signals, and eventually a dialogue commences, an evolving dialogue that can lead to some form of synthesis, in bridge terms a clear, unequivocal game bid. Bidding conventions, the innate ritual and process of the game, aid and abet this.

In psychoanalysis, analysts work with what they call counter-transference. This means the feelings generated in the analyst by what the patient is saying or communicating by body language. Bidding is similar to this. 'Why is my partner telling me this?' 'What is he really trying to say?' Psychoanalysis views human beings as operating on an ego–self axis, the ego as the functioning side of the person, the side which gets things done, the self as the aspirational side. In bridge this interplay exists as well. There is the urge to win, to triumph, an ego function, the wish for a 'good' game conforming to the rules, and the sense of honour and fair play which belongs to the self. Bridge is perhaps unique among card games in being able to satisfy both these needs.

Trouble can arise when partners are expected to fulfil an ideal role for the other, or are expected to interpret signals without equivocation. Mothers are meant to do this with children, implicitly, without question. Most former children seek to perpetuate this. Hence the attraction of bridge. The provider, or mother substitute, is partner, always there on cue. Needs will be met, will they not, partner? If they are not, then rage, paranoia, envy may come into play, all early attributes of the unsatisfied child. Partnerships can founder at this point, the rage at being let down, paranoia at being persecuted, envy of partner's 'deliberate' withholding.

Card playing can satisfy other psychological needs. It can be a defence against pain. Freud has a phrase: 'Acting out in place of remembering'. Cards in this way can be a substitute for the pain which actual remembering may bring. Dostoevsky was a famous example of 'psychic masochism'. Dostoevsky's true pleasure was in losing, which became a compulsive urge. For him the fear generated by cards was nothing compared to the fear he felt elsewhere – hence the attraction of gambling. Yet this very compulsion forced proved to be his salvation. It forced him into writing to pay gambling debts. Thus, in a roundabout way, he was putting the ego–self axis into operation. He found his purpose in life through writing, cards as destiny.

The Dutch historian and social philosopher Johan Huizinga, in his influential book *Homo Ludens* (1944), took the view that many of Western civilisation's major activities – law, warfare, philosophy, art – were based on the play factor. He gave a wide range of examples from philology, literature, comparative mythology, and history. He concluded that *homo ludens* (man who plays) is a more accurate label for the species than *homo sapiens* (man who reasons) since more members of the race, he averred, engage in play than in logical thinking. Play has assumed even greater importance nowadays. Technological innovations call for a more 'playful' response to problem situations. Lateral thinking rather than linear is an example of this. The playful element can be compared to the Jungian notion of the trickster, full of mischievousness, who works against the entrenched order, the staid and predictable.

The pleasure of cards for cards' sake, the perceived elegance of the game with its Aristotelian framework of time, place and action, its language of thirty-eight possible bids, give bridge an almost aesthetic quality. Indeed, the pleasure of card play may stem from such unconscious satisfactions. There is the chance to participate in a ritual governed by conventions or sets of rules, agreed by all present rather than imposed from without. Bridge, in this way, can seek to fulfil Dr Johnson's definition of the purpose of cards, namely 'generating kindness and consolidating society'.

Women in Bridge Today

—♠♥♦—
♣

In 1985, Joyce Nicholson, an Australian writer/publisher, sent a questionnaire to members of the International Bridge Press Association, seeking opinions as to why women did not achieve more wins at the top level of championship bridge. She got a response from 165 men and 63 women. Her conclusions were that women were disadvantaged by their upbringing, namely that women's lack of aggression, lack of competitiveness, lack of determination to win, lack of concentration and lack of stamina meant that the necessary killer instinct was not 'ladylike'. Also that women's heavy commitment to family responsibilities meant they lacked the single-mindedness necessary to reach the top. Secondly, they were influenced by men's attitudes and judgements, and their dependence on men, particularly financially, restricted their freedom and ability to take decisions (although seventy-four per cent of the women who replied described their husbands as very supportive). An additional factor emerging from her survey was that women did not play enough bridge in their early years when their education was preparing them to be good wives and mothers. Furthermore, women saw themselves as more tolerant of error and defeat, and less compelled to strive for perfection in what, even at the top level, was only a game. She published her findings in her book *Why Women Lose at Bridge* (1985).

Danny Roth in his book *Why Women Win at Bridge*, published in 1992, challenges Joyce Nicholson's book. Roth feels her arguments were flawed, and that she overemphasised the 'social' aspect of bridge. Roth points to the increasing number of top female bridge players in the world – the late Rixi Markus and Dorothy Truscott as two examples.

At international level bridge is divided into 'open' and 'women's' pools. Theoretically, women are eligible for either, but in practice few compete in the open game. Many top female players in America are now professionals, earning their living by playing with clients, both as partners and team-mates, but generally in the women's game. Top female partnerships nowadays spend just as much time as their male counterparts perfecting their bidding and their defensive signalling systems. In bridge, as elsewhere, women are now given more motivation to succeed and more choice about how to lead their lives. Much of this is due to the women's movement and women can now prosper in many formerly male preserves, such as bridge.

Roth takes the view that women are more tuned in to the notion of partnership. Men tend to be more individualistic, and more demonstrative, often trying to impress by playing to the gallery. Women prefer a simpler approach. This comes out particularly in deceptive card play. With many men, defensive card play designed to outwit declarer often succeeds only in fooling partner. Woman are usually more receptive to the need to help partner, and only when a woman player is sure that her partner cannot be confused will she focus her mind on deceiving declarer. The feminine propensity for caring for others emerges, especially in defensive signalling. A woman's meticulous attention to detail is often stronger then a man's, plus her ability to discriminate, whereas men are often victims of their own labyrinthine cleverness. As a whole, he feels that women are generally good at planning and looking ahead to possible future problems, an ability which stands them in good stead at the bridge table.

In 1989 a marathon duplicate bridge match was staged between men and women, placing one table in New York and the other in Paris. It was a charity event and money was raised by selling tickets which entitled the purchaser to play for one hour. Although some top-class players did participate, the vast majority, male and female, were ordinary club players. It was an extremely close affair. Play continued round the clock for a solid fortnight, during which 2,352 boards were completed. At the end, the men won by 200 International Match Points (IMPs), the equivalent of less that 0.1 IMPs per deal, a very slender margin. During the match, the lead changed hands a number of times.

Patrick West, the social historian, wrote recently:

> The love of numbers, calculation and competition are traits we associate with men more than women – there aren't too many women trainspotters or boxers. Does bridge satisfy the predator in the primeval male spirit, be it in codified and regulated form? The relative absence of women players in the higher echelons of the international bridge scene poses a question with wide ram-

ifications. Is it the function of nature or the product of nurture? Are women intrinsically less logical, rational and aggressive, or has society merely conditioned them that way? Can women ever be as good as men at the bridge table, not to mention the army, director's board, in front of the wheel and so on?

Cultural critics might note that since the Victorian era in particular, women have been coded by repressive bourgeois society into being submissive, emotional and exotic creatures, the very antithesis of the dominant, rational and prosaic male, who had been a determining force in this cultural creation. The sexual revolution of the late twentieth century has helped ameliorate this phenomenon, yet it still remains prominent.

The very pervasiveness of these gender codes is evidence to some of the intrinsic, biological reasons behind them. Neurologists have suggested that the reason lies in the physical make-up of the brain. One theory has it that in the human brain, one sphere deals with emotions, the other with reasoning. Some scientists have noted that in the female brain the collection of nerves attaching the two spheres together – the *corpus callosum* – is much larger and wider than the male's, thus women find it harder to differentiate between reason and emotion. In short they would find it hard to stay at the bridge table without associating a detrimental hand of cards with personal affront.

This theory of the brain is also responsible for other theories of behaviour difference between the sexes. It explains why women are better at languages and men better at driving, better at making decisions and judging distances, but as is well known, they are much more predatory, reckless and dangerous on the road. That old primeval hunter spirit triumphs.

The Social Function of Bridge

♠♥♦
♣

As a social activity, bridge reached its peak in the 1930s. It soon achieved a status as something people aspired to, it had its own social cachet, and the ability to play the game became one of the key social attributes. Studies of the spread in its popularity in the 1930s show how it filtered steadily downwards through the social strata. In London at the time, Mrs Grace Lapham, the head of the Child Training Institute, let it be known that more than twenty per cent of the requests she received for governesses insisted that they should play bridge. She quoted a satisfied parent commenting on the educative values of bridge for her child. 'By respecting his bids, you teach him to respect yours and a child who gets intelligent and interesting answers to his bridge questions will be more likely to come to his parents with his more important problems.'

Before 1930 bridge had been a game for the affluent, but by the early 1930s, at the start of the Depression, bridge was being played by the lower middle class and even by blue-collar workers, whose traditional card games had been pinochle and poker. Bridge was also making progress down the age gap with young teenagers increasingly following the lead of their parents and taking up the game.

Sales of playing cards were one of the few commodities that remained high throughout the Depression as newcomers learnt the game. Bridge publications no longer addressed just the *cognoscenti*, or the experts, but geared their articles more to the social player, the once-a-week player, or the ladies' afternoon bridge four. For instance, an article on *canapés*, which a bridge expert might assume to be about the technique of bidding developed in France by Pierre Albarran where a shorter suit is bid before a longer one, turned out in fact to be on cooking – advice on what hors d'oeuvres to serve at the bridge table. It is reminiscent of the invention of the sandwich in the eighteenth century by the 4th Earl of Sandwich, which also took place at the card table; Sandwich, an inveterate card player, was loath to stop playing, or leave the table, so he got his servant to bring him sustenance at the table itself – meat inside bread which still bears his name.

Another level of the appeal was the depth and complexity of the game. It provided intellectual stimulus in addition to its social function. Educated, literate people welcomed this complexity, while for those lower down the social ladder it could become a vehicle for self-improvement and social advancement. Bridge requires players to do the right thing, hence much of its middle-class appeal to the rule-conscious and convention-minded. Indeed, contract bridge arose at precisely the right moment for an expectant public. It took root first in the cultural atmosphere of New York bridge clubs. The wider public then began to hear of it by word of mouth. Their enthusiasm was communicated to others, and an ever-widening arc of public interest was formed. People on the fringe wanted to share the experience of those at the centre and in no time at all the game reached nation-wide proportions. History has precedents for this since card games run in fashions – piquet in the sixteenth century, ombre in the seventeenth, tarot games in the eighteenth, whist in the nineteenth, and bridge and poker in the twentieth. Canasta briefly threatened to usurp this reign in the 1950s, but the game, actually invented by bored ladies in Montevideo, Uruguay, irate at their husbands' constant poker playing, soon faded out. Bridge may well last longer than most and has changed remarkably little in its first sixty years.

Beginners at bridge feel hesitant about learning the game. They worry about its complexity. They feel they lack the necessary self-confidence, or even trust, to sit through the initial stages of trial and error needed to learn. Bridge always seems to have the status of being a difficult game, only for the experts. How often does the cry of 'Oh, I can't play as I'm not good enough' go up? The fear is that bridge rules are too complicated, that it will take years of experience to learn, let alone play well, and that a phenomenal memory is required, or uncanny powers of deduction, or the ability to maintain concentration over long periods. They worry about their lack of 'card sense', that combination of awareness of surroundings, intuition and feel – a sort of sixth sense that people say is central to the game. Rixi Markus's advice could be appropriate to a beginner: 'Face events with courage. Don't mourn over what is past. Every hand brings new hope, new chances. And the best motto is: "If the disaster had not happened, the good fortune might not have followed." Yes, you must have faith, as in life. Don't look back; so much lies ahead and there are so many hands to come.' Grown people sometimes feel they are too old to learn bridge, to learn new skills at a late stage in life, but they should heed her advice and that of Talleyrand: 'You don't play whist, young man? What a boring old age you are laying yourself up for.'

Rubber versus Duplicate

THE DIFFERENCE BETWEEN THE TWO FORMS OF THE GAME

A study in 1973 by Mrs William Warlick Jr from North Carolina, an instructor at the Psychology Department of Central Missouri State University, looked into the differences of temperament between these two types of players. She found that some rubber bridge players were put off duplicate because of the too stringent rules and the competitiveness. They feared public censure for any infraction of the rules they might commit. They felt they lacked the capacity to observe and understand human behaviour sufficiently. Furthermore, they believed that luck brought results as much as skill, and they doubted their ability, or even desire, to concentrate deeply for long enough periods. Rubber bridge was less ego-threatening.

Duplicate players, she found, possessed several important temperament traits, namely a tendency toward reflection, an awareness of others, profound concentration and philosophical introspection, plus an exceptional tolerance for criticism – all of these to a much greater degree than rubber bridge players. Her 'temperament survey' was administered to two groups of thirty-two regular players of each persuasion. Duplicate players were found to be more detached and impersonal, hence the deep concentration. Duplicate players felt their main attributes were a desire to play the game well, a sense of extreme competitiveness and a certain egotistic attitude of mind. For rubber bridge players, their attributes were social-mindedness and less interest in exactness and seriousness. Rubber bridge players described duplicate players as being strongly competitive and determined to play the game at its best. They described their own group as sociable and less serious.

There was a general tendency to equate 'better' players with duplicate players. Most respondents added that better players are able to read the behaviour of others more clearly. It was not always obvious why a player chose one sort of game. It may not always be known to the player himself, nor will it necessarily reflect the extent of his, or her, detachment or contemplativeness in other areas of life. In the end, probably each player chooses the game best suited to his or her particular temperament.

She also sent out two-page questionnaires about signs of 'deliberate or inadvertent cheating' that players had noticed in games. This included tone of voice, speed in bidding and passing, the manner of placing cards on the table during the play of the hand, card manipulation, body movements, sighing, smiling, frowning, facial expressions (eyes, lips, etc.), attempts to see opponents' cards and so on. She concluded that nearly every behaviour at the bridge table presented some kind of information relating to the hand held at that particular time. Information was given either deliberately or inadvertently. The problem arose as to what was deliberate or not. The giving of information outside the normal process of bidding was not necessarily a form of cheating, for instance, side remarks, gestures or voice intonations were not always to be regarded as giving unauthorised information.

Among rubber bridge players, sixty-one per cent stated they felt there was more cheating at duplicate. The reverse was true for duplicate players – sixty per cent indicated that more cheating occurs at party or rubber bridge.

Duplicate bridge players think inferior players cheat more, whereas rubber bridge players do not hold the same opinion. Neither duplicate nor rubber players enjoy a game at which cheating occurs, and both have feelings of guilt if they win as a consequence of cheating. However, rubber bridge players tended to watch for 'free' information from their partners' actions. She found that rubber bridge players tend to give information to their partners either deliberately or inadvertently.

Correctly reading and interpreting human behaviour is an ability possessed by the best players and very much part of the attraction of the game. Players seek to use their interpretations of actions, statements and tone of voice by others. A correct interpretation of partner's and opponents' behaviour indicates that a player has amassed extra information to which he would not be entitled if bridge were played with only a limited number of vocal expressions and nothing else. She also added that since we are human beings, we find it almost impossible to control our feelings of delight, disgust or perplexity during the bidding, or play, of a hand. Because of this, we give away so-called 'free information' whether we intend to or not.

Paul Soloway of Los Angeles, McKenney Trophy winner in 1968 and 1969 and member of the US international team, was one of the players who answered her questionnaire. He felt that opponents often conveyed information by facial expressions, tone of voice and speed in bidding and passing. However, he had never observed anyone attempting to transmit information by card manipulation or body movements (hands, fingers, etc.).

Although he considered a few players 'leaners' (they lean to the left or right to get a glimpse of an opponent's holding), he said he had seen relatively few deliberate attempts to see opponents' cards. Incorrect scoring also was relatively rare, and he added that it was almost impossible to tell whether or not such mistakes were inadvertent.

As far as seeing opponents' cards, Soloway did not have feelings of guilt. 'I bend over backwards to avoid it,' he said, 'but sometimes it is impossible.' He also made a conscious effort not to take inferences from his partner's actions, but said that it was impossible not to anticipate a problem in bidding or play.

Soloway felt that the form of bridge in which the most cheating occurs was rubber bridge – because the players do not know any better. He believed the main difference between rubber and duplicate players was competitiveness – the desire to win. This, he said, was what gives a player the 'killer instinct' necessary to be a top player.

Soloway also had several general comments:

> One of the first traits that struck me when I entered the bridge world was the competitiveness of the players. It seems that a lot of people who were active in sports have switched to bridge. Good 'game players' make good bridge players.
>
> Another trait was sensitivity, or the apparent lack of it. Most males are thick skinned, but I have seen needlers unnerve even the toughest player. This is a trait missing in most women.
>
> The part of the game most often overlooked is the psychology of reading one's opponents. I personally enjoy this aspect of the game the most. Being able to read if your opponent has a good hand or a bad hand is very important.

I am a bridge professional and thus play regional tournaments between thirty-five and forty weeks a year. I see many players in different parts of the country. Experience and constant practice have given me good table feel. I can often tell when an opponent has a good or bad hand or is raising with three or four trumps. Whether his partner is tuning in as well is hard to tell.

People are always sending out information but not everyone picks it up. Many people show disgust or approval without realising they are broadcasting their emotions – 'cheating' if you will. Most of this information, though, passes over everyone except the experienced player. The novice has little idea about what is really happening at the table.

The Italian Blue Team

♠♥♦
♣

The most famous team of all time was the Italian Blue Team. They dominated world bridge for fifteen years from 1957–72 in which they set an international record which will probably never be equalled: four consecutive European Championship wins, ten consecutive World Championships in the Bermuda Bowl and three consecutive World Olympiad victories.

They got their name from the 1956 Italian Trials when the Blue Team defeated the Red Team. They owed their success to devising one of the most accurate bidding systems ever known, the Roman System, and to making a profound and detailed study of the game. The Blue Team comprised Walter Avarelli, Giorgio Belladonna, Eugenio Chiaradia, Massimo D'Alelio, Pietro Forquet, Benito Garozzo, Camillo Pabis-Ticci and Guglielmo Siniscalco. Yet the real secret of their success was the leadership qualities of their non-playing captain, Carl' Alberto Perroux. The only time he was absent through illness they suffered a defeat, in the 1960 Olympiad at Turin.

Perroux retired in 1966. Even without Perroux they still won, although their supporters had many anxious moments. The artistry, the superb technique, were there as always, but the effortless ease which was a feature of their earlier triumphs was missing. Perroux was no longer there to inspire 'his boys', as he liked to call them. The key to his personality was, without a doubt, his gift of leadership.

Perroux had dictatorial powers. As 'Technical Director' he alone could choose Italy's team, or lay down their schedule of training or decide on all matters great and small. During the 1965 World Championships in Buenos Aires he made sure his team had a special players' dining room. This meant he could keep close control of his players, and that they could eat together and carry out, in private, post-match discussions on hands played, especially those where they had dropped points. A cardinal rule for the team which he maintained, though, was 'No recriminations'.

Perroux was a benign but ruthless disciplinarian, controlling his team from his headquarters in Modena, telling Forquet, for instance, a bank manager in Naples, to go to Rome to practise with Garozzo, a jeweller there. During actual tournaments, he made sure they lived ascetically and went to bed early. For other teams, international tournaments were a chance to combine work with pleasure, to play bridge by day and to enjoy the local amenities by night. Not so for the members of the Blue Team as the story of Forquet's honeymoon shows. Pietro Forquet was married on the eve of the 1964 Olympiad and his honeymoon coincided with it. All went well, matrimonially speaking, until the arrival of Perroux. As the Italians were due the next day to meet the British team, who were leading the tournament, Perroux decided that bridegroom and bride should not spend the night together and he sent Pabis-Ticci to sleep with Forquet and Pietro's bride to share a room with Signora Pabis-Ticci. Italy's next test was against the Americans, and again the young honeymoon couple had to separate for the night. Italy won the Olympiad, so perhaps Perroux's strategy was vindicated.

Asked to define the qualities that make a great player, Perroux listed the following: physical endurance, a gentle disposition towards a partner and the wisdom to recognise that the pair in the other room always play well, ruthlessness towards opponents who must be courteously and cordially destroyed, a measure of fanaticism in accepting a monastic life during championships and the rigours of constant practice at other times, plus a knowledge of mathematics, the memory of an elephant, the gift of intuition and a lively imagination. Finally, 'it is helpful to play bridge well'.

An effective captain needed authority, prestige, psychology and patience, he said. But if, as was true with Perroux, the members of his team had a genuine affection for their captain, there was less need for authority and prestige. Perroux said: 'I could always ask. I did not have to order.' The Blue Team had an extra incentive. Perroux again: 'There was a certain mysticism. We really felt that we were doing something important for our country.'

Occasionally 'misunderstandings' did occur. There is a story, possibly apocryphal, that Giorgio Belladonna and Benito Garozzo had a 'simple and harmless' arrangement that when one of them, as declarer, saw dummy for the first time he was to say 'Thank you' if the dummy was what he was expecting, and '*Grazie*' if the bidding had misfired. On one deal, after a long and involved sequence of asking bids and responses, Garozzo was sure that he had made all the right responses. Dummy was put down and, deep in thought as he planned the play, Belladonna forgot the 'system' and absent-mindedly murmured, '*Grazie.*' '*Grazie*?' screamed Garozzo, 'What do you mean, *Grazie*?'

The Blue Team will be remembered for their rapport and team spirit, unique in the annals of bridge.

Zia Mahmood

♠♥♦
♣

ZIA'S PRIVATE CHECKLIST BEFORE PLAYING A TOURNAMENT

1. Wake up.
2. Force my mind into a state of total alertness – aware of every out-of-tempo breath around the table; every change of mood; every kind of feeling.
3. Focus on the ever-changing people around me. Who are they? What do I know about them? Do we speak the same bridge language? How do I get my partner to play his best?
4. Think about the correct way to bid each hand, then go back and re-check. Make sure my reasoning was objective and my analysis not seduced by some flaw in my character.
5. Don't be lazy (my biggest problem) and work hard at even the most simple-looking hands. Appearances can be deceiving. Initial reactions are frequently accurate, but there's no harm in confirming that these impressions were indeed accurate.
6. Try not to let anything interfere with my mind's ability to work to its maximum. This is the hardest. It is so easy to be distracted, it's human to react emotionally to a disagreeable partner or opponent, or to disaster, or even to a spectator sitting too close to you.
7. Most of all, think only about winning – nothing less would do.

Bridge My Way, 1991

Zia Mahmood was born in Pakistan in 1947, and came from one of the top twenty families in the country. Bridge was virtually unknown there at the time. Men from such families were normally expected to go into business or politics. When Zia was still young, his father died unexpectedly in a plane crash. In the plane wreckage his briefcase was found with a sheet of paper inside detailing all his assets, which he had written down and carefully locked inside when he realised that the plane was going to crash. Zia's mother, an unconventional and remarkable woman, pursued her own career as a gynaecologist – this in a strongly Muslim country where women were usually expected to stay at home and raise the family. She would treat rich and poor alike, using the fees of the wealthy to subsidise her treatment of the poor.

Following Zia's father's death, she decided to take her two sons to England, both to continue her career and to put them through an English public school education, highly thought of at the time in Pakistan. They went to Rugby. Zia excelled at sports but did less well with traditions and rules. After school he trained as a chartered accountant but much of it was monotonous and boring. Life, he felt, had more to offer and he soon found his way into his familiar milieu of cards and women. He got an evening job as a croupier in a poker club. Yet he still managed to pass his accountancy exams, the second time round, at the age of twenty-two. His mother died suddenly soon afterwards, and he went back to Pakistan to help run the family newspaper business.

Pakistan then was quite a contrast to 1960s London. Social life for young people was very prescribed. Marriages were still mostly arranged and girls lived at home until they did get married. This was when bridge came into Zia's life. As with Goren, it was through meeting a pretty girl. 'At the time, I was trying to get better acquainted with an attractive young woman whom I knew only slightly. The good news was that she finally agreed to meet me. The bad news was that the venue was a bridge party. It wasn't my idea of a perfect date as I couldn't even play bridge, but it was better than nothing.' He had assured her that he knew about playing bridge. In three days he had to race through Alfred Sheinwold's *Five Weeks to Winning Bridge*, but the book gripped him anyhow. 'The big day arrived and, as you can imagine, I performed embarrassingly badly – though just about managed to save myself from complete exposure. But I was sufficiently intrigued by the game that my concentration was diverted from the girl – my reason for being there in the first place – to the intricacies of the game itself.' His liaison with the girl might not have prospered but he was hooked on the game. The essential spark had been lit.

He read whatever bridge books he could get hold of, aiming to learn more about play and technique, and about the unusual and interesting people associated with the world of bridge: 'People like Ely Culbertson, who had promoted the game by his eccentric behaviour, extravagant boasts and famous challenge matches. He had been to bridge what Cassius Clay was to boxing.' He was also impressed by the invincible Italian Blue Team, the *Squadra Azzurra*. He started to play most days with a group of friends. Like all beginners, he went through early frustration. 'I would finally master one point, only to find that there were many others to learn and conquer. But I remember the pleasure, the mixture of pride and satisfaction, after making a good play – a feeling no non-bridge player can understand.' He found he was becoming more and more obsessed, determined 'not just to learn the game but to master it and become an expert player. I was in a hurry, too, which didn't help. But learning was such fun that the time flew by painlessly, and I started to get better.' He was twenty-four and he never looked back.

Then, in 1975, the oil boom in the Middle East arrived and he and his brother went to Abu Dhabi to join in its rapid expansion. Yet by the end of a year, Zia was reluctant to stay on in Abu Dhabi. He became allergic to 'the regimen, the heat and, most importantly of all, the lack of bridge'. Whenever he had had to go to London on business trips, he had visited bridge clubs, and, despite playing for modest stakes, found that he won far more often than he lost. He wanted to play, and learn, the game full time. When he discussed these thoughts with family and friends, their reactions ranged from 'disapproving to horrified'. It didn't deter him. 'Being a life-long member of the Black Sheep of the Family Club, if I'm advised to do something, invariably I do the opposite. I decided to roll the dice, catching the next plane to London. I left my share of the business in my brother's more capable hands, telling him to invest it as he saw fit. I took £1,000 with me, £500 for the rent and £500 for a stake at the bridge club.' He still remembers his brother's parting words: 'If you're going to spend the rest of your life playing a game, then at least become the best.' His brother's words undoubtedly came true.

Zia wrote his book *Bridge My Way* in 1991, a very entertaining and informative book as we have seen from the checklist at the beginning. Here are some extracts:

People have different ways of preparing for a bridge match. I sleep. The more I sleep, the happier I am. And the happier I am, the better I play – simple. I like to wake up as close to game time as possible. In my opinion, a tired mind is the most important thing to avoid. You need to be fully alert at every moment. It is one of the facts of bridge life that the one second you spend daydreaming will be the one when you make a mistake.

There is no limit to improvement. An expert can learn something from a beginner, as much as from another expert. There's nothing demeaning in this fact. In bridge, *ego* is sometimes useful, but *hubris* is too dangerous a luxury. If a player listens to the views of others at these sessions, if he carefully registers and records his errors, listing them under category and type, he will improve.

I think it is useful to keep a record of your errors. You will soon discover your individual strengths and weaknesses, which probably will be concentrated in specific areas. Each person is different. Maybe your slam bidding lets you down; or your opening leads; or your competitive bidding – even all three. You can only cure something you have diagnosed, which is why I am stressing this point.

To become a complete bridge player, you need a mixture of qualities – some worked for, some acquired, and others innate. Card sense is an innate ability; but if you aren't born with a body full of card sense, you can still 'learn' about cards. The players with card sense enjoy a familiarity and ease with the cards. Often they 'know' how the cards lie. All the great players have it.

Another quality that is partly innate and partly acquired is table presence. Have you ever known that an opponent was going to make a particular bid even before he made it? Have you ever felt sure that someone, either your partner or an opponent, was about to play a specific card, and he did? Have you ever sensed that a key suit was going to break badly and been right? Or, have you wanted to double the opponents for no good reason, decided against it, and cursed later when they went several down? One inch under the atmosphere around every table, there's an invisible screen on which a movie is continually being played. Most people don't know it's there, but the successful player is one who can see it, hear it and feel it.

The pleasure of success is increased by comparison with the

agony of failure. This is one of the reasons why bridge is so endlessly fascinating. No matter how much you play, or how proficient you become, you can never be in total control.

Omar Sharif had this to say about Zia:

> Zia has long been a friend of mine and he is rated by many as the number one player in the world. In my opinion, however, his contribution has been much more than expertise because of the charisma and sense of fun that he brings with him to the game. He is the living proof that bridge is not a boring game for boring people but an exciting game that mixes all the most vital human qualities and emotions.

Omar Sharif

♠♥♦
♣

Omar Sharif was twenty when he made his first film, directed by a fellow Lebanese Christian living in Egypt. Sharif played opposite the well-known Egyptian film star Faten Hamamam, who later became his wife. Nevertheless, film-making was tedious with long waits between shots. To while away the time he would frequent a small bookshop in the centre of Alexandria, looking for books that would be 'amusing but not silly'. He had already read *Anna Karenina* and other Russian novels, and had very much enjoyed Thackeray's *History of Pendennis*, feeling he would like to play its hero. Then, one day, his eyes alighted on Charles Goren's *Better Bridge for Better Players*. Reading this book provided the distraction he needed. He was immediately intrigued by bridge. 'I felt like someone travelling for many hours through a long tunnel, then suddenly catching a glimpse of light and beautiful countryside, followed again by a period of darkness. I half-realized at this time an essential truth about bridge: that it is a very complex game, but in the complexity lies its beauty.'

In fact, he came from a card-playing family. His mother played cards with King Farouk's set, helped by the financial support of her rich, timber-merchant husband. At school Sharif 'hated swotting' – he passed his maths exam by working from first principles. 'It is a taste I have for working out puzzles – cards, bridge, maths. Bridge is like maths, it is all about logic, but with bridge every two or three minutes, every time you deal the cards, you have a new puzzle.' He always had this logical mind which he sees as essential for bridge.

Sharif later wondered whether he was attracted to bridge because it presented a problem that he couldn't easily master, so used was he up till then to easy success in other fields. Sharif, perhaps surprisingly, sees himself as a moody person. 'Picture me in the most beautiful salon, with gorgeous Louis XVI furnishing, with my closest friends or perhaps with a girl in whom I am extremely interested – in short, a situation in which everything combines to make me happy. We cheerfully discuss the most serious affairs, in truth the most trivial. Then suddenly a clap of thunder, a complete change of mood; for no reason I shall ever understand, I have an overwhelming desire to be alone. It's true; that's what happens.' His moodiness soon disappears when he is engaged in bridge – the sight, the touch, even the thought of the game excites him. Ever since he first picked up Goren's book it has filled a central part of his life. And bridge appeals, too, because it is the here-and-now, 'the battle raging in front of you, the conflict that has to be solved before anything else can happen'. Bridge in this way can be obsessive – it is a continuing confrontation with reality, a challenge that will not go away, that has to be faced.

Yet like all beginners, Sharif found the game difficult to start with and put a lot of effort into mastering it. 'I learned to play first by reading a book. And I've never taken a single lesson. But I did pay a high price while putting Goren's teachings into practice. Right away, I got in with the best players and, sure enough, they trounced me every time. They accepted me because the stakes were high and they won plenty of money from me. That was the price I had to pay to learn. The lessons were expensive but effective, because one day I was picked to take part in the World Bridge Olympiad, in New York, with the three best Egyptian players. I must admit that they were of average skill compared to the other international champions. But it was a start.'

For most of his adult years Sharif remained a bachelor, having divorced Faten, his first wife, in 1967. He once explained his prolonged bachelordom as follows: 'I have this incredible mother who was there all my life and is still there, so I don't have a need for a woman with me. In fact, I like my space. I like to have a girlfriend but I cannot sleep in the same bed with someone. I can make love, but then I must sleep alone.' In 1995 he married Nadiya Aja, a fifty-year-old well-off Saudi, and a keen bridge player herself, an essential requirement.

His film career really took off once he made his films with David Lean, *Lawrence of Arabia* and *Doctor Zhivago.* He moved from Egypt, partly because his increasing association with the international film industry and its Jewish links meant he was less favourably viewed in Egypt, and went to Paris, where he could be close to two favourite pastimes, horse-racing at Longchamps and European bridge tournaments.

Sharif developed the Sharif Bridge Circus in the late 1960s. Previously Sharif had played in friendly games with Benito Garozzo,

Giorgio Belladonna and Pietro Forquet of the undefeated Italian Blue Team, but not in competition. So Sharif borrowed the idea of the tennis pro circuit and set up his own professional bridge team to tour the United States and Europe. The Sharif Bridge Circus, which included the Italian players, was sponsored by Lancia cars. Their challenge matches were held in big hotels, an echo of the Culbertson–Lenz match, before hundreds of spectators, and drew enormous interest from radio, television and newspapers on both sides of the Atlantic. A second tour in 1970 included a spectacular event, a challenge match against the British players Jeremy Flint and Jonathan Cansino for £100 a hundred over a hundred rubbers (later reduced by time pressure to eighty rubbers). This lasted a whole week in London, six hours a day, and the match rivalled the Fischer–Spassky chess duels in publicity. In the end, Sharif's side won by 5,470 points.

Sharif says he prefers tournament bridge. 'What interests me is the intellectual challenge. With rubber bridge you cut for partners, so you can end up with an idiot, and you can't play elaborate enough systems . . . Bridge requires long, hard training and a great deal of intelligence. Winning isn't a matter of luck. A winner doesn't just happen. He's more gifted than the others, he's quicker on the trigger, he can solve game problems.' He particularly enjoys European settings, Juan-les-Pins, Deauville and London, where he regularly plays at the Macallan tournament. He recognises the obsessive side of bridge. 'There was a point when I became too keen. It was obsessive. I would play all the tournaments. I would not make certain films if they interfered with my bridge schedule. I dreamt about cards. I was driven by the competition. I was good at it and I wanted to be perfect. But bridge is like golf; you can never achieve perfection.'

His partners have varied. A favourite has been the French player, the opera-loving Paul Chemla: 'Chemla is nuts, like so many brilliant people,' Sharif once said. 'He's alive and fun to be with. He has tremendous flair, but he plays bridge very simply. All great players play the game simply. The great stars realise bridge is a logical game, and they keep it simple.' At tournaments Sharif is always surrounded by admirers, predominantly female. A typical scene would be to see him studying his cards while a mass of kibitzers, nearly all women, surround him. Sometimes he finds it hard to concentrate under such conditions, besieged for photos, autographs and handshakes after every hand. 'This great game of ours requires concentration,' he says, 'and sometimes I lose mine under these conditions.' Sharif tries to be affable and obliging to all. 'At times it can be quite amusing. At one tournament, a woman came up to me and said, "I really didn't want to meet you. I wanted to remember you always as Dr. Zhivago." '

Bridge fascinates Omar. 'Bridge grips you. Many games provide you with fun, but bridge grips you. It exercises your mind. Your mind can rust, you know, but bridge prevents the rust from forming. Bridge is my passion. There is the constant drive to improve. You want to play your best and you want to play with the best. There's no limit to the excellence you can achieve. Every time you deal there's something new – there's something different.' And he concludes: 'Here's a most interesting fact about bridge – you're never alone anywhere in the world when you're a bridge player. It's like having a special passport. You can go into a strange town, ask where the bridge game is, and immediately you're able to cut in for a rubber or two. Or if there's a duplicate game, the club manager will always go out of his way to find a partner for you.'

Appendix

THE ODDS AT BRIDGE

THE POINT COUNT

Probability of holding a precise number of high-card points (values expressed in percentages)

Number of points	% chance	Number of points	% chance
0	0.3639	19	1.0361
1	0.7884	20	0.6434
2	1.3561	21	0.3778
3	2.4624	22	0.2101
4	3.8455	23	0.1118
5	5.1864	24	0.0558
6	6.5542	25	0.0264
7	8.0282	26	0.0117
8	8.8922	27	0.0050
9	9.3560	28	0.0019
10	9.4051	29	0.0007
11	8.9446	30	0.0002
12	8.0268	31	0.0001
13	6.9143	32	0.000017
14	5.6934	33	0.0000035
15	4.4237	34	0.00000071
16	3.3109	35	0.000000098
17	2.3616	36	0.00000000927
18	1.6051	37	0.00000000062991

LONG SUITS

Most people would be surprised to learn that the chance of holding an eight-card suit is about 1 in every 200. Here is the full list.

Probability of having long suits

Longest suit in your hand	% chance
4	35.0805
5	44.3396
6	16.5477
7	3.5267
8	0.4668
9	0.0370
10	0.0017
11	0.000036
12	0.00000032
13	0.00000000062991

SUIT DISTRIBUTIONS

Probability of different suit distributions

Distribution	% chance	Distribution	% chance
4-4-3-2	22.5512	8-2-2-1	0.1924
5-3-3-2	15.5168	8-3-1-1	0.1176
5-4-3-1	12.9307	8-3-2-0	0.1085
5-4-2-2	10.5797	7-5-1-0	0.1085
4-3-3-3	10.5361	6-6-1-0	0.0723
6-3-2-2	5.6425	8-4-1-0	0.0452
6-4-2-1	4.7921	9-2-1-1	0.0178
6-3-3-1	3.4482	9-3-1-0	0.0100
5-5-2-1	3.1739	9-2-2-0	0.0082
4-4-4-1	2.9932	7-6-0-0	0.0056
7-3-2-1	1.8808	8-5-0-0	0.0031

Distribution	% chance	Distribution	% chance
6-4-3-0	1.3262	10-2-1-0	0.0011
5-4-4-0	1.2433	9-4-0-0	0.0010
5-5-3-0	0.8952	10-1-1-1	0.0004
6-5-1-1	0.7053	10-3-0-0	0.0002
6-5-2-0	0.6511	11-1-1-0	0.000025
7-2-2-2	0.5130	11-2-0-0	0.000011
7-4-1-1	0.3818	12-1-0-0	0.00000032
7-4-2-0	0.3617	13-0-0-0	0.0000000000062991
7-3-3-0	0.2653		

YARBOROUGH

This term is used for any hand at bridge that has no card higher than the nine. The origin of this derives from Lord Yarborough, an eighteenth-century English peer, who would offer his fellow whist players a bet of £1,000 to £1 that they would not get such a hand. Many took the bet believing it to be good odds, but the true odds are 1,827 to 1 – so the Earl was on to a good thing.

BIBLIOGRAPHY

Amory, Cleveland, *The Last Resorts*, Harper & Brothers, New York, 1952

Amory, Mark (ed.), *The Letters of Ann Fleming*, Collins Harvill, London, 1985

Appignanesi, Lisa and Forrester, John, *Freud's Women*, Weidenfeld & Nicolson, London, 1992

Beasley, Colonel H. M., *Beasley v Culbertson: The Official and Authentic Record of the International Bridge Match*, Hutchinson, London, 1933

Bowyer Bell, J. and Whaley, Barton, *Cheating and Deception*, Transaction Publications, London, 1991

Clay, John, *Culbertson: The Man Who Made Contract Bridge*, Weidenfeld & Nicolson, London, 1985

Cohen, Ben and Reese, Terence, *The Acol System*, Contract Bridge Equipment Ltd, Leeds, 1946

Cole, E. R. and Edwards, James, *Grand Slam*, Bodley Head, London, 1975

'Cut Cavendish', *The Complete Bridge Player*, T. Werner Laurie, London, 1906

Dahl, Roald, *Someone Like You*, Michael Joseph, London, 1954

Daniels, David, *The Golden Age of Contract Bridge*, Stein & Day, New York, 1980

Dunne, J. Patrick and Ostrow, Albert A., *Championship Bridge as Played by the Experts*, Whittlesey House, New York, 1949

Fisher, Nigel, *Iain Macleod*, André Deutsch, London, 1973

Fleming, Ian, *Moonraker*, Jonathan Cape, London, 1955

Francis, Henry G., Truscott, Alan F., Frey, Richard L., and Hayward, Diane (eds), *The Official Encyclopedia of Bridge* (Fourth Edition), Crown, New York, 1984

Frey, Richard L. (ed.), *Bridge for Women, by Peggy Solomon, Rixi Markus, Mary Jane Farell, Bee Gale Schenken, Helen Sobel Smith*, Doubleday & Company, New York, 1967

Goren, Charles H., *Better Bridge for Better Players: The Standard Book of Play*, Rockcliff, London, 1949

Goren, Charles H., *The Standard Book of Bidding*, Doubleday, Doran, New York, 1944

Goren, Charles H., *The Sports Illustrated Book of Bridge*, Time Incorporated, 1961

Halliday, Jon and Fuller, Peter (eds), *The Psychology of Gambling*, Allen Lane, London, 1974

Jacoby, Oswald and Morehead, Albert, *The Fireside Book of Cards*, Simon & Schuster, New York, 1957

Karpin, Fred L., *Psychological Strategy in Bridge: The techniques of deception and harassment in bidding and play*, Hart, New York, 1960

Mackey, Rex, *The Walk of the Oysters: The Curious History of Contract Bridge*, W. H. Allen, London, 1964

Macleod, Iain, *Bridge is an Easy Game*, The Falcon Press, London, 1952

Mahmood, Zia, *Bridge My Way*, Faber & Faber, London, 1991

Markus, Rixi, *Common Sense Bridge*, The Bodley Head, London, 1972

Markus, Rixi, *A Vulnerable Game: The Memoirs of Rixi Markus*, Collins, London, 1988

Maugham, Robin, *Somerset Maugham and all the Maughams*, Heinemann, London, 1966

Maugham, W. Somerset, *The Complete Short Stories*, William Heinemann, London, 1951

Mollo, Victor, *The Bridge Immortals*, Faber & Faber, London, 1967

Morgan, Ted, *Maugham*, Simon & Schuster, New York, 1980

Olsen, Jack, *The Mad World of Bridge*, Holt, Rinehart & Winston, New York, 1960

Ostrow, Albert A., *Bridge Player's Bedside Companion*, The Bodley Head, London, 1956

Parlett, David, *The Oxford Guide to Card Games*, Oxford University Press, Oxford, 1990

Potter, Stephen, *The Theory & Practice of Gamesmanship or The Art of Winning Games Without Actually Cheating*, Henry Holt, New York, n.d.

Ramsey, Guy, *Aces All*, Museum Press, London, 1955

Reese, Terence, *Reese on Play: An Introduction to Good Bridge*, Edward Arnold & Co, London, 1948

Reese, Terence, *The Expert Game*, Edward Arnold, London, 1958

Reese, Terence, *Story of an Accusation*, Heinemann, London, 1966

Reese, Terence, *Bridge Tips by World Masters*, Robert Hale, London, 1980

Reese, Terence, *Bridge at the Top*, Faber & Faber, London, 1977

Roth, Danny, *Why Women Win at Bridge*, Faber & Faber, London, 1992

Rovere, Ernest W., *Bridge Complete: A Comprehensive Text and Reference Book for Everyone, from Beginner to Expert*, Simon & Schuster, 1973

Sachen, William, *Bridge: A Guide to the Literature*, Garland Publishing, New York, 1984

Sharif, Omar, *Eternal Male*, Doubleday, New York, 1977

Sharif, Omar, *Omar Sharif's Life in Bridge*, trans. Terence Reese, Faber & Faber, London, 1983

Shepard, Robert, *Iain Macleod*, Hutchinson, London, 1994

Simon, S. J., *Why You Lose at Bridge*, Nicolson & Watson, London, 1947

Sims, Dorothy, *Psychic Bidding*, Vanguard Press, New York, 1932

Sims, Dorothy, *Curiouser and Curiouser: A Book in the Jugular Vein*, Simon & Schuster, New York, 1940

Sobel, Helen, *Winning Bridge*, Peter Davies, London, 1950

Treglown, Jeremy, *Roald Dahl: A Biography*, Faber & Faber, London, 1984

Truscott, Alan, *The Great Bridge Scandal*, Yarborough Press, New York, 1969

Truscott, Alan, *Grand Slams*, Unwin, London, 1986

Webster, H. T. and Calhoun, Philo, *Who Dealt This Mess?*, Doubleday, New York, 1948

Index